Theory
of
Film Practice

NOËL BURCH

TRANSLATED BY HELEN R. LANE
INTRODUCTION BY ANNETTE MICHELSON

SECKER & WARBURG
London

Theory
of
Film Practice
NOËL BURCH

Cinema Two

PN
1995
·B8513
C.2

Praxis du cinema by Noël Burch
first published by Éditions Gallimard, Paris, in 1969
Copyright © 1969, Éditions Gallimard, Paris

This translation, with Preface by the author, first
published in Great Britain 1973 by Martin Secker & Warburg Limited
14 Carlisle Street, London WIV 6NN
© 1973 by Praeger Publishers, Inc.

SBN 436 09704 4 (clothbound)
SBN 436 09705 2 (paperbound)

Printed in the United States of America

Contents

Introduction by Annette Michelson   v
Preface to the English-Language Edition   xvi

Part I   Basic Elements
1   Spatial and Temporal Articulations   3
2   Nana, or the Two Kinds of Space   17
3   Editing as a Plastic Art   32

Part II   Dialectics
4   The Repertory of Simple Structures   51
5   Absence of Dialectic and Complex Dialectics   70
6   On the Structural Use of Sound   90

Part III   Perturbing Factors
7   Chance and Its Functions   105
8   Structures of Aggression   122

Part IV   Reflections on the Film Subject
9   Fictional Subjects   139
10   Nonfictional Subjects   156

Index   168

ILLUSTRATIONS FOLLOW PAGE 76.

iii

Introduction

I t was just twenty years ago that André Bazin undertook to chart the course of film's *New Avant-Garde*, offering an endorsement of the conventions of our narrative cinema that was to produce the orthodoxy of the 1960's and its attendant strategy, *la politique des auteurs*.

We may use the abandoned concept of the avant-garde if we restore its literal meaning, and thereby its relativity. For us avant-garde films are those in the forefront of the cinema. By the cinema we mean of course the product of a particular industry whose fundamental and indisputable law is the winning, by one means or another, of public acceptance. This may seem a paradoxical statement to make, but it carries a corrective provided by the notion of innovation. The avant-garde of 1949 is just as prone to misunderstanding on the part of the mass public as that of 1925. . . . This avant-garde arouses no less hostility. On the contrary, it elicits more, because not soliciting misunderstanding, attempting as it does to work within cinematic norms it runs great risks: both misunderstanding on the part of the public and

the immediate withdrawal of the producers' support. The Patron Saint
of this avant-garde is and will remain Erich Von Stroheim.

This manifesto, published in the tenth issue of *Les Cahiers du
cinéma*, was framed in reply to a short essay by Hans Richter on "The
Film as an Original Art Form" that posited a future for a tradition
represented by the past work of Eggeling, Leger, Duchamp, Man
Ray, Picabia, Ruttman, Len Lye, Cocteau, and Richter himself, citing the continuing efforts of Maya Deren, Frank Stauffacher, James
Broughton, and Curtis Harrington. To those names one might at that
time have added those of Kenneth Anger and Harry Smith. Neither
Bazin nor Richter were then in a position to sense the imminence
of a new era initiated by the work of Stan Brakhage and Robert
Breer—nor that of the mature Resnais, the young Godard. Richter
had, obviously, some awareness of a possible continuity and, rather
than accept Bazin's characteristically tactful description of him as
the sole survivor of a noble line, he pointed with discernment and
generosity to younger artists then working in obscurity to create
options in cinema consistent with the aspirations and achievements
of advanced painting and music in this century.

Bazin's reply, then, laid the foundation for that revision of the
canon that was to animate the critical orthodoxy of the postwar
period and continue well into the 1960's. And it is within and against
the context of this orthodoxy that one must read and understand
Theory of Film Practice. Its impulse, its method, and the judgments
generated by them work toward the confirmation of those options
eliminated in Bazin's revisionist view of the *avant-garde*. That view
was, of course, the quite natural response of a man overjoyed at the
thought that cinema was no longer to be considered "the inheritor of
painting and music," but could take its place as "the competitor of
the novel"—this at a time when the creative energies at work in novel-
istic enterprise were particularly low. For those unconcerned with
advanced and innovative art, the position of Bazin, articulated with
that remarkable delicacy and authenticity that distinguish him from
all his epigones, afforded a particular sense of ease regained.

One hears it in the long sigh of relief publicly exhaled by Andrew
Sarris:

I have always felt a cultural inferiority complex about Hollywood. Just
a few years ago, I would have thought it unthinkable to speak in the

same breath of a "commercial" director like Hitchcock and a "pure" director like Bresson. Even today, *Sight and Sound* uses different type sizes for Bresson and Hitchcock films. After years of tortured reevaluation, I am now prepared to stake my critical reputation, such as it is, on the proposition that Alfred Hitchcock is artistically superior to Robert Bresson by every criterion of excellence, and further that, film for film, director for director, the American cinema has been consistently superior to that of the rest of the world from 1915 through 1962. Consequently I now regard the *auteur* theory primarily as a critical device for recording the history of the American cinema, the only cinema in the world worth exploring in depth beneath the frosting of a few directors at the top.

The dramatically confessional tone celebrates a shift of perspective as a shift of power. One thinks of Pound's reevaluation of the classical canon:

I took my critical life in my hand some years ago when I suggesteed that Catullus was in some ways a better writer than Sappho, not for melopoeia, but for economy of words. I don't in the least know whether this is true. One should start with an open mind. The snobbism of the Renaissance held that all Greek poetry was better than any Latin poetry. . . . I doubt if Catullus is inferior to Sappho. I doubt if Propertius is a millimetre inferior to his Greek antecedents; Ovid is for us a storehouse of a vast mass of matter that we cannot now get from the Greek.

The rhetorical strategies are strikingly similar; the difference lies, of course, in their respective contexts, and in the functional, practical quality of Pound's criticism—its sense of the useful and his concern with the *future* of poetry. In the decade that intervened between Bazin's formulations and their adoption by American criticism, that consciousness of an alternate aspiration or tradition that forms the context of Bazin's statement had been expunged. The American disciple commits himself to a curatorship from which that dimension of historical awareness that informs the criticism of the Master with a certain exquisite tact is missing. In the decade since that American commitment, we have seen the erosion of the film industry and the forms generated and sustained by it. We have seen, as well, Bazin's critical and theoretical position undermined by history, assailed, and, in the very review he founded, replaced by a resurgence of a more radical aesthetic aspiration in the politically radicalized climate of 1968 and after.

Bazin had argued for a cinema of "transparency," for a style grounded in mimesis, positing "faith in the image" as generating the kind of spatiotemporal continuity that would guarantee the integrity of dramatic action as the vehicle of the phenomenal world's "ambiguity." Reading his early major critical pieces on the American Cinema and the Italian Neorealists, one finds him responding to that renewal of energy in the immediate postwar period as a man of his time and in a manner that exactly parallels that of American criticism of the day, though with infinitely more sophistication and grasp of cinematic form and style. The resemblance of basic stance and expectation, above all, the identity of the presuppositions informing these critical reactions, is striking when one compares his work with the strictly contemporaneous efforts of James Agee and Robert Warshow.

Here is Bazin on Rossellini's *Paisa*, a film that he, like Warshow, considered exemplary:

> The mind has to move from one fact to another, like jumping from rock to rock in order to cross a river. The foot may hesitate in choosing between two stones, or may miss it or slip. So with our mind. Because the essence of the stone lies not in the fact that it permits the traveler to cross the river without getting his feet wet. Facts are facts, our imagination makes use of them but their primary function is not to be useful. In the standard cinematic script the fact is attacked by the camera, broken up, analyzed, reconstituted; it retains its nature as fact, of course, but is enveloped in abstraction, like a brick of clay. Facts, in a Rossellini film, take on meaning not in the manner of a tool whose function is determined in advance like its form. Facts follow each other, and the mind is forced to perceive that they resemble each other and that in resembling each other, they come to mean something which was contained within them. . . . But the nature of the 'image-fact' is not only to be involved with other facts in the relationships invented by the mind. . . . Considered in itself, each image being only a fragment of reality preexistent to meaning, the screen should present an equal concrete density.

Bazin, working in the lively, intellectual climate of postwar Paris, was able to fuse his theoretical heritage and analytic powers in a critical venture whose quality, breadth, and power are incomparable with that of any American film critic of his time. The manner in which specific insights are generated or supported by a synthesis of phenomenological method and Catholic sensibility constitutes, in and through its contradictions, a still fascinating chapter in the intellectual history of the period. The notion of "ambiguity" derived from the literature of existentialism is supported and confirmed by a certain natural piety. The texts to be studied are Simone de Beauvoir's supplement to Sartre's *Being and Nothingness*, published in this country as *The Ethics of Ambiguity*, Sartre's own literary criticism— and particularly his early essay on Mauriac, turning its iconoclastic impulse upon the notion of God as Artist and Artist as God—and, finally, Merleau-Ponty's single essay on the aesthetics of film. Informed by a Catholic piety lingering undissolved in the climate of postwar Paris, Bazin's theory is hierophantic in its general thrust, in its desire to found a cinema that would stand in asymptotic relation to an "essential" Reality. It requires an effacement of style, of that "shadow" intervening between the eye and an Ultimate Spectacle. For that spectacle of "Creation," Bazin proposed, in fact, the Artist as Witness.

Seizing, then, upon the work of Renoir, Welles, and Rossellini, Bazin, in a really brilliant insight, presented the effect produced by depth of field (as in *La Règle du jeu* and *Citizen Kane*) as working to expand and intensify the possibilities of "ambiguity." Expanding and intensifying the illusionism of that spatial continuum in which the beholder's gaze and attention is, to use Bazin's own phrase, free to move, to choose, to miss, and to slip, Welles' depth of field and Rossellini's long shots permit the beholder to encounter and explore the visual field. The viewer, unguided by an assertive style, proceeds in time to apprehend the *données* of that field, by implication rehearsing through the experience of film viewing the existential situation of being-in-the-world, "choosing in ambiguity."

It is interesting to note Bazin's use, as an ultimate supporting argument (or rhetorical strategy) of a political metaphor: The depth of field that underscores this ambiguity guarantees the more "democratic" ordering of phenomena presented. Not subjected to the "subjective" emphases of a more assertively edited footage or the metaphorical thrust of the montage style, the material is not in any way subject to "hierarchization" or "distortion." The spectator re-

tains his "democratic right," as it were, to make meaning from within
that cinematic manifold, that recording of reality, of those "facts,"
the naked and modest revelation of which, the director, in his loving
respect for "things themselves," presents. With a certain justice, one
can speak of Bazin's critical and theoretical work as providing an
aesthetics of postwar Christian Democracy, and of Warshow's as
both reflecting and reinforcing American liberalism in its Eisenhower
phase, its native empiricism intact, its sociological bent "uncor-
rupted" by any theoretical impulse.

In this period of the 1950's, Eisenstein quite naturally becomes the
target of liberalism's reordering of the past: His assertive, analytic
style is seen as the ultimate assault upon the integrity of a preexistent
"reality" and as the ultimate form of cinematic *hubris*. Interestingly
enough, Eisenstein had used the same political metaphor to support
his own case for the style of montage so antithetical to that of the
Realist and Neorealist revivals. In proposing the "montage of attractions," he posited the rapid, percussive style of *October* as isomorphic
with the triadic process of the dialectic (each shot opposed by
another shot contrasting in composition, directionality, tone, rhythm,
pace, and tonal values, with these oppositions generating a fresh
moment of significance). He argued, too, for the "democratic" freedom of the spectator, the active quality of his film-viewing experience
as involved in the constant apprehension of the dialectic of contrasts
and of metaphors extended to every parameter of film. That incessant
process of radicalization that animates his work from *Strike* to *The
General Line*, the last film made before his departure to Europe
and America, is intended to represent a particular step forward.
"In distinction from orthodox montage according to particular
dominants, *The General Line* was edited differently. In place of an
'aristocracy' of individualistic dominants we brought a method of
'democratic' equality of rights for all provocations or stimuli, regarding them as a summary, a complex."

Our two major theoreticians—Europeans, both—had elevated their
chosen cinematic styles into filmic ontologies and then proceeded
to elevate those filmic ontologies and the experiences afforded by
them into paradigms of ontological awareness as such. Bazin posited
the response to the spatiotemporal continuity of Realism and Neo-
realism to its mimetic function as that of existential freedom viewed

as choosing in ambiguity; Eisenstein offered to his spectators the experience of revolutionary consciousness unfolding in the apprehension of the dialectic. The two men joined in common recognition of the cognitive experience as central to the strategies and ends of art. As we know, in this they are not alone; they restate, each for his time and for the rapidly developing medium, the century's concern with art as an "orphic explanation of the world." In so doing, they proposed as well—as if in concert, as if united through the magic of a Kuleshov effect—the terms of a debate on *the politics of illusionism*.

There is a sense in which the speed and inevitability of film's development will quickly and inevitably render most criticism obsolete. Its radical novelty and uniqueness lie in the unparalleled malleability of the temporal medium that gives us an unprecedented grasp upon the nature of causality itself. It is this that confounds the noblest attempts to constitute its ontology. In his own filmic ontology, Bazin had precluded the interest and the importance of the processes of abstraction and reflexiveness then at work. He had, moreover, precluded critical examination of the terms of its illusionism by and through the art itself. However, for some of us, coming to think of film in the Paris of the late 1950's and early 1960's, and for myself, then an art critic, there was a sharp sense of Bazin's work as being brilliant in its critical insights yet fundamentally unacceptable in its more general totality, in its presuppositions, and in its implications. Fundamentally antipoetic, resolutely antimodernist, Bazin's taste and theory tended to sever film (as the primary commitment to the "fundamental and indisputable law" of public acceptance "within the American industry" would naturally sever film) from one's experience and expectations of advanced painting and music and from the innovative theatrical movement then at its extrordinary height. All this was, one felt, offensive to one's taste. It demanded a disaffection with respect to the work of the generation of 1925, an assumption of its inevitable and irreversible decline that was at variance with one's sense of history—and of film history—as inflecting and inflected by the course of aesthetic innovation in this century. And, by 1962, there was a small body of French film—in particular the early work of Godard—that argued the bankruptcy of this reading of history. Perhaps one has to have lived through that particular moment we know as *"la nouvelle vague"* to sense the manner in which Godard and Resnais redefined cinematic aspiration, undertaking—as in *Last Year at Marienbad* and *My Life to Live,* —to transcend the antitheses established in the the critical literature between the style of montage and the style of spatiotemporal continuity. The long, sinuous tracking shots and the purposive disjunctiveness of mismatches in *Marienbad* resolved those antitheses within a single fresh masterwork, confounding the critical impulses that had dissociated them.

For some of us, then, and for Noël Burch in particular, this moment, anticipated by the work of Bresson, Tati, and a few others, inaugurated the possibility of a renewal and redirection of critical energies and an end to cinema's alienation from the modernist tradition. It is in this context that *Theory of Film Practice* must be read. It is the work of a young American who had chosen, as a teen-ager in the early 1950's, to live in France and work in film. Burch's intensive involvement with the medium develops as part of that same chapter of postwar cultural and intellectual history, sensed and lived with an intensity of commitment to the poetic principle rare in film critics of any period. His primary experiences and impulses are those of a filmmaker, and he is almost alone among the critics of that time in a lack of concern with extra-aesthetic sources or supports for criticism and theory. He does not share the concern (which Bazin, as a *Normalien,* bequeathed to his inheritors) with the manner in which aesthetic discourse may be grounded in current or traditional philosophical inquiry.

His discourse is primarily critical, animated by a restless and empirical voracity of aesthetic experience. *Theory of Film Practice* is at every point derived from and confirmed by the perception that film develops not through the constraints and conventions of an industry, but in opposition to them. One does not find in this book the vestiges of a phenomenological stance elevated into a filmic ontology, but rather one finds a concrete investigation into the possibilities of formal analysis that may eventually constitute a serious basis for the phenomenology of film. Burch's method is analytic and descriptive, in a manner unique to film criticism in that time and place. Not surprisingly, it is related to the best of contemporary art and music criticism, committed to the investigation of their newly developing forms in relation to each other.

Inscribed within these essays, written in 1967, is an intellectual and cultural history of a period that was to close one year later. They trace the preoccupations of someone operating quite outside the purlieu of French academic life and the traditional philosophical culture of the Parisian *aggrégé*. Burch offers a number of aesthetic judgments, methodological options, and presuppositions animated by a commerce with the liveliest in French culture of the 1950's and 1960's: its literature, its music, its theater—and its cinema.

Constantly we encounter, as intellectual themes, an aesthetic reference, a compositional paradigm, the example of serial musical composition as it flowered then. A first generation of composers trained in the immediate postwar period had inherited the perfected logic of serial composition, formulated by Schönberg and refined by Webern. The work of Pierre Boulez and Jean Barraqué and the criticism of Michel Fano and André Hodeir extend the compositional principle to each parameter of musical structure, following the organization of pitches and timbres with those of duration, attack, and so forth. We confront, through Burch's critical reference, a radicalization of the series in the music of the 1950's. The rigor, totality, and authority of that radicalization process have, of course, their closest and most illustrious precedent in Eisenstein's own incessant radicalization of the montage style, his own extension of its authority thirty years previously to all the filmic parameters and its consequent culmination in the style of "intellectual montage." It is, I think, Burch's commitment to an aesthetic of poesis that animates his abiding presupposition that a work must be "rigorous in every respect." We are continually referred to the notion of a work that is "organically coherent," a film in which "every element works with every other," of the logic of that coherence as being, finally, the manifestation of that poetic sovereignty of the Imagination that constitutes it. And the will to entirely organize and account for the elements constituting a given work, the will to integrate chance and contingency *as* chance and contingency, to "organize delirium" itself, as Boulez had proposed, is the most immediate critical manifestation of the new *dialectic* proposed in this revivification of the cinematic as a radically synthetic art.

This revivification will require an extensive redefinition of the contours and locations of the filmic parameters. Thus, the space off screen is patiently explored, its part in the radically synthetic constitution of the filmic object is stressed; off-screen space is, for the first time in critical literature, rendered fully *visible, accessible*. A fresh evaluative view of history as a history of developing forms eschews the notion of the pantheon, proposes its own paradigms. French film is privileged, and so is the film of Japan. "American slapstick comedy," on the other hand, "represents the only major collective contribution made by the American movie industry to the art of film comparable to the contributions made by the French primitives and perhaps even more comparable to that of the Soviet masters." And, within the larger, historical and local areas, readjustments and rehabilitations are in order. Thus, we begin with the detailed analysis of Renoir's early *Nana* as constituting (together with *La Règle du jeu*) the core of his immense achievement, and we are given the early *Cronaca d'un amore* as Antonioni's masterwork of cinematic structure. And, paralleling the particular insights that inform an analysis of Siegel's *Baby Face Nelson* is the unremitting analytic precision expended upon the reparation of the supreme critical injustice done to the work of Marcel Hanoun, the most neglected of film masters, the man whose career speaks more eloquently than any other of the constraints, the waste inherent in the film industry and its mass public.

The coming chapter in the history of filmic practice and its theory in France is unthinkable without a radical transformation of that situation by its film-makers—just as film-making in this country has been transformed by the sustained heroism of some generations of independent artists, for whom no place was ever made, as was made for their French contemporaries, in a subsidized film industry of the postwar era. The hesitations of French film, the inconclusiveness of the time since May, 1968, the problematic quality of Godard's work, his recent development (and the manner in which a progressive political radicalization has impelled him to reinvent, as it were, the aesthetic strategies of his American independent contemporaries), all provide the clearest testimony to the necessity for that change.

Theory of Film Practice, completed in 1967, attempts to inaugurate a fresh view of cinematic history, and also marks the conclusion of an historical period. This period of general filmic renewal coincided with a personal youth and growth, and I was fortunate to share in all of these. Burch's intransigence, his accent of urgency, are those of the shared discoveries and enthusiasms, the reciprocal confirmations and debates of that youth, invested, as one reviews them through their theorization, with a particular authority. His voice puts forth a claim for total structural rigor and organicity, insisting, as Descartes did, that "the intellect is a passion"—or that the demands of criticism, when most stringently made, ratify and sustain the sovereignty of the Imagination.

ANNETTE MICHELSON

New York
January, 1973

Preface to the English-Language Edition

I wrote this book in 1967. It originally appeared as a series of ten articles in the *Cahiers du cinéma*, the substance of which was drawn from lectures given at the Cours Littré, a cramming school for future film students and the incubator, as it were, of l'Institut de Formation Cinématographique (IFC), founded later that same year by Jean-André Fieschi, Daniel Manciet, and myself.

Those lectures—and articles—were extempore formulations of ideas that had preoccupied me with increasing urgency during my previous fourteen years of sporadic activity as a film-maker. Not unnaturally, though perhaps unfortunately, I seized upon that unexpected opportunity to express them in print with the conviction not only that they had achieved fruition but that they were to be my last word in the matter: At the time I regarded myself as a film-maker, a "creative artist," first and foremost and this incursion into the field of "theory" as a passing indulgence. This no doubt explains why the book, in my present view, grossly overreaches itself, why I find it in many places superficial, supercilious, and, above all, needlessly and unenlighteningly peremptory.

The subsequent research that I was able to conduct with Fieschi and our students at the IFC during its four-year existence taught me a number of things—among them, that my film-making, teaching, and writing were indissoluble parts of the same epistemological search—and, although I do not believe that they actually negate the basic premises of this book, they would certainly enable me to situate and formulate them better today. In particular, the techniques of analysis that I have since developed would have helped me avoid the elusively vague descriptions and downright errors that plagued the two French versions (articles and book). Most of these have, I think, been now either eliminated, corrected, or, in two cases where I felt that their absence would have perturbed the development of my arguments too deeply, designated as errors and maintained as "imaginary examples"—a procedure I consider to be justified within the confines of a text that, despite a veneer of "objectivity," was primarily a film-maker's statement of how he at one time wanted to make films and would have liked to see others make them. To what extent this is a productive attitude the reader will have to judge for himself.

To be more specific in my criticism, I would say that the book tends to decline more or less steadily as it progresses, especially from Chapter 8 on. The fundamental classifications set forth in the first four chapters and the sixth were closely related to my own experience as a film-maker—had, and still have, a *material grounding*—while the two feature-length films analyzed in Chapter 5 were the two works that I had studied most closely up to that time. Unfortunately, the spurious need that I felt to make the book a definitive statement led me on, especially in the last two chapters, to write about matters upon which I had reflected only very superficially, and, although I feel that the basic insights set forth regarding the form-subject relationship are not exactly wrong—and can, as experience has proved, serve to set readers on more fruitful paths—they certainly have for me today an aura of irresponsibility about them.

In order that the book may better serve readers—whether future film-makers or merely serious film-lovers—I should like to use this Preface to clarify a few general notions that recur prominently throughout the book in which I am afraid are often rather ill-defined terms. Perhaps this will help to define a proper critical perspective on this early attempt to inaugurate a phenomenological approach to film art and make it easier to disregard much of the deadwood and deal with the material that is still alive. For, in view of the present embryonic development of phenomenological analysis as applied to the narrative film, this text still seems to be capable of opening horizons for the thinking film-maker and the student of film history and aesthetics.

One of the terms employed most frequently—perhaps too frequently—in this book is "form." At the time of writing, my approach to the concept was undoubtedly loose and hazy, even though I still believe I was guilty of no actual abuse of the word. However, in order to firm up both this detail of terminology and, I think, the book's over-all tonus, I should like to suggest here a simple but very seminal approach to the concept borrowed from lectures given by André Hodeir on *musical* form at the IFC: *The form of a work is that mode of being which ensures its unity while tending to promote, at the same time, the greatest possible diversity.* This comprehensive definition should, I think, if applied to the chapters that follow, enable us to avoid the pitfalls of a mechanistic interpretation of the propositions that I have set forth—and that I readily admit seem at times to elicit such a reading. In the light of it, my analysis of Marcel Hanoun's *Une Simple histoire* should be seen to lay bare a model in which this mode of being may be detected as operative at every level: narrative, psychological, and dramaturgical as well as purely "technical." And this is how I would like the reader to approach the more fragmentary remarks regarding the "form" of many of the other films mentioned in the book.

A second point, especially important to this English-language edition, is that the above-mentioned "technical" aspect of film, to which I give special attention, was most often referred to in the original French as *écriture* or *facture*, words that have generally had to be rendered as "style" and "texture." These words must be read as having more precise referents than is generally the case in English, always implying as they do to specifically material options of a "technical" nature (*facture* means texture in the articulative sense, *écriture* is *graphic inscription* as much as "style"). The cognate word "technique" has been largely avoided, partly because of the confusion, often encountered where films are concerned, between technique (essentially the director's) and technology (the cameraman's, sound engineer's, and so on) and partly because of the arcane ghetto to which traditional criticism has tended to relegate "the mere mechanics" of film-making, as opposed to such "primordial" and "universal" factors as the "human" dimension, the "sense of reality," and so on. Although no special emphasis is placed upon the fact in this book, my entire approach was, even then, implicitly predicated on the conviction that the illusionist approach to film-making—comparable to what Brecht condemned in theater as "identification" and what the nineteenth century called "the pathetic fallacy" and which is in fact the *raison d'être* of what I call "the zero point of cinematic style"—contains a fundamental principle of alienation that degrades both film-maker and spectator. Today a better understanding of the "semantics" of artistic progress has made it possible to reread Brecht without taking literally his belief that politically committed—non-alienating—art must, by definition, convey a manifest political *message* (information), and, by coupling his theoretical writings with Eisenstein's, to examine the "crest line" of film-making in terms that were defined thus by the latter:

> It draws the spectator into a creative act in which his own personality is not dominated by that of the author, but fully develops in harmony with the author's conception, just as the personality of a great actor fuses with that of a great playwright in the process of creating a classical image on the stage.*

In Eisenstein's view—as in my own—a complete reading of artistic process, including the conscious perception of form, is a liberating activity. As for the dialectical conception of film form that I unknowingly borrowed from another essay by Eisenstein, I feel today that, although it is in no wise an erroneous approach, it may not constitute the universally productive hypothesis I once believed it to be, which may have been one of the reasons for Eisenstein's own seeming abandonment of it. A film's mode of being is all but infinitely complex, due to the uniquely *composite* nature of filmic material (which I attempt to define in this book). I think that the following pages are useful in that they try to isolate a few of the

---

* Sergei Eisenstein, *Notes of a Film Director* (New York: Dover, 1970), rev. ed.

vectors of this complexity and propose models of how they function. Taken in its most elementary sense (which was how Eisenstein certainly took it), "dialectics" may convey a meaningful image of the conflictual organization to which these elementary parameters have been subjected by nearly every consequential film-maker in his or her search for "unity through diversity." However, it is probable that more sophisticated, specific concepts will have to be developed, possibly combining the semiological and phenomenological approaches (as I was incapable of doing here), if we are to render full account of the audiovisual art, the manner in which it has been perceived in the past and may be perceived in the future. It is this project that I hope to further with two books now in preparation, the one a study of the concept of form in Japanese cinema, the other a history of the development of Western film language from 1895 to 1935, books to which I hope readers will find the present volume as useful an introduction as it has been an indispensable preparation for the author.

I wish to thank Annette Michelson for her helpful criticisms during the preparation of this somewhat revised English edition.

Noël Burch

London
January, 1973

I

Basic Elements

1

Spatial and Temporal Articulations

The terminology a film-maker or film theoretician chooses to employ is a significant reflection of what he takes a film to be. The French term *découpage technique* or simply *découpage*[1] with its several related meanings is a case in point. In everyday practice, *découpage* refers to the final form of a script, incorporating whatever technical information the director feels it necessary to set down on paper to enable a production crew to understand his intention and find the technical means with which to fulfill it, to help them plan their work in terms of his. By extension, but still on the same practical workaday level, *découpage* also refers to the more or less precise breakdown of a narrative action into separate shots and sequences *before filming*. French film-makers, of course, are not the only ones to have a term for this procedure. Both English- and Italian-speaking film-makers have a similar term for this final version of the script—called a "shooting script" in English and a *copione* in Italian—though they always speak of "writing" it or "establishing" it, thereby indicating that the operation the word describes is no more important in their minds than any other in the making of a film. A third French meaning of *découpage*, however, has no English equivalent. Although obviously derived from the second meaning of a shot

3

breakdown, it is quite distinct from it, no longer referring to a process taking place before filming or to a particular technical operation but, rather, to the underlying structure of the *finished* film. Formally, a film consists of a succession of fragments excerpted from a spatial and temporal continuum. *Découpage* in its third French meaning refers to what results when the spatial fragments, or, more accurately, the succession of spatial fragments excerpted in the shooting process, converge with the temporal fragments whose duration may be roughly determined during the shooting, but whose final duration is established only on the editing table. The dialectical notion inherent in the term *découpage* enables us to determine, and therefore to analyze, the specific form of a film, its essential unfolding in time and space. *Découpage* as a structural concept involving a synthesis is strictly a French notion. An American film-maker (or film critic, in so far as American film critics are interested in film technique at all) conceives of a film as involving two successive and separate operations, the selection of a camera setup and then the cutting of the filmed images. It may never occur to English-speaking film-makers or English-speaking critics that these two operations stem from a single underlying concept, simply because they have at their disposal no single word for this concept. If many of the most important formal break-throughs in film in the last fifteen years[2] have occurred in France, it may be in part a matter of vocabulary.

An examination of the actual manner in which the two partial *découpages*, one temporal and the other spatial, join together to create a single articulated formal texture enables us to classify the possible ways of joining together the spaces depicted by two succeeding camera setups and the different ways of joining together two temporal situations. Such classification of the possible forms of temporal and spatial articulations between two shots might seem to be a rather academic endeavor, but to my knowledge no one has previously attempted such a classification, and I believe that it may well open up some important new perspectives.

Setting aside such "punctuation marks" as dissolves and wipes, which may be regarded as mere variations on the straight cut, five distinct types of temporal articulation between any two shots are possible.

The two shots, first of all, may be absolutely continuous. In a certain sense, the clearest example of this sort of temporal continuity is a cut from a shot of someone speaking to a shot of someone listening, with the dialogue continuing without a break in voice-over. This is, of course, precisely what happens whenever a shot is followed by a reverse-angle shot. Although the term "straight match-cut," as is made clear later on in this chapter, refers more specifically to spatial continuity, it is also another example of absolute temporal continuity. If shot A shows someone coming up to a door, putting his hand on the doorknob, turning it, then starting to open the door, shot B, perhaps taken from the other side of the door, can pick up the action at the precise point where the previous shot left off and show the rest of the action as it would have "actually" occurred, with the person coming through the door and so on. This action could even conceivably be filmed by two cameras simultaneously, resulting in two shots[3] that, taken together, preserve an absolute continuity of action seen from two different angles. To obtain as complete a continuity in the edited film, all we would have to do is cut the tail of shot A into the head of shot B on the editing table.

A second possible type of temporal relationship between two shots involves the presence of a gap between them, constituting what might be called a *temporal ellipsis* or *time abridgement*. Referring again to the example of someone opening a door filmed by two cameras (or by the same camera from two different angles), a part of the action might be omitted when these two shots are joined together (in shot A someone puts his hand on the doorknob and turns it; in shot B he closes the door behind him). Even the most conventional films frequently use this technique as a means of tightening the action, of eliminating the superfluous. In shot A someone might perhaps start up a flight of stairs, and in shot B he might already be on the second or even the fifth floor. Particularly when a simple action such as opening a door and walking through it is involved, it might be emphasized that the ellipsis or abridgement can occur in any one of a large number of possible variations; the "real" action might span some five or six seconds, and the time ellipsis might involve the omission of anything from a twenty-fourth of a second to several seconds, and might occur at any point in the action. This is equally true in the case of absolute temporal continuity; the transition between shots may occur anywhere. A film editor might maintain that in both cases there is only one "right" point at which to make a straight match-cut or abridge the action, but what he really means is that there is only one place where the shot transition will not be consciously noticed by the viewer.[4] This may well be. But if we are seeking a film style that is less "smooth," that actually stresses the structures that it is based upon, a whole range of possibilities remains open.

This first type of temporal ellipsis involves, then, an omission of a time-span that is not only perceptible but *measurable* as well. The occurrence and the extent of the omission are necessarily always indicated by a more or less noticeable break in either a visual or an auditory action that is potentially capable of being completely continuous. (A continuous temporal-auditory action, verbal or otherwise, occurring in conjunction with a discontinuous temporal-visual action, as in Jean-Luc Godard's *Breathless* and Louis Malle's *Zazie dans le Métro*, is, of course, not at all precluded.) In the previous examples of going through a door or going up a flight of stairs we become aware of the existence of a temporal discontinuity or gap as a result of the spatial continuity having been forcefully enough maintained to allow the viewer to determine mentally that some portion of a continuous action has been omitted and even enable him to "measure" the actual extent of the omission. (Temporal *continuity* can likewise only be measured relative to some other *uninterrupted* visual or auditory continuity.) Thus, if a shot transition takes us from one location to another, more distant one without there being any way of relating the two distinct spaces (such as a telephone or some other means of communication), the temporal continuity between them will remain indefinite unless it is preserved through the use of such clumsy devices as successive close-ups of a clock-dial or some convention such as cross-cutting, an emphatic alternation between two actions occurring in two distinct spaces.[5]

A third type of temporal articulation and a second type of abridgement are possible, the *"indefinite ellipsis."* It may cover an hour or a year, the exact extent of the temporal omission being measurable only through the aid of something "external"—a line of dialogue, a title, a clock, a calendar, a change in dress style, or the like. It is closely related to the scenario, to the actual narrative and visual content, but it nonetheless performs a genuine temporal function,[6] for, even though the time of the narrative obviously is not the same as the time of the film, the two time spans can nevertheless be related in a rigorously dialectical manner. The reader may object that the boundary between the "measurable" ellipsis and the "indefinite" ellipsis is not clear. Admittedly a segment of time abridged in the process of splicing together two shots showing someone walking through a door can be measured rather accurately—namely, as that part of the action that we know must be gone through but do not see, whereas we are less capable of measuring "the time it takes to climb five flights of stairs." However, "the time it takes to climb five flights of stairs" still constitutes a unit of measurement, much as "one candle power" is the amount of light furnished by one candle; this is not at all the case, on the other hand, when we realize that something is occurring "a few days later," as in an indefinite ellipsis.

A *time reversal* constitutes another type of possible temporal articulation. In the example of someone walking through a door, shot A might have included the entire action up to the moment of going through the door, with shot B going back to the moment when the door was opened, repeating part of the action in a deliberately artificial manner. This procedure constitutes what might be called a *short time reversal*, or an overlapping cut, such as Sergei Eisenstein used so often and to such striking advantage—as in the bridge sequence in *October (Ten Days That Shook the World)*—and such as certain avant-garde film-makers have used (see also François Truffaut's *La Peau douce* and Luis Buñuel's *The Exterminating Angel*. At this point, however, it is worth noting that time reversals, like time ellipses, are commonly used on a very small scale, involving the omission or repetition of only a few frames, as a means of preserving *apparent* continuity. The preservation of an appearance of continuity is, of course, what is always involved in any conventional use of time abridgement. What we are referring to now, however, no longer involves simple mental deception—that is to say, making an action that is not visually continuous convey a "spirit" of continuity—but the actual physical deception of the eye. When it comes to "match-cutting" two shots showing someone walking through a door, for perceptual reasons which are quite beyond the scope of this book), a few frames of the action may be omitted or repeated in order that the filmed action may seem more smoothly continuous than would have been the case had the shot been picked up *precisely* where the previous one left off.

The flashback is a more usual form of time reversal. Just as a time ellipsis can span either just a few seconds or several years, so too can a time reversal. The fifth and last type of temporal articulation thus is the *indefinite time reversal*, which is analogous to the *indefinite time ellipsis* (the exact extent of a flashback is as difficult to measure without outside clues as is the extent of a flashforward) and the opposite of a *measurable time reversal*. The reason why the flashback so often seems such a dated and essentially uncinematic technique today is that, aside from its use by Alain Resnais and in a few isolated films such as Marcel Carné's *Le Jour se lève* and Marcel Hanoun's *Une Simple histoire*, the formal function of the flashback and its precise relationship to other forms of temporal articulation have never been understood. Like the voice-over, the flashback has remained little more than a convenient narrative device borrowed from the novel, although both have recently begun to assume other functions.

But might not this inability to measure the exact temporal duration spanned by either flashback or flashforward point to some basic and previously overlooked truth? Are not jumps forward and backward in time really identical on the formal organic level of a film? Are there not ultimately, then, only four kinds of temporal relationships, the fourth consisting of a great jump in time, either forward or backward? Alain Robbe-Grillet obviously believes this is so, and in that sense, his and Resnais's *Last Year at Marienbad* perhaps comes closer to the organic essence of film than it is currently fashionable to believe.

*   *   *

Three types of articulation between the spaces depicted in two successive shots are possible—apart from, and independent of, temporal articulations, even though they have obvious analogies to them.

A first kind of possible spatial relationship between two shots involves the preservation of spatial continuity in a manner similar to that in which temporal continuity is preserved, *although this spatial continuity may or may not be accompanied by temporal continuity*.

The door example in all three variations is an instance of spatial continuity; in each case, the same fragment of space fully or partially seen in shot A is also visible in shot B. Any change in angle or scale (matching shots, that is, taken from the same angle but closer or farther away) with relation to the same camera subject or within the same location or the same circumscribed space generally establishes a spatial continuity between two shots. That much is obvious. It seems to follow that there is only one other form of possible spatial articulation between two shots: spatial *discontinuity*—in other words, anything not falling into the first category. This discontinuity, however, can be divided into two distinct subtypes bearing a rather curious resemblance to the two distinct subtypes of time ellipses and reversals. While showing a space different in every way from the space visible in shot A, shot B can show a space that is obviously in close *proximity* to the spatial fragment previously seen (it may, for instance, be within the same room or other closed or circumscribed space). This type of spatial discontinuity has given rise to a whole vocabulary dealing with spatial orientation, and the fact that such a vocabulary should be necessary serves to emphasize how essentially different this type is from an obvious third possibility, complete and radical spatial discontinuity.

This vocabulary dealing with spatial orientation brings us to a key term, one of some concern to us here: the "match" or "match-cut." "Match" refers to any element having to do with the preservation of continuity between two or more shots. Props, for instance, can be "match" or "not match." On a sound stage one can often hear remarks such as "these glasses are not match," meaning that the actor was not wearing the same glasses or was not wearing glasses at all in a shot that has already been filmed and is supposed to "match" with the shot at hand. "Match" can also refer to space, as in eye-line matches, matches in screen direction, and matches in the position of people or objects on screen. There are also spatiotemporal matches, as in the door example, where the speed of movement in the two shots must "match," that is, must *appear* to be the same. To clarify this notion of "match" or "match-cutting," a brief history of how it developed is in order.

When, between 1905 and 1920, film-makers started bringing their cameras up close to the actors and *fragmenting* the "proscenium space" that early cinema had left intact, they noticed that, if they wanted to maintain the illusion of theatrical space, a "real" space in which the viewer has an immediate and constant sense of orientation (and this was, and still remains, the essential aim for many directors), certain rules had to be respected if the viewer was not to lose his footing, to lose that instinctive sense of direction he always has in traditional theater and believes he has in life. This was the source of the concepts of eye-line match, matching screen direction, and matching screen position.

Eye-line match and matching screen direction concern two shots that are spatially discontinuous but in close proximity. When two shots show two different persons supposedly looking at each other, person A must look screen right and person B screen left, or vice versa, for if both look in the same direction in two successive shots, the viewer will inevitably have the impression that they are not looking at each other and will suddenly feel that he has completely lost his orientation in screen space. This observation on the part of the second generation of film-makers contains a basic truth that goes far beyond the original goal of matching. Only the Russian directors, however (before Stalinism brought film experimentation to an abrupt halt), were beginning to glimpse what this really implied: that only what happens in frame is important, that the only film space is screen space, that screen space can be manipulated through the use of an infinite variety of *possible* real spaces, and that disorienting the viewer is one of a film-maker's most valuable tools. We will come back to this idea later.

As a corollary to eye-line match, film-makers also discovered the principle of matching screen direction: Someone or something exiting frame left must always enter a new frame showing a space that is supposedly close by or contiguous from the right; if this does not occur it will seem that there has been a change in the direction the person or object is moving in.

It was also noticed, finally, that in any situation involving two shots preserving spatial continuity and showing two people seen from relatively close up, their respective screen positions as established in the first shot, with one of them perhaps to the right and the other to the left, must not be changed in succeeding shots. To do so risks confusing the viewer's eye, for he invariably will read any shift in screen position as necessarily corresponding to a shift in "real" space.

As the techniques for breaking down an action into shots and sequences were developed and refined, these continuity rules became more and more firmly fixed,[7] methods ensuring that they would be respected were perfected,[8] and their underlying aim, to make any transition between two shots that were spatially continuous or in close proximity *imperceptible*, became increasingly apparent. The introduction of sound brought an increased emphasis on film as an essentially "realistic" medium, an erroneous conception that soon resulted in what we might call the "zero point of cinematic style," at least in so far as shot transitions were concerned. The Russian experiments exploring an entirely different idea of *découpage* were soon considered outdated or at best only marginally important. "Jump cuts" and "bad" or "unclear" matches were to be avoided because they made the essentially *discontinuous* nature of a shot transition or the *ambiguous* nature of cinematic space too apparent (the overlapping cuts in *October* were viewed as "bad" matches, and the *découpage* of Alexander Dovzhenko's *Earth* was thought to be "obscure"). Attempting thus to deny the many-sided nature of the cut, film-makers eventually had no well-defined aesthetic reason whatsoever for cutting from one shot to the next, often doing so for reasons of pure convenience, until by the end of the 1940's some of the most rigorous directors (Luchino Visconti in *La Terra trema*, Alfred Hitchcock in *Rope*, Michelangelo Antonioni in *Cronaca di un amore*)[9] began wondering whether cuts were necessary at all, whether they should not be purely and simply eliminated or used very sparingly and endowed with a very special function.

The time has now come to change our attitude toward the function and nature of cinematic articulation, both between individual shots and in the film over all, as well as its relation to narrative structure. We are just beginning to realize that the formal organization of shot transitions and "matches" in the strict sense of the word is the essential cinematic task. Each articulation, as we have seen, is defined by two parameters, the first temporal, the second spatial. There are, therefore, fifteen basic ways of articulating two shots, that being the number of possible combinations of the five temporal types and the three spatial types of transitions. Each of these possibilities, moreover, can give rise to an almost infinite number of permutations, determined not only by the extent of the time ellipsis or reversal but also, and more importantly, by another parameter that is capable of undergoing an almost infinite number of variations too: the changes in camera angle and camera-subject distance (not to mention deliberate discrepancies in eye-line angles or matching trajectories, which are less easy to control but almost as important). I am not saying that these are the only elements that play a role in a transition between shots. But other elements such as camera and subject movement, frame content and composition, and the like can define only the particular nature of a given match and not the function of articulations in general. As regards the content of the film image, it may be interesting to know that a close-up of a man's expressionless face followed by a shot of a bowl of soup creates the impression that the man is hungry; but this relationship between the content of two shots is a *syntactical* one that merely helps us determine the *semantic* relationship between them. Although film remains largely an imperfect means of communication, it is nonetheless possible to foresee a time when it will become a totally immanent object whose semantic function will be intimately joined with its plastic function to create a *poetic function*. Although camera movements, entrances into and exits from frame, composition, and so on can all function as devices aiding in the organization of the film object, I feel that the shot transition will remain the basic element in the infinitely more complex structures of the future.

One of the possible forms that this over-all organization of film articulations might take can already be foreseen, for the fifteen types of shot transitions can give rise to patterns of *mutual interference,* resulting in yet another controllable set of permutations. At the moment of transition, the articulation between two shots might seem to fit into any one of the five temporal categories and any one of the three spatial categories, but then something in shot B or some other subsequent shot might *retrospectively* reveal that the transition actually belongs in an altogether different temporal or spatial category, or perhaps even both. Examples of this procedure exist even in relatively conventional film-making. In a scene in Hitchcock's *The Birds,* Tippi Hedren, who has lingered too long at the home of the local schoolteacher, telephones her fiancé. The first shot shows her in a medium close-up. The next shot shows the teacher starting to sit down in an armchair, blocking part of the frame at the beginning of the shot. Because of the alternation between shots to which we have become accustomed in similar scenes, and more importantly because of the absence of any other clue to the spatial orientation, we have the impression the camera is aimed at some other part of the set; hence there appears to be preservation of temporal continuity (Tippi Hedren continuing her conversation off screen) along with spatial discontinuity. When the teacher is finally seated, however, she reveals the part of the set in the background that she has previously blocked from view, and we see Tippi Hedren in a medium-long shot at the telephone. Spatial continuity had in fact been preserved as well (it is a matching shot from the same angle). Our first impression of the situation was an erroneous one, and we are belatedly forced to correct our initial misconception. This is a much more complex process of awareness, to say the least, than that implied in the "invisible" match. The exact nature of the relationship between the two shots remains vague for several seconds and becomes obvious only sometime after the transition has occurred. The variable duration of this interval may furnish another parameter.

Another frequently employed technique involves having a distant shot of someone followed by a closer one, with this second shot subsequently turning out to be occurring at some other time and perhaps even in some other place. Although this procedure is commonly used in flashbacks and time ellipses, it has hidden potentialities that allow more complex formal structures to be created (as in *Une Simple histoire*).

It is, however, important to note that this sort of disorientation presupposes a "coherent" spatial and temporal continuity, a previously created context built around immediately comprehensible relationships between shots.[10] A more systematic,[11] more structural use of the disorientation created by these "retroactive matches" would depend on establishing some sort of dialectical relationship between such matches and others that are immediately comprehensible, a dialectic in which the "deferred" match might perhaps still be an exceptional device but would no longer remain a gratuitous or merely stylistic "gimmick."

Still other possibilities can result from the nonresolution of these "open" matches, films that would have this very ambiguity as their basis, films in which the viewer's sense of "real" space would be constantly subverted, films in which he could never orient himself. Resnais's *Last Year at Marienbad* and Jean-Marie Straub's *Nicht Versöhnt*, especially in their use of indefinite time ellipses and reversals, already provide examples.[12]

I have just briefly outlined a set of formal "objects"—the fifteen different types of shot transitions and the parameters that define them—capable of rigorous development through such devices as rhythmic alternation, recapitulation, retrogression, gradual elimination, cyclical repetition, and serial variation, thus creating structures similar to those of twelve-tone music. None of this is as abstractly theoretical as might be imagined.

As early as 1931, Fritz Lang's masterpiece *M* was entirely structured around a rigorous organization of the film's formal articulations, starting with sequences in which each shot is temporally and spatially autonomous, with time ellipses and changes in location playing the obviously predominant role, then gradually and systematically evolving toward the increasing use of the continuity cut, finally culminating in the famous trial sequence in which temporal and spatial continuity are strictly preserved for some ten minutes. In the course of this progression a certain number of "retroactive matches" also occur, the most striking of which takes place when the gangsters leave the building in which they have captured the sadistic child-murderer. Lang repeats a shot, already used several times, of a housebreaker seen through the hole in the floor he has made to get into a locked bank. The thief asks for a ladder so he can climb out. A ladder is thrown down and he clambers out, only to discover that it is the police and not his gangster friends who are there waiting for him. We then realize that the time between the mob's departure and the arrival of the police has been completely skipped over in a time ellipsis, that instead of occurring immediately after the departure of the thief's pals this shot in fact happens a good deal later than we initially thought.

A more recent film, Marcel Hanoun's little-known masterpiece *Une Simple histoire*, is entirely structured around principles similar to the one I have been describing. Although these principles are arrived at in Hanoun's case in a purely empirical manner, they are nevertheless applied with utmost rigor. *Une Simple histoire* will be examined in detail in another chapter.

The contemporary film narrative is gradually liberating itself from the constraints of the literary or pseudo-literary forms that played a large part in bringing about the "zero point of cinematic style" that reigned supreme during the 1930's and 1940's and still remains in a position of some strength today. It is only through systematic and thorough exploration of the *structural* possibilities inherent in the cinematic parameters I have been describing that film will be liberated from the old narrative forms and develop new "open" forms that will have more in common with the formal strategies of post-Debussyian music than with those of the pre-Joycean novel. Film will attain its formal autonomy only when these new "open" forms begin to be used organically. What this principally involves is the creation of a truly consistent relationship between a film's spatial and temporal articulations and its narrative content, formal structure determining narrative structure as much as vice versa. It also implies giving as important a place to the viewer's disorientation as to his orientation. And these are but two of the possible multiple dialectics that will form the very *substance* of the cinema of the future, a cinema in which *découpage* in the limited sense of breaking a narrative down into scenes will no longer be meaningful to the real filmmaker and *découpage* as defined here will cease to be experimental and purely theoretical and come into its own in actual film practice. It is this cinema of the future that the following pages will hopefully help to bring forth.

Notes

1. From the verb *découper*, "to cut into pieces."
2. As of 1966.
3. Two meanings of the word "shot" should be distinguished, depending on whether it is shooting or editing that is being referred to. During shooting a shot refers to whatever is filmed after the camera starts and before it stops; during editing it refers to whatever is included between two "cuts" or shot changes. Two words are in fact needed, but to my knowledge no language makes such a distinction.
4. See my remarks below on the "zero point of cinematic style."
5. That this is no more than a convention is quite amply demonstrated by an episode in the television series "The Man from U.N.C.L.E.," which consisted

of two separate actions cross-cut together; on the one hand we witnessed Ilya Kouriakin's misadventures as a prisoner of an Arab tribe, obviously extending over a period of several days, and, on the other hand, Napoleon Solo's adventures, taking place within a period of only a few hours.

6. This has only recently become apparent, principally because this kind of ellipsis has ceased to be systematically indicated by dissolves.

7. The principal ones have been mentioned here. Also worth mentioning is the rule about changing a camera angle by at least thirty degrees (or not at all), which stems from the perceptual nature of the matched shot change (see Chapter 3).

8. Also worth citing: the cutaway, the rule of the median line, and the manner in which actors' movements can be slowed down or speeded up so that long shots and close-ups of the same subject match (see Chapter 3).

9. It is worth pointing out that this preference for prolonged shots was subsequently abandoned by all three directors, corresponding (in Antonioni's case at least) to an increased awareness of the extremely important function a shot change can fulfill.

10. The author refers readers to Eisenstein's concept of the "montage unit" as set forth in Vladimir Nizhny, *Lessons with Eisenstein* (tr., Jay Leyda and Ivor Montagu [New York: Hill and Wang, 1969]), a book with which he was unfamiliar at the time of writing.

11. Bresson's *Une Femme douce*, which appeared just before the publication of this book, has a formal texture entirely based on this kind of match—and it indicates the limits inherent in a systematic use of "deferred" or "retroactive" matches.

12. Robbe-Grillet's *L'Homme qui ment* (*The Man Who Lies*) obviously goes much farther in this direction.

2

Nana, or the Two Kinds of Space

To understand cinematic space, it may prove useful to consider it as in fact consisting of *two different kinds of space*: that included within the frame and that outside the frame. For our purposes, screen space can be defined very simply as including everything perceived on the screen by the eye. Off-screen space is more complex, however. It is divided into six "segments": The immediate confines of the first four of these areas are determined by the four borders of the frame, and correspond to the four faces of an imaginary truncated pyramid projected into the surrounding space, a description that obviously is something of a simplification. A fifth segment cannot be defined with the same seeming geometric precision, yet no one will deny that there is an off-screen space "behind the camera" that is quite distinct from the four segments of space bordering the frame lines, although the characters in the film generally reach this space by passing just to the right or left of the camera. There is a sixth segment, finally, encompassing the space existing behind the set or some object in it: A character reaches it by going out a door, going around a street corner, disappearing behind a pillar or behind another person, or performing some similar act. The outer limit of this sixth segment of space is just beyond the horizon.

What role do these spatial segments play in the formal development of a film?

This question could be answered in the abstract, but it seems pref-
erable to refer to a film that is a model of the exhaustive use of
off-screen space and its systematic opposition to screen space, Jean
Renoir's masterpiece *Nana*, a key film in the development of a cinematic language.

Beginning with its first great dramatic scene, when Muffat meets
Nana, the entire visual construction depends on the existence not
only of an on-screen space but also of an off-screen space that is
fully as important. How is this sense of off-screen space established?

In *Nana*, as in any film, the spatial segments are defined first of
all by entries into and exits from frame. More than half the shots
in Renoir's film begin with someone entering the frame or end with
someone exiting from it, or both, leaving several empty frames before or after each shot. Indeed, we might say that the entire rhythm
of *Nana* depends on these exits and entrances, their dynamic role
becoming all the more important in that, except for a half dozen or
so dolly and pan shots (to which we shall return later), the film
consists almost entirely of shots during which the camera does not
move. Obviously only four of the six spatial segments previously
described are brought into play to any important degree: the area
behind the camera, the area behind the set, and, most importantly,
those areas bordering screen space on the right and left. The upper
and lower segments are used for entrances and exits only in a few
rare shots taken from an extreme upward or downward angle or
along a staircase. I have said that these segments are "defined" by
movements into or out of frame. By that I simply mean that one
or another of the spatial segments in question takes shape in the
viewer's imagination every time an entrance or exit occurs into or
out of that segment. Toward the beginning of the film, there is a
shot in which Muffat, rushing toward Nana's dressing room, meets
young Georges, Nana's new conquest, as he leaves her dressing room
in a sort of ecstatic daze. The shot in which their paths cross is an
extremely brief one, lasting barely a second. The two men, seen in
a medium shot against a bare wall, are caught in mid-flight, Muffat
entering left and Georges right; their paths cross like two arrows,
without their even glancing at each other, and they exit on opposite

sides of the screen. The essential part of the action in this shot (the trajectories of the two men) takes place *off screen*, although in such a brief span of time—the moment preceding and following each entrance and each exit—that it borders on the instantaneous; this action *simultaneously* defines the left and right segments of off-screen space.

Renoir also attempts to use exits and entrances as a way of defining the spatial area "behind the camera" and "behind the set," a rare practice at the time *Nana* was made. He brings this area into play almost as often as he does those spatial segments contiguous to the four frame borders. Entrances and exits, through doors located near the center of the frame, preceded or followed by an empty screen, frequently occur in the film (particularly in Renoir's treatment of Nana's grand salon and boudoir). It is thus principally the *empty frame* that focuses our attention on what is occurring off screen, thereby making us aware of off-screen space, for with the screen empty there is nothing as yet (or nothing any longer) to hold the eye's attention. Of course, an exit leaving an empty frame behind makes us aware of a certain definite area of off-screen space, whereas a shot that begins with an empty frame does not always allow us to foresee which side of the screen someone will suddenly enter from or even if anyone will enter at all (as my comments on Yasujiro Ozu later in this chapter will indicate). At the same time, the principles governing matching screen direction and camera angle are of some help to us in certain cases, mainly in those involving the eventual entry into frame of a character whose direction of movement has been hinted at in an earlier shot—which in *Nana* is, however, far from always being the case. In any event, as soon as a character has actually entered the frame, his entry *retrospectively* calls to mind the existence of the spatial segment from which he emerged. Conversely, as long as the frame remains empty, all of the surrounding space is appreciably equal in potential, and the spatial segment from which the character emerges takes on *specific* existence and *primordial* importance only at the actual moment the person enters screen space.

Renoir also introduces another innovation in his use of space: His actors exit by brushing past the camera much more often than was customary in 1925, thus defining the space located behind it. More

generally, however, one might wonder how to "classify" exits *along
a diagonal*, since ordinarily access to the space behind the camera
involves passage through either right or left spatial segment, except
in the relatively rare case when the character exits "through" the
camera, blocking the lens, and then perhaps unblocking it in the
following shot as he "comes out of the other side." Probably
99 per cent of all frame exits and entrances have a *dominant
direction*, and this is obviously so in the case of any entrance or exit
that takes the form of brushing past the camera. Only a device such
as an exit through one of the frame corners in a shot taken from a
strictly vertical downward angle is really ambiguous in this respect.

There is also the case of the character's head jutting out of frame
as he stands up, whereupon he exits from the frame altogether, either
to the left or to the right; this variation, however, brings the two separate segments into play *successively*, that segment bordering the
upper frame line first, then that bordering either the left or right
frame line. Obviously any "horizontal" combination of this sort
may be used.

A second way in which a film-maker can define off-screen space
involves having a character look off screen. In *Nana*, an entire sequence or some part of it (the principal example being the scenes
at the race track) frequently starts with a close-up or a relatively
tight shot of one character addressing another who is off screen.
Sometimes the gaze of the character speaking is so intense, so fraught
with meaning, that the character off screen (and therefore the imaginary space that he occupies) becomes as important as, if not more
important than, the person who is visible in frame and the actual
screen-space. Nana's servants are constantly sticking their heads
through doors to find out what is going on in the space we cannot
see behind them, and both the invisible space thus defined and the
invisible persons who occupy it are at least as important as what
the viewer actually sees on screen. Finally, looking toward the camera
(which is not the same thing as looking directly into the lens, for this
latter sort of gaze gives the illusion of being aimed at the viewer and
not at the space behind the camera and is seldom used except in
commercials and for theatrical asides) defines the space behind the
camera where the object of this gaze presumably is located.

A third way of defining off-screen space, this time in relation to a stationary and silent shot, involves framing a character in such a way that some part of his body protrudes out of frame. The set itself, of course, extending as it necessarily does all around the frame, also brings off-screen space into play in a similar way, although in this case it is a totally nonfunctional way. Off-screen space is, after all, purely imaginary, and only something that is the particular and *principal* focus of attention can bring it into play. It is not until a disembodied hand enters the frame to pluck the egg cup out of Muffat's hands as he absentmindedly toys with it that we become consciously aware of off-screen space. Up until that moment, the Count's legs, extending out of sight beyond the lower frame-line, or the shelves that probably extend beyond to the left, do not concern us in the same way. It is important to realize that off-screen space has only an intermittent or, rather, *fluctuating* existence during any film, and structuring this fluctuation can become a powerful tool in a filmmaker's hands. Renoir was one of the first to have fully realized this. Shots in which a hand is thrust into frame occur frequently in *Nana*, as when a man's hand (his body being otherwise invisible) enters the frame to offer Nana a drink in the dance-hall scene. In a certain sense, what is involved here is a rather special case of a frame entrance. However, because much of the person's body remains off screen, the off-screen space is more emphatically present than if his entire body had suddenly appeared in frame. This third way of defining off-screen space includes yet another subdivision that is completely *static*—for instance, in the shot where Nana's head and torso are cut off vertically by the left frame line throughout her long discussion with Muffat in the dance hall.

Off-screen space may be divided into two other categories: It may be thought of as either imaginary or concrete. When the impresario's hand comes into frame to take the egg cup, the space he occupies and defines is imaginary—we do not know, for example, to whom this arm belongs. When in a subsequent shot the camera reveals the full scene, with Muffat and the impresario side by side, the space becomes concrete *retrospectively*. A similar process occurs in any situation involving the use of shot and reverse shot, with the reverse shot converting an off-screen space that was imaginary in the initial shot into concrete space. This off-screen space might conceivably remain imaginary if no wider shot, no shot taken from another angle, or no camera movement is introduced revealing the person to whom an arm belongs, to whom an off-screen glance is directed, or the exact off-screen segment toward which an exiting character has headed. (The anonymous arm in the dance-hall scene is an example, for we never see whose arm it is, or the space that this person occupies, at least not explicitly.)

By contrast, in the remarkable scene in which Vandeuvre comes to Nana to chide her for her relations with young Georges, the transition from a medium shot of the two of them sitting side by side to a long shot showing the Count sitting by himself in the same place at the extreme right of the frame evokes an off-screen space that is altogether concrete in nature, for just prior to this shot we could see that Nana was sitting less than two feet from him, just beyond the edge of the new frame. Moreover, the Count continues to look in Nana's direction and continues to talk to her, thereby causing us to be very much aware of this fragment of off-screen space. Although the Count does rise and pace back and forth frame center, his chair remains where it was, and the preceding shot had clearly established that it is next to Nana's; we therefore continue to be quite conscious of this off-screen space. But we are soon to discover that this space has undergone a change without our knowing it. We think we are quite familiar with this space; we believe we know Nana's exact position and therefore precisely which section of space off screen right she occupies as Vandeuvre strides back and forth across the carpet. He finally exits right and then joins her in the next shot, entering this space from the left; the shot reveals that Nana in the meantime has sprawled out on a couch we had not previously seen (at least not in this sequence, which amounts to the same thing, so immense is our capacity for forgetting things during a film;[1] for this reason the structuring—and restructuring —of cinematic space can be achieved only within the limits of one particular sequence). We realize in retrospect that our initial conception of this off-screen space was erroneous, that the space being established was not what we thought it was, that it was, to use the terms of this discussion, not concrete but *imaginary*.

It should be apparent by now that we are once again dealing with one of the dialectical[2] dimensions of film form. Moreover, it is of some interest to establish parallels between this kind of retrospective awareness of the true nature of off-screen space and the delayed awareness of the spatiotemporal nature of a match. It is a dialectic in which a number of extremely complex possibilities are implicit, particularly when we consider that not only does the use of such devices as movements into or out of frame, off-screen glances, and partial framing (or the use of any two or three of these simultaneously) determine whether the space in question is imaginary or concrete but also that this space can be either predictive and imaginary or retrospective and concrete (through the use of spatial "ellipses" similar to the one just described in *Nana*, for instance), all quite independently of the spatial segment or segments actually brought into play, this latter factor multiplying the possibilities enormously in and of itself. But this ambiguity can also apply to the relationship of screen space and off-screen space itself. It is possible to see off-screen space without our being aware that it is off screen (as when the camera is aimed at a mirror with the mirror frame not visible), realizing that fact only after the camera pans or after someone in frame has moved. It is also possible to assume that someone or something present in a previous shot is somewhere off screen in the shot we are now viewing, whereas the person or object is actually in frame, but concealed by the play of shadows or colors (examples may be found in Ozu's *Duckweed Story* and Valerio Zurlini's *Cronaca familiare*). Obviously this happens relatively rarely and involves a paradox, almost a play on words (it being by definition impossible to "see" off-screen space). But it is important to be aware that inversions of this sort are possible (although perhaps occurring in some other form), because this helps establish the limits within which this particular parameter can evolve.

One might perhaps wonder what purpose an analysis of the kind I am undertaking can possibly have. Even if it is readily conceded that systematic oppositions of off-screen and screen space constituted one of Renoir's essential tools and that a film made over forty years ago is a success largely because of this opposition, any attempted classification of the possible relationships between these two kinds of space is nonetheless apt to be considered sterile and pedantic today. Have I not simply been describing how *every* film is made? Any film, admittedly, employs movements into and out of frame; any film, admittedly, suggests an opposition between screen space and off-screen

space through the use of such devices as off-screen glances, the shot
and the reverse shot, partially out-of-frame actors, and so on. Yet,
from *Nana* on, only very few directors (the greatest ones) have used
this implicit dialectic as an explicit means of structuring a whole
film.

At this point a clarification is in order. If *Nana* seems such an important film today, it is not merely because it marks the beginning
of the extensive use of off-screen space but, more importantly, because it marks the first *structural* use of it. For many years the silent
film regarded as using off-screen space most significantly was Ewald
André Dupont's *Variety*. Why? Because during a fight scene that
soon became famous, Emil Jannings and his rival roll on the ground,
leaving the screen momentarily empty. A hand with a knife in it
then enters the frame from below and immediately plunges out of
frame again to deliver the fatal blow. Jannings then rises up and into
frame all by himself . . . and several generations of film historians
applauded this "magnificent understatement." From that moment
on, off-screen space came to be used almost exclusively as a way of
suggesting events when directors felt that simply showing them directly would be too facile. Erected into a veritable aesthetic system,
this principle was carried to its ultimate limits in Nicholas Ray's
first (and best) film, *They Live by Night*. In this gangster movie, all
violence systematically occurred off screen or was simply "elided,"
thus creating what was undeniably a very odd sort of "intense understatement." However, this rather crude distinction between what
is actually visible and what is left unseen utterly fails to take into account the complex vectors that *directional* and *diversified* oppositions
between screen space and off-screen space can provide in the way of
an aesthetic tool, as certain other directors had discovered.

Yasujiro Ozu, one of the greatest of pre–World War II Japanese
directors, was the first film-maker after Renoir to have understood
how important the existence of two distinct kinds of space is. He
was also perhaps the first director to have really understood the
value of the empty screen and the tensions that result from leaving
it empty.

Although Renoir often has his actors in *Nana* move into or out of
an empty shot, the screen remains empty for no more than a few
frames, just long enough for the actor to make a definite entrance or

exit. A certain visual monotony admittedly results from Renoir's frequent use of this technique, even though its repeated use does play a primary structural role in this masterpiece, as I have already pointed out. Ozu was doubtless the first to vary the *relative length of time* in which the screen was left empty, sometimes leaving it empty before an entrance, but more frequently after an exit. He began to use this procedure extensively in his last silent film, *Duckweed Story* (1935), and, even more importantly, in his first sound film and masterpiece, *The Only Son* (1936). It unfortunately became a kind of tic in many of the last works of his old age, which are, on the whole, more academic and stilted than his earlier, prewar films.

In *The Only Son*, the empty screen is used as a means of creating a whole maze of off-screen spaces, often made concrete in an entirely original way by showing some purely decorative, almost abstract, nonlocalized detail within the set or location, these shots generally occurring just after someone has exited from a shot or before a character enters the next shot. Ozu's use of this technique reaches a pinnacle in a relatively wide-angle shot (about a medium shot), following a perfectly conventional dialogue scene, in which the camera focuses on a fairly nondescript corner of the set for nearly a minute! Throughout this prolonged shot, a series of discrete off-screen sounds suggests all sorts of vaguely possible off-screen action, finally modulating into the noise of a factory and bringing on the next scene, which takes place in a vacant lot next to the factory whence the sounds are coming. This amazing shot quite clearly illustrates a basic principle: The longer the screen remains empty, the greater the resulting tension between screen space and off-screen space and the greater the attention concentrated on off-screen space as against screen space (the time required to exhaust our attention depending on how simple a scene the screen shows, a perfectly black or white screen constituting the obvious limit). Throughout *The Only Son* and his other films immediately following it, Ozu uses this tension as a variable parameter, the duration of empty screen shots varying from several twenty-fourths of a second to quite a few seconds. The variations in tension thus created provide him with a formal means of structuring his *découpage*. Their range is enormous and perfectly perceptible to the practiced eye.

Another film-maker for whom the empty screen and the off-screen space it establishes have a crucial importance is Robert Bresson. This is particularly obvious in A Man Escaped and Pickpocket. The shot in A Man Escaped in which Fontaine kills the sentry is a quite striking example. A rather tight shot shows Fontaine in three-quarter profile hugging the wall just short of the corner, on the other side of which the sentry is standing. Mustering all his courage, Fontaine moves forward, exits frame right, immediately circles around and re-enters, crosses the frame again, and re-exits to the left just beyond the corner of the wall. The screen now remains empty and quite neutral as the sentry is presumably killed (there is no sound from off screen, however), and then Fontaine enters once again.[3] Just as in the shot where Georges and Muffat cross each other's path in Nana, what we have here is a situation that essentially depends on bringing off-screen space into play, but in a complex and "syncopated" manner. This and other similar uses of off-screen space might be ascribed to Bresson's alleged reluctance to show distasteful scenes, but, as Au Hasard Balthazar and Mouchette have demonstrated, in actual fact he is not all that squeamish, and plastic values have always been the crucial ones determining his use of a technique, as is amply proved by the manner in which he organized the movements into and out of frame in this particular shot.

In Pickpocket the empty screen plays a much broader role. Here, Bresson achieves what might be called an orchestration of space, rigorously controlling the moments when the screen is left empty and the duration of these moments and establishing the precise extent of the surrounding off-screen space through his use of sound (the shots in which the pickpocket leaves his room, then exits from frame, with the sound of his footsteps then being heard as he makes his way down the stairs come particularly to mind).

Generally speaking, there are cases, especially in the silent film, where the relative length of time during which the screen is left vacant either before or after an exit or entrance itself determines, independently of sound, how large an area of off-screen space is established, even though this off-screen space may never actually be seen. The same holds true for the glance of anyone in frame looking toward someone off screen, whether the latter is standing still or moving. Off-screen sound, however, always brings off-screen space into play, regardless of whether or not it occurs in conjunction with any of the spatial modalities thus far described. When sound alone is involved, either as background noise, music, or an off-screen voice coming from an undetermined direction, it brings the surrounding space as a whole into play. Even when there is no indication of the *direction* a sound is coming from (and today, of course, stereophonic sound, on a strictly auditory level, provides *some* indication of direction), we are able to tell approximately how far away it is, and this *distance* factor provides yet another parameter, though it is one that as yet has seldom been explored.

Thus, whether through the use of sound, through the variation of the length of time the screen is left empty, or by means of off-screen glances, it is possible not only to bring now one and now another of the six spatial segments into play but also to indicate the extent of the off-screen space. The "unit" for measuring it, though indirect, is quite precise: One may not be able to determine that an off-screen actor is exactly thirty feet from the frame line, but it can be determined that it takes him four seconds, or else twenty frames, to reach it, and that fact makes it possible to control this particular parameter.

Michelangelo Antonioni is another great orchestrator of movements into and out of frame, particularly in his first film, which remains his masterpiece, *Cronaca di un amore*. It has often been noted that there are only two hundred or so separate shots in the entire film; most of them are very long, and all of them give proof of an absolutely unprecedented degree of visual organization. The principal structural factor in the film is movements into and out of frame, used mainly for rhythmic effect but also serving to bring into play, in an extremely complex manner, the spatial segments immediately adjacent to the frame lines, particularly those on the right and left. The bridge party sequence comprising two or three shots and running for some three minutes is built around Clara's repeated entries and exits, on the one hand, and those of a plump, ludicrous-looking woman with her dog cuddled in her arms, on the other. Because of the camera movements and the characters' movements off screen, these entrances and exits always occur at unexpected places and unexpected moments. In other sequences of the film, Antonioni often prolongs an exit by having someone on screen look off screen in the direction of a person who has just left, thereby bringing that segment of off-screen space to life. This is especially true in the admirable sequence shot of the lovers as they plan the murder on the bridge, a sort of elaborate circular pan, the lovers entering and exiting in turn, with these movements into and out of frame occurring at constantly varying distances from the camera, thus creating a hallucinatory rhythm underscoring the nature of the quarrel between the lovers, which simultaneously separates them and binds them together.

In his later films, Antonioni uses the empty frame quite extensively, in a manner somewhat reminiscent of Bresson. In *La Notte*, however, he introduces on several occasions a totally novel technique, whereby the "real" dimensions of whatever is visible on the empty screen are impossible to determine until the appearance of a human figure makes the scale obvious. As the husband goes up to the floor of the apartment building he lives on, for instance, the first thing we see is some kind of corrugated surface, the actual size of which is impossible to determine. When he then steps into the shot through the elevator door (which is not identifiable as such before it opens), his entrance not only leads to a change in the nature of the off-screen space (the spatial segment "behind the set" being specifically brought into play), but also modifies the actual area defined by the shot, for the space suddenly proves to be much smaller in scale and the camera much closer than had been apparent when the screen was still empty. Later, lying stretched out on a couch waiting for his wife to return, Marcello Mastroianni raises his eyes and looks out of the window (off screen). A shot of some sort of rectangular surface follows. His previous eye movements suggest that this surface, of as yet undetermined scale, is something he is looking at through the window, but when Jeanne Moreau walks into this new shot at the very bottom of the frame she looks very tiny. We then realize that the rectangular surface is actually the huge façade of some windowless, multistoried building. These two instances in which the awareness of the true scale of a shot does not occur until some time after it has begun are obviously analogous to the examples of the "retroactive" or "deferred" match described in Chapter 1.

A third method used by Renoir as a means of linking together screen space and off-screen space consists of framing only a part of an actor's body. This technique has become banal today as a way of situating a reverse angle shot (for instance, the back of a head on the edge of the screen); but, at the same time, the Japanese in particular have used it to create admirable effects of composition, obviously inspired by traditional Japanese graphic art.[4]

One other problem we must consider is camera movement, deliberately left for the last here, because it is much more resistant to analysis in terms of "two kinds of space" than are static shots. To return to *Nana*, there are, as I have already pointed out, only a half dozen or so camera movements in the entire film; therefore, their appearance tends in each instance to be a very special occasion. Only in two cases, however, do they seem to have been explicitly conceived of in terms of relating on-screen space to off-screen space. The first instance is a long dolly backward, starting from the pillows on Nana's bed,[5] with the camera gradually revealing her enormous boudoir as it backs away, off-screen space being involved here precisely because the function of the shot is to reveal the part of the room that was initially invisible. The second instance is the shot in which the camera tilts slowly up from Muffat's legs to reveal his full torso as he discovers Georges's dead body.

Any camera movement obviously converts off-screen space into screen space or vice versa. This is not the essential purpose, however, of all camera movement. It is often used to create what is essentially a *static composition* around one or several moving actors, as in the shot in Orson Welles's *Othello* in which the camera dollies backward following Iago and Othello as they walk on the ramparts, off-screen space coming into play only when Iago gets ahead of Othello and exits before him.

It is perhaps because the Russians, Alexander Dovzhenko in particular, sensed the multiple implications present in camera movements (only two of their many possible functions have been illustrated) that in some of their films they severely limited them and thereby made their use all the more striking. In Dovzhenko's *Earth* the few camera movements perceptible as such involve only slight "nudges" of the camera, which very explicitly reveal an off-screen space directly adjacent to the space in the original composition. I feel that, if a rigorously dialectical relationship between off-screen space and screen space is to be created, camera movements should participate in it in the manner suggested by the early Russians. Not that camera movements need always be as rare as they are in *Earth* (or in *Nana*), nor need they always participate in the spatial dialectic—thus suggesting yet another possible dialectic, that between camera movements that actually participate in the creation of some relationship between the two kinds of space and those that do not.

It is interesting to compare this notion of placing striking limitations on the use of camera movement with the formal conception underlying that other masterpiece of the French silent film, Marcel L'Herbier's *L'Argent*. This film, made in 1927, was the first to systematically use camera movement to establish the basic rhythm of the film's *découpage*, thereby anticipating by twenty years Welles's and Antonioni's film styles at their most sophisticated. Enormous stylized sets designed by Lazare Meerson invite L'Herbier's camera to dolly around frequently, unfolding new vistas of off-screen space at every turn. Spatially, the film is in a constant state of flux; this, plus the fact that the editing of the film is fully as rigorous as the camera handling, gives it an altogether original dynamic dimension. And, though I persist in believing that an analysis of camera movement in terms of the "two kinds of space" is scarcely an easy task, a close reading of *L'Argent* might perhaps provide a key.

As we have seen, the possibilities of articulating the relationships between screen space and off-screen space in an orderly fashion, of organizing them structurally above and beyond the simple orchestration of movements into and out of frame (which in itself is very seldom attempted), are even more complex than were the possibilities implicit in the structuring of the spatiotemporal articulations between shots. These possibilities become even more complex when we consider that the articulations of imaginary and concrete space described above also have a part to play. The analysis herein of this vital parameter has perhaps not been as exhaustive as that of the types of shot transitions. Nevertheless, the two types of space could conceivably be articulated in accordance with the same "para-serial" principles applicable to shot changes (repetition, alternation, elimination, progressive proliferation, and so on). Although it is true that a thoroughgoing and fully organic structuring of an entire film on the basis of these principles exists at present only as a theoretical possibility, the work of a Bresson or an Antonioni[6] already indicates that someday such a plastic organization will no longer be a purely speculative notion.

Notes

1. And my own capacity for making up things after the film is over. A student of mine has recently pointed out that the scene is much simpler than this, that in fact Nana never moves. I have left this false description in nevertheless, as the idea it illustrates still seems to me important, and as I am sure one could find—or make!—a sequence to bear it out. (See also the false example from Bresson's *A Man Escaped* in this same chapter.)

2. My notion of a dialectical film form developed several years before I had read Eisenstein's essential text "A Dialectical Approach to Film Form" in *Film Form*. Rather than cross swords with those Marxian film specialists who have upbraided me for my "irresponsible" use of the dialectical idea, I refer them to Eisenstein's analysis.

3. This description too is completely inaccurate. Fontaine actually only exits from frame once. I became aware of this during a re-viewing of the film just before submitting the final draft of the French manuscript. I nevertheless decided to leave this passage unchanged, thereby providing a deliberate example (there are doubtless inadvertent examples elsewhere in the text) of the viewer's faulty recollection of a film, a phenomenon quite intimately related to the way in which he perceives a film, which is a subject that deserves thorough study in itself. Aside from the problems it can create for a critic or analyst of films, I would like to point out the very positive effect this sort of faulty recollection can have on the creative faculty. The shot as it is described here does in fact exist in a short film made by myself, in which I incorporated the shot, as I remembered it, as an "homage" to Bresson.

4. Some compositions of this sort (the love scenes in *Hiroshima mon amour* and *Une Femme mariée*, for example) bring off-screen space into play only to a very slight degree (more so, however, than if the whole body were visible in frame). Moreover, there could conceivably be similar situations in which the viewer's awareness of off-screen space is momentarily intensified by having one of these "sculptural fragments" suddenly move, leaving the frame entirely, or having the rest of the body move into frame with it— which suggests yet another dialectical possibility.

5. These pillows are first seen in a mask shot that opens out as the dolly begins. The mask shot and the iris, even though infrequently used nowadays (see, however, François Truffaut's *Jules and Jim* and Charles Laughton's *The Night of the Hunter*), provide a very interesting way of transforming certain sections of screen space into off-screen space. In the light of the dialectical perspective proposed here, these techniques might recover their rightful place.

6. One might also add Vera Chytilova's admirable *O necem j iném (Something Different)*; this film would have provided just as apt a chapter title as Renoir's *Nana*.

3

Editing as a Plastic Art

Thus far, I have examined the general nature of a filmed image and the articulations between such images without really considering what they actually look like. While still maintaining my "structural" approach, I might now examine both the image and the shot transition as concrete visual phenomena.

The Screen Image

I might first venture to point out how the way in which we see differs from the way in which a camera sees, an ambitious and somewhat risky endeavor, which many others, notably Karel Reisz in his excellent *Technique of Film Editing*,[1] have undertaken before me. However, since I am attempting to redefine the components of film form, I cannot avoid dealing with this particular problem, despite the difficulty involved.

We may approach it by considering a phenomenon that occurs as frequently in film as in real life: reflections on a glass surface. Let us see what the top of a pinball machine looks like when viewed from an angle. If the intensity of light on both sides of the sheet of glass is more or less equal, we will have no trouble making out what is taking place below it, and, if we are absorbed in a game in progress, we will see only that game; the glass will seem perfectly transparent. If, however, it should occur to us to examine the sheet of glass more objectively, we will notice that a reflection of the surroundings is superimposed on our view of the game going on underneath it, that both images are more or less equal in intensity, and that if the reflected image of the surroundings is at all complex the game in progress under the glass surface will now strike us as being practically "illegible." It is actually an unconscious mental process (selection) and a physiological process (focusing the eye) that enable us to differentiate successfully the two superimposed images, rejecting the one that does not interest us.

Let us now film this same situation without taking any special precautions. The resulting film image will show these two images superimposed, and when this superimposition is projected on the screen, we would succeed in eliminating the image that in principle does not interest us only with the greatest difficulty. The image of the game in progress beneath the glass would have become absolutely "illegible." If we wish to re-create the same effect we experienced watching the scene with the naked eye, we must attach a polarizing filter to the front of the lens to tone down the reflection or mask the reflected background, if this is possible.

Why is it impossible to distinguish between these two images once they have been captured on film and projected on a screen? This is because everything projected on a film screen has exactly the same intrinsic "reality," the same "presence." Once projected on the flat surface of the screen, the two superimposed images become one and indissoluble, mainly because the screen has only two dimensions and therefore any shape projected on it is equally "present," just as much "before our eyes" as any other shape. Even the parts of the image that are out of focus are perceived as quite distinct, visible, tangible entities, as what might be called "clumps of fuzziness." Another example might clarify this even further. Let us consider the following situation: While setting up a shot, a director of photography notices that there is a lamp or some other prop behind an actor, perhaps even several yards behind him, but just above his head. Even if the object in the background is going to be shown in such soft focus that its contours will be very indistinct, the director of photography will insist that the lamp be moved, because it will seem to be growing out of the actor's head. And he is quite right. Were we to be confronted with the same scene in life or were we to stand in the same place as the camera, we would not be at all disconcerted by the lamp; it would not strike us as being some monstrous excrescence; we would probably not even notice it. Yet, on the screen, this juxtaposition of objects would immediately leap to the eye, for when we view a screen we see everything at once; every form and every contour seems equally prominent visually (while sometimes we are completely oblivious to the head of a person sitting just in front of us and blocking as much as a fourth of that same screen!). Because of this fact, the problem of "legibility" arises more commonly and above all in more specific terms when we are observing a film image than when we are observing a real-life situation.

Our contention that all the elements in any given film image are perceived as equal in importance obviously runs counter to a fondly cherished notion of nineteenth-century art critics later embraced by a number of twentieth-century photographers: the belief that the eye explores a framed image according to a fixed itinerary, focusing first on a supposed "center of compositional focus" (generally determined by the time-honored "golden rectangle"), then traveling through the composition along a path supposedly determined by the disposition of its dominant lines. Eisenstein himself was quite taken with this notion, and the visual portion of his analysis of the introduction to the battle on the ice in *Alexander Nevsky* is based on this supposition. Such a conception is as outdated in art criticism today as composition according to the golden rectangle is in the art of painting. Even if the nineteenth-century eye did indeed see things in this way, the modern eye apparently does not. Any film image obviously includes some elements that call attention to themselves more strongly than others do, a case in point being that someone who is speaking will generally be noticed first. This is indeed true, but we are nonetheless also aware of the compositional whole, of which the person speaking is but a part, and we are aware in particular of the actual rectangular frame, even if the background of the image is uniformly black, white, or gray. For to "look" has to do with a mental process, whereas to "see" has to do with the physiology of the eye. And, when we view a film, as when we view a painting or a photograph, *seeing* is no longer dependent on *looking*, as is nearly always the case in a real-life situation; the selectivity involved in looking no longer affects the nonselectivity involved in seeing in the slightest.[2]

For all this to be the case, there is, however, one essential condition: The viewer must be seated at the proper distance from the screen. If he is too close, so close that his field of vision does not include the whole screen, his eyes must change focus as the centers of visual interest shift, and he will never be able to grasp the total visual effect created by the framed image. If, on the other hand, he is too far away, the image will be so schematic that he will see only these centers of interest, within a frame that is smaller than that seen in the view-finder by the film-maker when he shot it (the view-finder image, we must remember, takes in the eye's whole field of vision), and the initial principles underlying the composition will thus be distorted (just as in painting, a particular composition cannot be successfully executed on every scale, each composition seemingly having a scale best suited to it). With these as well as other considerations being taken into account, it has been mathematically determined that the optimum viewing distance is approximately two times the width of the screen. The fact that under present circumstances it is quite impossible for every viewer in a theater to be at that precise distance from the screen (nor even within a reasonable approximation of it) does nothing to invalidate this principle, but simply indicates that the movie theaters of the future will have to be built differently.[3]

Once a film-maker has become aware of the nature of the film image, as outlined here, what conclusions should he draw? First, to state the obvious, the frame must always be conceived of as a total composition. Yet the possible ways of composing any given shot are as various as the temperaments of individual film-makers, and the problem of composition in general is beyond the scope of this book. On the other hand, a far smaller number of film-makers are aware of, let alone concerned with, the possibility—or even the obligation, if they are at all sensitive to the imperative need to deal organically with the raw materials of film-making—of organizing the transitions —that is, the articulations between shots as a function of the total composition of each successive shot—thereby creating a structural framework capable of incorporating the formal elements discussed thus far as well as those to be dealt with in future chapters.

Static Articulations

Generally speaking, the first film-maker to concern himself with abstract cinematic form as concretely embodied in "figurative" film-making was Sergei Eisenstein. And he is also one of the relatively few film-makers to have actually set down his formal preoccupations in writing.

Eisenstein's analysis of his first masterpiece, *The Battleship Potemkin*, emphasizes the film's over-all structure, based on the five-act pattern of classical tragedy, on poetic caesura, and on the golden rectangle, first of all; then, taking the well-known Odessa steps sequence of the film as his example, he discusses the plastic organization attained through editing.

The editing of this sequence, Eisenstein tells us, is based on oppositions between the dynamic content of the various shots (rapid movements as against slow movements, ascending movements as against descending movements) and on oppositions between shot sizes (and therefore between the number of objects and people included in each shot). The altogether extraordinary aesthetic tension of this historic film sequence is created through the interplay of these formal contrasts.

When he analyzes the religious procession in *The General Line*, Eisenstein introduces a new concept, which he calls "polyphonic montage," a kind of musical interweaving of the different "voices" of the sequence (enthusiasm, ecstasy, shots of men singing, shots of women singing); variations in shot size are also involved.

One of Eisenstein's greatest discoveries, which, however, he appears to have written about only incidentally, is his approach to editing as a function of the composition of each successive shot, particularly in situations involving a series of shots showing the same subject from a number of different angles.

To understand what this entails, we have only to recall a school of painting that originated only a few years before Eisenstein shifted his artistic preoccupations from painting to theater and cinema. I am referring, of course, to Cubism, and more particularly to an aspect of Cubist experimentation best typified, perhaps, in the various studies of stringed instruments undertaken by Juan Gris around 1912 (although examples from Italian futurism would also be relevant here). If we examine a painting such as *Violin and Guitar* (1913), we find that what may be regarded as the central motif is made up of three tightly "framed" representations of the fingerboard and, between two of these, a "close-up" of the sounding-board. And, while it would be greatly oversimplified to reduce the painting to this multiple view of an object, to the extent that this motif *is* that, it may be regarded as a premonitory illustration of the aesthetic strategy involved in cutting together shots of the same subject from different angles, as Eisenstein was to develop it some ten years later. Now, it may be postulated that part of the pleasure afforded by the Gris painting derives, not from simply seeing an object depicted from several viewpoints simultaneously, but rather from the process by which the eye compares each aspect with the others, identifying "objectively" common features in their new perceptual guise, setting differences against similarities—in short, discovering continuity in discontinuity, and vice versa. Now, because of the way in which the eye remembers shapes, two shots of the same subject taken from two different angles can result in the same sort of aesthetic satisfaction when they are intercut. More specifically, variations in contours or areas from one shot to the next—relative to the fixed coordinates provided by the frame lines—can set up a play of tensions and permutations that will be highly satisfying to the eye, thanks to their complexity and coherence, and also quite capable of being structured.

That there is a structural potential here is quite evident, though we must admit that the above-mentioned satisfaction is rather vague in nature. That this sort of pleasure does correspond to quite concrete factors seems to be confirmed by the existence of the so-called thirty-degree rule. This rule, empirically established during the 1920's, has it that any new angle on the same camera subject must differ from the previous angle by at least thirty degrees.[4] Film-makers had noticed that any angle change of less than thirty degrees (and thus not counting moving the camera closer or farther away with no change of angle—what the British call a "concertina") resulted in a "jump" that made the viewer vaguely uncomfortable. This feeling of malaise is doubtless due to the tenuous, ill-defined character of such a cut; the new shot is not sufficiently distinct from the preceding one, especially if both are taken from similar camera-subject distances. Yet one could just as easily say that this discomfort results from the utter visual pointlessness of this kind of cut, that the viewer's feeling of vague annoyance stems mainly from the fact that his eye is frustrated, for it demands that, if there is any change at all in the configuration that it sees, this change must be a noticeable one and the resulting tensions must be pronounced and obvious.

We might briefly point out that, although this rule teaches us something very important about the nature of a shot change, it nonetheless is not sacrosanct; changing the angle by less than thirty degrees has already become part of the modern film-maker's vocabulary, for, as we have already indicated in our discussion of eye-line matches and screen-direction matches, malaise or discomfort can provide an altogether useful element of tension, as is demonstrated by Godard's *Breathless* and many of Sam Fuller's films, which abound in jump cuts, usually occurring at moments of extreme violence.

We have said that Eisenstein was probably the first film-maker to have conceived of frame composition as a function of the over-all relationship between a film's separate images. In *October*, the series of low angle shots of the cathedral towers consists of simple reversals of diagonal lines, while the sequence of the suspended bicycles employs a simple but very attractive set of variations on gleaming round forms set against a black background. *The General Line* contains a series of ultra-rapid flashes of the cream-separator's spout creating spatial relationships that are somewhat more complex in nature, involving contrasts between the spout seen with a more or less pronounced degree of foreshortening and the same spout seen "undistorted" in full profile. Equally effective albeit more elementary are the multiple reversals of direction of a train of carts being towed through the fields by the all-powerful tractor. But perhaps the most perfect example of this method of spatial recomposition is to be found in the opening sequence of Eisenstein's suppressed film *Bezhin Meadow*. The sequence centers around the body of a dead woman lying prone on a cart as her son weeps for her and the father stands looking on. Each of the elements of this "tableau" recurs in every succeeding shot, yet they have been so radically rearranged each time they reappear as to constitute a totally new variation on the initial space. Unfortunately, it is quite impossible to analyze this sequence in great detail, for the film has come down to us only in the form of the frame enlargements that are all that remain of it. Yet we may still perhaps regard it as Eisenstein's mature achievement in this particular direction. *Ivan the Terrible,* on the other hand, contains interesting contrasts of a quite different sort. The scene in which the boyars are waiting for news of Ivan's hoped-for death opens with three close-in shots of small groups of anxious faces. In the background of each shot is the same brightly lighted icon, differently placed in the frame. There is similarity of composition with respect to the figures, dissimilarity with respect to the icon. It is fairly clear that these shots in no way "match" among themselves (the relative positions of the figures and the icon have obviously been tampered with to achieve satisfactory recombinations from shot to shot). Such tampering violates one of the sacrosanct rules of spatial "continuity," and usually it results in that sense of disorientation and malaise that we have discussed. But this is not at all the case here. Why? Simply because Eisenstein has here managed to create a very unusual sort of cinematic space: It exists only in terms of the totality of shots included in the sequence;[5] we no longer have any sense of a surrounding space endowed with independent existence from which a sequence of shots has somehow been excerpted. Rather, we see a space that exists in the same many-faceted, complex way that Braque's billiard table exists; we see a setting that is the sum total of all the perspectives of it embodied in the successive shots, a setting whose cohesion is created by the harmonious articulation of the shots. This obviously is a rare and difficult achievement. Several similar "bad" matches in Ivan's "death chamber" used for analogous compositional reasons (they stem mainly from a concern with the pictorial harmony of each individual shot) merely create a feeling that something is "wrong." The spatial unity of the room is too definitely established before and after these isolated matches for us to feel that they are anything but gratuitous violations of that unity. Yet the previously described shots of the boyars show the way, suggesting how shot spaces can be coherently articulated so that space becomes "open," and proving that the more carefully planned the permutations of objects from shot to shot are, the more apparent this "openness" will be.

Akira Kurosawa is one of a number of contemporary film-makers who have been strongly influenced by this concept. This is most clearly apparent in the first part of his remarkable *High and Low*. For about an hour, the action unfolds almost entirely within a rich industrialist's bay-windowed living room, where a manhunt for the kidnaper of the son of the industrialist's chauffeur is being organized. The wide screen serves to emphasize the principle of visual organization implicit in most of the "matches," based as they are on constant variations in the screen positions of the many characters from one shot to the next: the industrialist, his family, his servants, and police officers, present either all together or by turns in the room. These permutations, moreover, are often combined with a process of selection. In a first shot we might have, for instance, from left to right, characters A, B, C, and D. In the succeeding shot, by choosing the proper camera angle and tampering a bit with actual positions, we might have D at the extreme left of the screen, B at the extreme right, and everyone else off-screen. C, B, and A might then reappear in the subsequent shot in this new order from left to right, and so on. Kurosawa's treatment of people as *interchangeable units*, a conception that goes far beyond the conventional notions of matching screen positions, allows a rather elaborate, almost serial organization of shots, an organization that provides the actual spoken dialogue as it unfolds with a base line, so to speak, either underlining it or counterpointing it in a manner that might be described as dialectical.

Let us go back in film history once again and refer to yet another example of a visual organization based on the permutability of similar or identical shapes—in this case again the human body, which functions as a constant, regardless of what individual character is on screen at any given moment. This principle of organization can be seen in the first part of *Boule de suif*, Mikhail Romm's first film (1934), set entirely within a particularly restricted space, the inside of a stagecoach. In order, doubtless, to avoid the visual monotony inherent in such a situation as this, where half a dozen people are riveted to their seats carrying on a conversation (which, moreover, is soundless, since this is one of the last films of the silent era), Romm relies on a *découpage* in which very few shots are ever repeated, in itself a remarkable achievement and one that reveals how aware Romm was of the need for a constant variation of visual space. Not only does he constantly vary the identity, size, eye-line direction, and number of faces in each shot; he also continually counterpoints faces shown in sharp focus and faces shown in soft focus: At times a face shown in close-up, screen right, may be in sharp focus while two faces in the background remain in soft focus, at times a face in the background in the center of the frame may be in sharp focus while two faces only partly in frame are in soft focus, and so on. The variations that may result when this parameter interacts with the four cited above are obviously enormous, and Romm takes full advantage of them.[6]

Thus far I have discussed only the visual relationships between shots involving an actual cut, situations, that is, in which our eye recalls what it saw in shot A and compares it with what it sees in shot B; the structural tensions that result from such a comparison provide the essential justification for this type of editing. A dissolve, however, is fundamentally no different as a visual entity; it merely provides a slightly different way of juxtaposing two spatial compositions, for the momentary superposition of two images concretizes a visual relationship similar in most respects to the "imaginary" relationship existing between two shots linked by a straight cut. This fact is often forgotten now that the dissolve has become a "punctuation mark" capable of linking any two shots together so as to indicate the passage of time. However, such use of the dissolve is in fact a relatively recent convention.

When the dissolve was first discovered in the early years of silent film, it was used more freely; it rarely had any specific "meaning" and was hardly ever employed to indicate the passage of time. Because there were titles for that very purpose, dissolves were not needed. For many years in the silent era, dissolves were used as a means of securing a "soft transition" from a close-up to a long shot (or vice versa) within a single perfectly continuous sequence. More generally speaking, they were used to create plastic, rhythmic, or poetic effects (Abel Gance, Germaine Dulac, Jean Epstein, and Marcel L'Herbier providing notable examples of this). Even after the introduction of sound the dissolve continued to be used in a very free way for a variety of purposes. In *Applause* (1929), for example, Rouben Mamoulian used dissolves as a way of getting from a shot of a character on the telephone to a shot of the person on the other end of the line. It was not until a number of years later that the current convention whereby a dissolve invariably indicates a passage of time became firmly established.[7]

Several contemporary young directors have recently reacted against the overfacile use of this convention and simply eliminated dissolves altogether in many of their films (Godard, Resnais, Hanoun). Bresson, on the other hand, while seemingly continuing to assign a conventional meaning to dissolves, in fact uses them as a structural element, as both a rhythmic and a plastic entity, thereby adopting the silent film-makers' freer approach. What strikes one in this respect in his *Diary of a Country Priest*, *A Man Escaped*, and *Pickpocket* is Bresson's concern with making the dissolve into an autonomous formal device, using it as a means of concretizing the relationship between two compositions based on the same or identical materials as well as that between shots based on completely dissimilar materials. In *Pickpocket* particularly, the differences in angles from which the hand is seen stealing into a pocket as one image dissolves into another and the way in which the position of the hand shifts in the frame from one shot to the next are only a further development of the kind of editing discovered by Eisenstein and explored by Romm, Kurosawa, and others. There is, of course, an important difference in rhythm between a dissolve and a cut: In a dissolve, the superposition is not instantaneous and "imaginary" but occurs over a span of several seconds; it is less abrupt, flows more easily, and, above all, "occurs before our very eyes." But, on one level of phenomenological analysis, they are identical.

Before abandoning this discussion of the possible relationships created through "static matches," a word might be added about the juxtaposition of two totally dissimilar shots—two shots, that is, that have no similar visual elements. Is it possible to structure such a relationship other than "semiotically"? The problem involved here is a very delicate one. I feel that any plastic relationship resulting from the juxtaposition of two shots of this sort can be discussed only in terms of specific instances and cannot be analyzed in general terms, even in the vague way used above to analyze the possible articulations between shots that include some common elements. This is, however, a problem that every film-maker should be aware of and seek to resolve in his own particular fashion, even if only in a purely empirical and practical way.

Dynamic Articulations

In the preceding pages of this chapter I have restricted myself to a discussion of the possible ways of creating graphic relationships between shots that are essentially static at the moment that the cut is made. But one can also cut, of course, from one shot to the next when some essential part of one or the other of them is in motion. Is it possible to organize this type of shot change, either independently of the types of structures to which two completely static shots lend themselves or in conjunction with them? The principles governing these types of structures should be equally applicable to any two shots containing moving elements. The actors' movements in Kurosawa's *High and Low*, for instance, do not affect the structural principles previously outlined at all.

Once again, Eisenstein was the first to be concerned with this aspect of "dynamic cutting." We have already seen that one of the basic structural elements of the Odessa steps sequence in *The Battleship Potemkin* is the contrast between ascending and descending movements. In this case, however, the directions of real movements and of these movements as they appear on the screen correspond; the ascending movements of the people of Odessa making their way up and the descending movements of the soldiers coming down the steps are both filmed in such a way that these respective directions are faithfully reproduced on the screen.[8] In *Strike*, on the other hand, there is a series of shots showing how a group of mischievous workers send the spying foreman sprawling with a nudge from a heavy wheel dangling from the end of a crane. In the first shot the wheel swings from right to left; a second shot shows the same wheel moving in the opposite direction, and the foreman's fall is likewise seen from opposite angles. Eisenstein was well aware that this was a rather radical violation of the principles governing matching screen direction, but he nonetheless felt the need for linking these shots together in this way, without the insertion of cutaways, because of the aesthetic effect, the feeling of jarring, violent speed that results from this match.

Although an isolated instance at that period, it nevertheless pointed the way to the structures that might result from changing the screen direction of movements that are quite obviously continuous in what is supposedly the "reality" being filmed. In modern cinema, a striking example of a sequence of shots based on this principle occurs at the beginning of Jean-Pierre Melville's *Bob le flambeur*. Bob enters the Place Pigalle early in the morning, and, as he walks through it, he is seen from several very different angles, each shot including a municipal water-sprinkling truck making its way around the square. Owing to the difference in angles, the sprinkler's direction of movement is not at all the same from shot to shot: At times it moves from left to right, at times from right to left, at times away from the camera, at times toward the camera, and the beauty of the sequence stems directly from this broken pattern, from these apparent shifts in screen movement as opposed to the real (or supposedly real—here too one must often cheat) trajectory that we automatically reconstruct in our minds. The apparent implication here is that a film audience's perception has somehow evolved from the time in which a change in screen direction was automatically equated with a change in real direction, a reaction that brought about the "rule" governing matching screen directions. In actual fact, however, the situation is not that simple. Just as *Ivan the Terrible* contains, as I have pointed out, apparent mismatches in screen position that perform a plastic function (and therefore do not "bother" us), as well as other matches that are jolting, so too "mismatches" in screen direction are a "valid" technique only when the accompanying sense of disorientation results in a perceptible structure. In the brilliant nymphomaniac sequence in *La Notte*, Antonioni shows the girl kicking the door of her room shut. But the latch does not catch, and the door abruptly swings back away from the camera. In the following shot, a close-up taken from inside the room, the door (cut on its movement) is now seen swinging back toward the camera again. This second shot could conceivably create the impression that the door had changed direction in "real" space. The actual trajectory of a door as it swings back is so familiar to us, however, that we have no trouble re-establishing the real nature of the movement—we immediately apprehend it as one continuous move-ment that has been "rendered" as if it were discontinuous. These two shots thereby stand out as the components of one of the two strong matches around which the sequence pivots, the second being the following match: a transition from a straight-on close-up cen-tered on the girl to a medium shot in which she is on the far right side of the frame, a transition completely ignoring the principles gov-erning the "concertina" and resulting in a second abrupt break in the flow of the sequence. It is worth pointing out the obvious analo-gies between the manner in which we apprehend the deliberately omitted portion of a continual temporal process (ellipsis) and the mental process that occurs when we compare a movement as it ap-pears on the screen with that movement as we assume it occurred in "reality." This, of course, is not the first analogy of this sort we have come upon in the course of our analyses, nor will it be the last. Cor-respondences of this kind doubtless indicate the fundamental cohe-siveness of the various cinematic parameters as well as how these parameters might eventually be organically interrelated to set up a vast series of permutations so complex in nature as to be totally beyond anything presently imagined.

Another type of dynamic articulation juxtaposes an internally static image at the end of one shot with an image in motion at the beginning of the subsequent shot. Flashes of static shots alternating with extremely rapid tracking shots, a technique some members of the French avant-garde of the 1920's were extremely fond of, is a rather crude example of this type of structure. Orson Welles's version of *Othello* is an altogether more satisfactory one. A large number of scenes in the film are built around cuts involving the following two types of shots: A first shot may show a motionless actor who sud-denly begins to move just before the shot ends, only to be seen standing still once again in the second shot without having com-pleted the movement he has previously begun, this movement's final phase having been abridged in the transition; or, in another variant, an actor might be completing a movement at the beginning of the second shot, even though he was motionless at the end of the first. When it occurs as frequently as it does in *Othello*, this type of tran-sition creates a rather special rhythm and a very flexible structure that can be varied by alternating the two sorts of matches or by a threefold combination of these matches, straight continuity cutting, and other types of temporal abridgement. It goes without saying that this type of shot transition can be used in conjunction with the various sorts of static matches already described, as is often the case in this film.

Similar relationships between static and moving shots are also possible when they contain quite dissimilar elements; directors such as Juan-Antonio Bardem and Michael Cacoyannis have a predilection for this kind of shot change. But this technique seems too facile, not organic enough, too mechanical, when compared to shot changes involving "brief ellipses" in the action that add a "vertical" dimension to the "horizontal" opposition between the spaces defined by the two shots.

Thus far, we have discussed only one of the two vectors of movement: direction. There is also speed. Apparent screen speed varies in direct proportion to the camera's distance from the subject. If we film a man raising his hand in a medium shot, then film that man doing the same thing at the same speed in close-up, the gesture will now appear to be much faster than it was in the medium shot, for in the same time that it takes a hand in a medium shot to travel across a fraction of a foot of screen space, it will have traveled several feet of screen space in a close-up. Accepted practice, an expression of that "zero point of cinematic style" we have already mentioned, requires that the apparent screen speeds of two shots be matched by tampering with "real" speeds. Clearly we are dealing here again with a situation involving a discontinuity as opposed to a continuity, and the film-maker can in fact use these differences in apparent speed for dialectical purposes; in this instance as in all others involving cutting on movement it is not difficult to imagine how a dialectic of this sort could be combined with a dialectic of direction.

At this point, one can only note that the analysis contained in this chapter is a good deal less exhaustive, less systematic, and above all more pragmatic than the discussion in the last two chapters, perhaps because the subject dealt with here is far broader and much more intangible than the relatively simple questions of the spatiotemporal articulation of shots and the relation of off-screen space to screen space. It is extremely difficult to describe, much less classify, any of the phenomena we have been discussing in this chapter: Classification might not even serve any useful purpose in this context, for editing as a plastic art is so complex a subject that those of us concerned with film probably do not yet have the means with which to undertake serious analysis of it. For the time being, any investigation in this field must necessarily take a pragmatic form, the making of films. Contemporary and future film-makers who are aware of these problems will discover far more rewarding, more complex, and more rigorous ways of organizing "matches" functionally than any outlined here, and the examples cited here will then seem quite naïve in retrospect. But perhaps they will at least serve to open the discussion.

Notes

1. Karel Reisz and Millar Gavin, *Technique of Film Editing* (New York: Hastings, 1967).
2. What is described here, however, is the "good gestalt" of an ideal viewer. Further research has shown that the film-goer often tends to see filmed images very much as he sees life: unframed, *lumpen*, with the figures completely blotting out the ground. The pinball example is in fact an extreme case significant only on an elementary level.
3. These comments were written before the release of Tati's *Playtime*. Even if they still hold true for films in general, they are not applicable to Tati's film, the first in the history of cinema that not only must be seen several times, but also must be viewed from several different distances from the screen. In its form, it is probably the first truly "open" film. Will it remain an isolated experiment? Masterpieces somehow eventually assert their authority and become models.
4. In the Gris painting, it will be noted that this rule is "respected" only as regards the first and third representation of the violin (counting from the right): The difference in "framing" between the third and fourth images is minute; the difference factors are more specifically pictorial. I mention this in order to stress the limitations of any comparison between Eisensteinian editing and Cubist representation.
5. Carl Dreyer's *The Passion of Joan of Arc* is built entirely around this simple idea and constitutes a perfect introduction to this fundamental concept.
6. It is also worth noting that, in the film as a whole, there is a complete opposition between the first part and the second part, which takes place entirely inside an inn, the camera remaining rather distant from the action, the depth of field being kept at a maximum, very short focal-length lenses and low angles being used throughout, in anticipation of what was to be the characteristic style of the early Orson Welles films. Curiously enough, this split into two parts is not without analogies to *High and Low*, for the sec-

ond part of Kurosawa's film abandons the apartment in which the first part of the action takes place and shifts to the streets and slums of Tokyo, which change of setting brings about a radical change of style.

7. The reasons for this standardization are intimately bound up with the establishment of the "zero point" of film-making defined earlier. This particular manifestation of that development would make a fascinating subject of study from the point of view of film perception.

8. This is true only in part. Actually, this sequence is a large-scale development of the concept of "montage units," that is, a dialectic of "good" and "bad" matches, inaugurated in *Strike* and theorized by Eisenstein in his teaching— see *Lessons with Eisenstein* by Vladimir Nizhny (New York: Hill and Wang, 1962).

II

Dialectics

4

The Repertory of Simple Structures

Frequent mention has been made in the first part of this work of a dialectical conception of cinematic form. It must be emphasized once again that this is not so much a specifically Hegelian process as a conception principally and perhaps somewhat improperly borrowed from serial music, from what the contemporary French composer and theoretician Jean Barraqué has called post-Webernian "musical dialectics": the organization of the various musical parameters (pitch and duration of sound, instrumental attack, timbre, and even silence) within musical space. As has already been pointed out, cinematic parameters of a similar nature exist. Thus far, I have been concerned largely with examining the most important of these parameters from the point of view of *découpage* (the spatiotemporal characteristics of the match, the relationships between screen space and off-screen space, and plastic interactions between shots), the very nature of which suggests the possible forms that their dialectical organization might take. It might be pointed out in passing that there are still other parameters of this sort, obviously lending themselves to a similar sort of organization: variations in shot size, in camera angle and height, in direction and speed of camera and subject movement within the shot, and, naturally, in *the duration of a shot*. Duration, however, confronts us with a basic problem, if only because an examination of it reveals, once and for all, the limits of my analogy with serial music. For, while there are in fact general analogies between the dialectics of serial music and those of film, there is also a fundamental difference: the fact that these cinematic dialectics cannot be expressed or written down in purely arithmetical terms as musical structures ultimately can be. And yet, if there is one cinematic parameter that would seem to be quite easily reducible to its mathematical equivalent, it is the duration of a shot expressed in seconds and frames. It has even been suggested that these time spans could be built up into something like "tone rows." Nevertheless the daily experience of any film-maker (as well as the few sporadic attempts that have been made to organize the durations of shots in patterns independently of their content) shows quite clearly that the viewer's estimate of the duration of a shot is conditioned by its *legibility*. Roughly speaking, it is a direct function of legibility; an uncomplicated two-second close-up will appear to be longer than a long shot of exactly the same duration that is swarming with people;[1] a white or black screen will appear to be longer still. For this reason, the organization of *perceptible* durations is a process that in the final analysis is as complex and necessarily as empirical as that of organizing ellipses; and, for the same reason, any given cinematic rhythmical pattern measured simply in seconds and frames will never be experienced in the same way as a musical pattern, unless it consists of nothing more than a simple alternation of black and white frames. If the images involved are at all complex, this rhythmical unit remains little more than a pure abstraction and is not at all perceptible as a coherent pattern.

Despite this, the possible ways of structuring this double phenomenon of duration and legibility constitute a problem that every great film-maker has tackled, each in his own way. Alain Resnais, perhaps, has been the one most consciously concerned with it. He was probably the first to realize that the wide screen, rather than forcing the film-maker to use only relatively prolonged shots (because of the greater difficulty the viewer has "reading" each shot in this format), on the contrary considerably *expands* the possible range of relationships between duration and legibility. In *Marienbad*, he deliberately alternates very prolonged shots with very short shots, with some of these latter involving flashes of only a few frames. In a more general way, Resnais is one of the few *auteurs* (together with L'Herbier, Eisenstein, and, above all, Gregory Markopoulos[2]) to have realized that the relationship between duration and legibility in itself constitutes a dialectic and that simply finding a duration adequate to the legibility of each shot is not what is important; the creative factor lies, rather, in varying the ease or difficulty with which a shot can be "read" by making certain shots too short to be "comfortably" grasped (thus creating a "tension" through frustration) or so long that they can be read and reread to the point of absolute satiety (thus causing a "tension" through boredom).[3] These constitute the poles (or rather the vectors) of a true dialectic of durations capable of generating visual rhythms ultimately as complex as those of contemporary music.

Besides these parameters having to do with the *découpage* of a film, other potentially dialectical parameters exist, which can, I think, be listed with some degree of thoroughness because they are so clearly bipolar in nature.

The first of these are the *photographic parameters*, the most important of which are perhaps softness and sharpness of focus, as well as their corollary, the extent of the depth of field. I have already dealt with the part these parameters play in the composition of Romm's *Boule de suif*. However, the first film-makers to have experimented with this theme to any appreciable extent were Germaine Dulac, Jean Epstein, Abel Gance, and Marcel L'Herbier, a group often referred to as the French impressionists or first French avant-garde. Their concern with contrasts in focus led them to reduce artificially the extended depth of field imposed on them by the diaphragm openings of the lenses used at the time. They employed gauze or plates of glass rubbed with Vaseline to that end, even using this latter trick to introduce areas of soft focus into a shot in which everything else at the same depth is sharply in focus (for instance the first scene in L'Herbier's *El Dorado* in which Eve Francis, sitting on a bench facing the camera in the middle of a row of girls, is quite noticeably in soft focus while her neighbors are in sharp focus). These film-makers were just as concerned with transitions from soft to sharp focus, which they attained chiefly by having their actors move in depth, an effect intensively explored by nearly every one of the great Russian directors, Eisenstein, Dovzhenko, Romm, and Boris Barnett in particular.

In Japan, Ozu was equally intrigued by the possibilities of contrasts between soft and sharp focus, and *The Only Son* contains a series of shots that is astonishing in this respect. We first see two people seated facing each other, profiles toward the camera. A pillow in the foreground is in sharp focus while the characters in the background are in soft focus. As the conversation continues we see each of the two characters in turn full face in a shot and reverse shot, after which the camera returns to its initial angle. But now the pillow is in soft focus while the two people are seen sharply. This symmetrical structure, although an elementary and isolated example, already is evidence of a concern that we might describe as dialectical and that we come across in several other instances in this film and in others by Ozu. Evidences of this concern for the relationship between soft and sharp focus can be found in the work of many of the greatest contemporary film-makers as well, notably in that of Antonioni and Resnais, but chiefly in that of Bresson, where the two parameters are often strongly opposed, either for purely compositional reasons or, less frequently, for structural reasons, often in association with entrances and exits and an empty frame.

The other photographic parameters, at least in so far as black-and-white photography is concerned, have to do with actual light values, that is, with contrast and with tone, or brilliance, as it is called in television. A mixture of photographic styles systematically employed within a film, almost always in conjunction with an alternation in settings, between interiors and exteriors, as in *Last Year at Marienbad* (but also in numerous mass-audience films such as *Divorce Italian Style*), between past and present (as in *Hiroshima mon amour*), between dream and reality, summer and winter, and the like occurs fairly frequently. Another example is Joseph von Sternberg's first film, *The Salvation Hunters*, which is divided into three parts (exteriors, interiors, and exteriors, successively), each associated with an extremely characteristic photographic style. Such alternations (or gradations) in contrast and tone might conceivably be built up into autonomous structures, ones not necessarily occurring synchronously with changes in setting, thereby establishing a kind of complex dialectic within and between individual shots. It might be added that, even though this as yet may not have been done either in an all-black-and-white or an all-color film, it has nevertheless been undertaken in films involving a mixture of the two.[4] Experiments involving a mixture in the same film of black-and-white images and color images go back to the origins of film-making. The "primitives" (Méliès comes particularly to mind) sometimes tinted their films, either entirely or only in part. Abel Gance's masterpiece, *Napoleon*, went even further in this direction, as in the sequence in which Napoleon looks out over the sea from the top of a cliff, which introduces into a black-and-white context a series of shots all tinted differently, thus producing a remarkably striking visual effect. These experiments were more or less abandoned after the advent of color film,[5] but they have been taken up again in the last fifteen years by some of the younger film-makers. In *Night and Fog*, Resnais alternates color and black-and-white sequences; this depends, however, on yet another alternation, that between "documents from the past" and shots taken "in the present." Probably one of the first serious attempts at creating a structure centering around these two poles, a structure functioning independently of the narrative structure although dialectically related to it, is Monique Lepeuve's short film *Exemple Étretat*. This young film-maker has made several experimental films dealing with many fundamental problems of cinematic form and language, and, in this particular case, black-and-white images, monochromatic images in every tonality, and polychromatic images using every color in the spectrum as a dominant color or having no dominant color at all—in short, images exploiting every aspect of color taken in its largest sense—alternate in rapid succession. The editing of this film, moreover, sets up a complex underlying rhythm, another of whose elements is a mixture of live location shots and old picture postcards. One final element, a half-spoken, half-sung (and, on one occasion, whistled) commentary, which seems alternately to cleave to the images and draw apart from them, crowns the structure of a film that, brief and modest as it is, nevertheless represented an important step toward a much more complex use of film dialectics than the simple ones we have been discussing.

Before describing a third type of dialectic, we might linger for a moment on a particular type of contrast between color and black-

and-white, one that illustrates a procedure that has more general applications and may in fact play a very important role in any dialectical structure. This procedure consists of emphasizing one of the two poles of a parameter by using it rarely or perhaps only once, a concept that has rather striking analogies to a technique used in post-Webernian serial music whereby a certain note or register is emphasized. Rather than systematically alternating shots or sequences in color and ones in black-and-white throughout a film, certain film-makers have introduced a single sequence or even a single shot in color into what is otherwise a purely black-and-white context (for example Agnès Varda in the precredit sequence of *Cleo from Five to Seven* and Marcel Hanoun in the sequence at the race track in *Le Huitième jour*). Doubtless the most startling use of this technique is to be found in Kurosawa's *High and Low*, where a single pair of color shots unexpectedly appears on screen, ostensibly to show a column of smoke whose color (red) is necessary as a plot device, but in actual fact its very sudden, almost gratuitous, appearance is a striking signal marking the beginning of the third section of the film, which is treated in a very different style from the two preceding ones.

It is apparent, finally, that there exists a series of auditory parameters that correspond to these photographic parameters and that can be (and often have been) organized into dialectical structures. However, these auditory parameters are so important that I prefer to treat them in a separate chapter.

Let us now go on to the third classifiable type of dialectic (although here my endeavor to be "encyclopedic" might well be questioned). This third type might be called *organic dialectics*. The simplest of these dialectics, obviously, is the opposition between an image and its absence (which has as its corollary the opposition between the presence and the absence of a sound track, as used throughout Godard's *Deux ou trois choses que je sais d'elle*, for instance). We are dealing here with a type of dialectical relationship that is different from those examined previously in that it is reduced to its two poles; it is limited, that is to say, to a simple alternation (even though a kind of subdialectic may be present within the pole constituted by the absence of an image, in the form of every possible gradation in tone between a black screen and a white screen), for no matter how illegible an image may be it still remains an image. The absence of an image on the screen traditionally constitutes a simple "punctuation mark" used to "signify" the passage of time in the same way a dissolve does. Academic film theoreticians have maintained that a dissolve suggests a shorter lapse of time than does a fade-out to black, a view that has no basis in perceptual reality and merely expresses a willful desire to attribute some inherent, organic value to a perfectly arbitrary convention. Film-makers such as Dovzhenko, Jean-Pierre Melville, and, above all, Bresson, while continuing to use the blacked-out screen as a punctuation mark, have nonetheless also sensed the possible structural value of the fade as compared to the essentially more plastic value of the dissolve. But it has been chiefly the young experimenters of the American "underground" cinema who have really endeavored to use the presence and absence of an image as poles equal in value, organizing whole films around this opposition. Stan Brakhage in *Reflections on Black* and Bruce Conner in *A Movie* both use long passages in which a dark screen plays a far more active role than that of a mere punctuation mark. But it is Ken Jacobs's *Blond Cobra* that I have principally in mind. Though a rather frivolous film in other respects, it includes very long sequences in which the screen remains completely black (as a result of a character having blocked the camera lens), while the voice of the inimitable Jack Smith tells one wild story after another. As the film unfolds, the "threat" of the black screen is felt more and more acutely each time a character approaches the camera (and the film-maker exploits this to the hilt, the film having been shot in some kind of garret and at "point-blank range"). It is this "threat" that ultimately provides this rather rudimentary dialectic with whatever interest it has.

We must now discuss two "triads" that on first reflection would seem to play a fundamental role in cinematic dialectics. The first of these involves backward motion and forward motion pivoting around the stationary image; the second consists of fast and slow motion centering around normal film velocity, with each of these two "triads" giving rise to two dialectical possibilities. Jean Epstein created a sort of aesthetic philosophy of film with these parameters as a foundation in his last theoretical writings, for he seems to have regarded them as the very cornerstone of film art. This bias caused him to put forward a number of ideas that strikingly foreshadow certain very contemporary concepts, especially those having to do with discontinuity, but in my view his theories are a bit too far removed from actual practice to be really relevant. Aside from their use as embellishments of the narrative (fast motion for "slapstick" effects, slow motion for "poetic" effect), there have been very few serious attempts to employ this series structurally, and even in these few instances fast or slow motion has had the conventional connotation. Only a few experimental films and Vertov's *Man with a Movie Camera* can be cited as examples of such an attempt. As a matter of fact, despite their deliberately spare and nonnarrative use in certain Kurosawa films, the effects that result from these parameters are too "expressionistic," too "magical" (rather like those created by distorting lenses) to function successfully independently of a narrative framework and can be approached structurally only on this narrative level.[6]

On the other hand, the opposition between the two poles constituted by the moving image and the stationary image has been used frequently for some years, sometimes in a more or less dialectical manner. Chris Marker made *La Jetée* entirely from stationary images (although this case in fact involves something else again—the use of photographs as a material, which will be discussed below), and the presence within that context of a single shot in which something actually moves (the girl opening her eyes) acts as the film's center of gravity. Truffaut in *Jules and Jim* and many of the younger English directors use the freeze frame as a kind of punctuation mark or as visual gags; the results are somewhat uneven.

Another organic dialectic, however, has proved to be relatively rich in possibilities: the opposition of live and animated shots. The probable inventor of this technique, Émile Cohl, was also the greatest pioneer of the animated film. His animated sequences were often bracketed by live sequences, but of principal interest here is the way in which he often introduced live figures into his brilliant cascades of graphic metamorphoses. In Walt Disney's hands, this principle became badly distorted, leading to such films as *Saludos Amigos*, in which the "realistic" relief and perspective of the animated sequences merely destroy the contrast effect so successfully employed by Cohl in his opposition of animated and live scenes. More recently, however, American and Czech animators have their similar techniques in a more modern and deliberately structural fashion. The outstanding example is Karl Zeman's masterpiece, *The Fabulous World of Jules Verne*, which contains an extremely varied mixture of the live and the animated throughout. In it Zeman used, perhaps for the first time, a medium shot of a live scene followed by a long shot of the same scene *manifestly* shot in animation (as against the "special effects" in *King Kong*, for example, which aim at creating an *illusory* continuity of materials). Zeman has continued to explore this mixture of live and animated actions in the features he has made since, but he has never equaled either the formal rigor or the poetic tension of this first film. This area nevertheless has a great many possibilities as yet unexplored, though Zeman's tendency to use a pastiche of graphic styles should be avoided if these are to lead anywhere.

Except for isolated examples such as Cohl's work, this concept of organic dialectics is relatively recent, unity of material and style having been an almost universally respected rule (inherited as it was from the traditional arts) until the advent of television. It might be added that this has been one of the greatest contributions made by the latter medium. By breaking down the barriers between genres and in particular by quite naturally introducing a mixture of the "live" and the "staged," television has encouraged the creation of new forms and new structures based on a deliberate mixing of genres and the materials inherent in them and has begun to explore the multiple dialectics that can result from such mixtures. In France, André S. Labarthe, the coproducer (with Janine Bazin) of the *Cinéastes de notre temps* series and its principal artistic director, is one of the film-makers to have best sensed these possibilities. In many of his programs (for example, on Gance, Godard, Roger Leenhardt) Labarthe attempts to structure the breaks in tone and style implicit in the alternate use of filmed interviews and other "raw" documents, on the one hand, and film-clips from the work of the film-maker in question, on the other, thus seeking to create a *discontinuous* essay form[7] to replace the often flat continuity of the classical documentary, an approach not unlike the discontinuous techniques of modern music. The program on Godard in particular employs a dialectic wherein obvious breaks in style and materials contrast with imperceptible "deferred" or "retroactive" transitions, thus exploiting the ambiguous relationship between the mock-improvised style of Godard's films and the straightforward interview style (Godard converses with Labarthe in a car, while the streets seen in a cutaway through the windshield are those of Godard's film *Alphaville*). Within cinema as opposed to television, it is Godard himself who has most thoroughly explored melanges of styles and materials, and a large number of his films have used these mixtures as an essential structural element. The extremely simple structure of *Vivre sa vie*, consisting of separate sequences set off by titles (an original mixture of materials in and of itself in a sound film), depends on oppositions between the various styles of the sequences: real as versus fake interviews, fake documentary style accompanied by voice-over, fake newsreel footage, and so on. *Une Femme mariée*, which formally is a good deal less schematic, uses sudden (and numbered) interjections of real (?) *cinéma-vérité* sequences into a staged context, which in turn reaches at times a degree of abstraction that constitutes a third level of formal material; the film, moreover, is punctuated throughout by the sudden appearance on screen of advertising posters and slogans. The result of all this is a vast "time collage" in which these stylistic breaks are intended to serve as an organizing principle. The rhythm of the film is not entirely satisfactory, however, and the actors were perhaps not very well chosen for the dual roles assigned them. This collage technique was later used more successfully by Godard in *Pierrot le fou*, where it became an integral part of a more rigorous dramatic framework (which had its own dialectic between "action" and "narration," to be examined in more detail later). In this film, each sequence, though not strictly compartmentalized as in *Vivre sa vie* or *Une Femme mariée*, nonetheless illuminates the central narrative framework in a number of quite specific ways, generally through an explicit reference to a particular genre (musical comedy, the gangster film, the television interview, melodrama, the comic strip, the nightclub act, and so on). This alternation is thus not only an essential structural element in the film but also one of its subjects.

Although Godard uses a whole range of relationships between the camera and his characters, he very seldom films his actors without their being aware of it. The only use of the candid-camera technique with which I am acquainted in his work occurs in his second film,

Une Femme est une femme. As Susan Sontag has said, "It is not that Godard makes improvised films, it is just that he likes to give them the *look* of improvisation." Agnès Varda, on the other hand, has created in *Opéra-Mouffe* a unique example of a rigorously dialectical opposition between spontaneous "live" shots and "staged" shots, the link between the two types being provided by shots that are apparently spontaneous though actually planned beforehand. The strict compartmentalization of sequences, and above all the enormous range of differences in their relative durations, provides the essential framework around which the organization of this other dialectic hinges. The precise coloration that the dialectical relationship between the live and the staged assumes becomes all the richer because it extends over a range of expression reaching from "crude realism" (unrehearsed live images) to deliberately heightened, poetic "unreality" (planned images) with a rather delightfully ambiguous sort of *"fantastique social"* (apparently spontaneous but actually prearranged scenes) falling in between.[8]

Various attempts of this sort have since been made in featurelength films; Vilgot Sjöman's *I Am Curious (Yellow)* comes particularly to mind, constituting as it does a totally new dialectical reworking of the old gimmick of the film within a film. Certain techniques used in television programs (as discussed in Chapter 10) also come to mind.

Finally, although Godard successfully uses famous paintings as punctuating devices in his films, in much the same way[9] that he uses advertising posters, no other examples involving the satisfactory integration of painting into a dialectic of materials occurs to me. That, however, does not hold true for still photographs. William Klein in his *Float Like a Butterfly, Sting Like a Bee,* the anonymous editor of *October in Paris,* and, above all, the very talented Peter Emmanuel Goldman have all juxtaposed still photographs and live shots of the same scene in a rather striking way at times. In their work, transitions from one form of visual representation of an action to the other result in a very unusual sort of poetic and rhythmic vision.

The dialectics of film style begin at the level of individual shots and matches, as we have seen, although they may well result in structures underlying whole sequences and entire films. As for "photographic" dialects, they can function as easily between sequences as between shots. Of the "organic" dialects, some tend to function more between sequences—that is to say, they tend to follow a film's *narrative line*, as opposed to its *découpage* or plastic organization (were we to adopt the traditional distinction, which is rather incompatible with the views expressed here). Another extremely important type of dialectic must now be considered as well, one intimately connected with a film's narrative skeleton and therefore with the concept of a sequence, except in so far as certain contemporary filmmakers are endeavoring to make the individual shot as basic a narrative unit as the sequence. This is the dialectics of "narrative time," in other words the organization of the extended temporal jumps or ellipses, either forward or backward, dealt with in Chapter 1. It was apparently not until quite late in film history, notably with the flashbacks in Carné's *Le Jour se lève*, that the dialectical possibilities of narrative time were noticed. The articulation of flashbacks (or flashforwards) around an action unfolding in a film's "present tense" provides the most obvious means for structuring narrative time. But it is only recently that organic development of a simple linear progression in narrative time has been attained, by means of the complex dialectical structures that will constitute the subject of the next chapter.

The film best representing the contemporary attitude toward the flashback (its function, that is, in a nonchronological narrative that nonetheless refers to an implicit time-scale) is Jean-Marie Straub's *Nicht Versöhnt*. The history of modern Germany serves as the film's standard of temporal measurement, and its central dialectic is based on the manner in which sequences move forward or backward in time in relation to that standard. A completely different and infinitely more fertile approach is that used in *Marienbad*, whereby each sequence (or rather each sequence shot) refers to one or several other sequences in what is perhaps the past, perhaps the present, or perhaps a future "tense." This dialectic of ambiguity with its several variables[10] in itself engenders complex structures that are independent of the film's narrative structures (thematic variations on the statue, the woman at the balustrade, and so on) or its plastic values (the organization of camera movements, shot size, ellipses, and so on). The dialectics of time are too basic and involve too

many other problems concerning the so-called form-content dichotomy for us to explore them in any greater depth within the limits
imposed by this brief inventory of the principal simple dialectics.

Whether one sets apart the dialectics of time as a separate series of
relationships or whether they are included as part of the dialectical
interactions between sequences, these latter in any event constitute
a final major type of simple structure. These dialectical relationships
between sequences are many and are a basic tool of film-makers.

Most screen writers, even the most commercially minded, know
that it is best to create *some* kind of contrast between successive
sequences, whether in duration, tempo, tone, or a combination of all
three. Very few film-makers, however, attempt to structure their
work in an *abstract* way by using these parameters. *Opéra-Mouffe* has
already been cited in this chapter as a striking example of variations
in the nature and duration of sequences, and in the first chapter we
noted Fritz Lang's *M*. But the film-maker most concerned with problems of duration is undoubtedly Robert Bresson, particularly in his
Diary of a Country Priest and subsequent films. Starting with predominantly short sequences, *Diary* progressively evolves to a point
where long sequences predominate (the sequences, that is to say, do
not actually last longer, longer sequences simply occur more frequently). The shorter sequences, moreover, are associated with a
voice-over narration and with a supple, flowing rhythm, involving a
great deal of compositional movement and reframing; the long sequences, on the other hand, are in synchronous sound and visually
composed largely through the use of the shot and reverse shot technique. *The Trial of Joan of Arc*, by contrast, is much more regular in structure; what counts primarily here is the duration of
successive shots as well as sequences, and even of the intervals sep-
arating the beginning or end of a line of dialogue from the beginning or end of a shot or sequence.[11] The film's entire underlying
rhythm stems from these variations. In Bresson's films—so uniform
in mood—conflicts and even variations in *tone* have little place. In
current film practice these conflicts or variations in tone usually
tend to resemble the alternation between melodrama and slapstick
found in Renoir's *Diary of a Chambermaid*, a film from his American period, though usually the contrasts are not quite so jarring. A
few years earlier, Renoir had very successfully exploited this param-

eter in *La Règle du jeu*, a beautifully orchestrated film famous precisely for its subtle mixture of tones and "genres."

Mr. Hulot's Holiday provides an even more important example. Here the contrast between sequences, simultaneously involving duration, tempo, tone, and setting (interiors or exteriors, night or day) is under constant, meticulous control, determining the whole progression of the film and constituting its principal source of beauty. Aside from the broken rhythm of the gags, so perverse and yet so perfect, the principal rhythmic factor is an alternation between strong and weak moments, between deliberately action-packed, screamingly funny passages and others just as deliberately empty, boring, and flat. When the pretty girl's companion shows her an absolutely empty seascape, visible from the window of her room, and says, "Sometimes people fish down there, but there's nobody there today," boredom is being put to good use. Similar scenes aimed at creating a feeling of real boredom go on for quite some time, but it is created in such carefully controlled "doses" that it plays a special rhythmic role in the film's over-all structure. There come to mind (among many other possible examples) the empty beach accompanied by the off-screen sounds of the restaurant dining room, the episodes of the child with his ice cream, the couple looking for seashells, etc.

In the whole history of cinema, this film, along with *Zéro de conduite*, has perhaps best succeeded in fulfilling the structural possibilities inherent in taking each sequence as a cellular unit, as an irreducible entity independent of any over-all spatial or temporal dialectic.

We have now only to mention a large number of other dialectics that are quite difficult to categorize: those concerning dialogue, the style of acting, the décor, make-up, and costumes—everything, in short, relating to the *explicit content* of images and sounds.

One of the most remarkable examples of a particular structure of this kind is to be found in Joseph von Sternberg's masterpiece, *The Blue Angel*, one of the greatest films in the history of cinema. In a certain sense, we are dealing here with the dialectics of sound, as the structure in question depends on whether the noise of what is happening out in the music hall is audible or inaudible during scenes occurring in the dressing rooms. The crucial strategy here is the use of a pair of doors constantly opening and closing in a marvelously complicated pattern; snatches of music, bursts of applause, and scraps of dialogue drift in as the doors are open and are cut off as they shut, each time in a different relation to the editing scheme. A structure of variations results that is exemplary in its rigor. Sometimes one of the doors (which one?—they all look alike and the space these dressing rooms define is one of the most totally abstract in cinema, analyzable only in terms of what each successive "composition" reveals) opens off screen, there is a sudden burst of music, followed by a shot of the door, which is then closed again. Sometimes a door opens on screen, the shot then shows something else, and it closes off screen. At times, the door opens or closes at the junction of two shots; at times, the door is opened or closed without affecting the ambient sounds—another unseen door perhaps has remained open. Jannings's return to "The Blue Angel" near the end of the film provides a kind of recapitulation of the structures employed in depicting his two previous visits to the nightclub. The very first scene in the classroom when Jannings opens the window, thereby allowing the "celestial" sound of the children's chorus to enter, is also a subtle prefiguration of this underlying pattern; moreover, it is the last time Jannings will be in control of events. The formal structure thus closely relates to the dramatic progression lying at the very heart of the film, Jannings's transition from an active to a passive role. (See also Chapter 9.)

The largest variety of structures of this sort is to be found in *Marienbad*, where they involve both lines of dialogue and dramatic incidents (either repeating them exactly, or with some variation, or recalling, alluding to, or prefiguring them) and décor (the progressive proliferation of furniture and ornamental motifs on the walls of the hotel room as well as its progressive increase in scale).

Yet another type of dialectic based on a film's décor occurs in one of Kon Ichikawa's most intriguing films, *The Actor's Revenge,* a work that employs a whole range of set styles, from a plain black background to totally realistic interiors, including painted backcloths and other essentially theatrical scenic devices between these two extremes. In a highly ambiguous sequence (halfway between dream and reality) a sort of thick, yellowish fog slowly clears to reveal the same fog painted on a theatrical backdrop. The film, moreover, uses theatrical conventions such as a *Doppelgänger* of the hero and the mixture of the comic and the tragic (devices possibly borrowed from Jacobean theater, consistently employed here in a thoroughgoing dialectical manner).

As for the style of acting, Alain Robbe-Grillet in *Trans-Europ-Express* performs an interesting experiment, juxtaposing scenes played by nonprofessionals and scenes played by professionals. This provides another structure, which is not yet fully developed here, and rather simplistically mirrors one aspect of the film's dramatic line, which itself is a bit simplistic. The film nevertheless is an indication that this structure may well develop into something quite complex, whereas the mixtures of amateur and professional actors that occur so frequently in Italian films have always been chaotic and seem to lead nowhere.

Robbe-Grillet's whole body of films (like several of his novels) employs structures evolving out of some form of itinerary or journey. His use in *Trans-Europ-Express* of the Paris-Antwerp run is dialectical, at least in our sense of the word used here, as is the double trajectory Michel Mitrani employs in his television film based on Samuel Beckett's *All That Fall*. In this latter film, the over-all schematic path of the action is first seen in a single shot taken from a helicopter, and that action is then played out in detail in the remainder of the film.

The task of defining the concept of structure or dialectics in general has been left until the end of this chapter, for its true nature is chiefly revealed through the multiplicity of forms it takes and its principal interest perhaps lies in the fact that it enables us to see how all kinds of investigations and experiments that might at first appear to be completely foreign to each other actually converge. It will be noticed that I have used the phrase "structure or dialectics." I have done so because I feel that in film the two concepts are more or less interchangeable, for structures almost always seem to occur in dialectical form—that is to say, a structure necessarily evolves within a parameter defined by one or more pairs of clearly delineated *poles*. Even a structure involving a progression or itinerary, although less simple internally perhaps, has two poles—a point of departure and a point of arrival (Paris and Antwerp in *Trans-Europ-Express*, for example). Generally speaking, then, a structure exists when a parameter evolves according to some principle of progression that is apparent to the viewer in the theater, or perhaps only to the film-maker at his editing table, for, even though there may be structures that are "perceptible only to those who have created them," they nonetheless play an important role in the final aesthetic result. Although the concealed forms present in *Wozzeck*, forms that Alban Berg hoped would always remain imperceptible to the listener, have often been enlisted to bolster up a certain philistine attitude, they nevertheless constitute a highly revealing precedent for film. As an art, film undoubtedly is closer to opera (at least opera as Berg conceived it) than it is to "pure" music, to which reference has perhaps been made too frequently.

It has recently occurred to me, moreover, that what we refer to as *structure* is perhaps no more than an extension of a concept that Russian and Anglo-Saxon film theoreticians continually dwelt on— namely, *rhythm*. Though I indicated at the beginning of this chapter that rhythm in film cannot be reduced to a succession of pure durations as is the case in music, I am tempted at this point to conclude that cinematic rhythm is defined by the sum total of all the parameters thus far enumerated and is therefore incredibly complex. For this precise reason, the temptation to reduce this enormous complexity to a simple analogy with music must be strictly avoided (and admittedly this has not always been done in the course of this discussion), if we are ever to grasp the essence of film form.

As should be obvious, and as a more thoroughgoing analysis would show, the structural principles noted thus far in a number of masterpieces are never applied in as systematic or as rigorous a manner as might seem to be the case from a general description such as that offered here. The rhythmic contrasts between the short and long sequences (and the accompanying contrast in styles of *découpage*) in Bresson's *Diary of a Country Priest* are certainly not of a mathematical rigor, and the film displays a large number of "deviations" from the norm established. Such deviations can themselves be built into even more elaborate formal patterns, though no example comes readily to mind except for my own unfinished film based on Georges Bataille's *Bleu du ciel*. Every sequence in this project followed what was perhaps an overly rigid principle of *découpage* (involving, for instance, a succession of shots and reverse shots in which the shot size progressively changed), which was violated at one or several key points in accord with another basic pattern that was itself a simple structure.

If we look back on this chapter, it may appear to be quite sketchy and schematic, for an enormous amount of ground had to be covered in a brief space. This reasonably complete inventory of simple structures nonetheless had to be drawn up before I could proceed to examine in greater detail a few of the complex dialectics that can result from them.

Notes

1. This, of course, is not the only cause of image illegibility: It can result from any form of visual interference such as reflections or fuzziness of image or a distracting element on the sound track—or even the width of the screen (as I indicate in my remarks on *Marienbad* below).
2. Markopoulos's great innovation consists in his alternation of unbearably prolonged shots and one-frame flashes, and even more importantly in his insertion during the most beautiful moments in films such as *Twice a Man* and *Himself as Herself* of one-frame close-ups, these close-ups consisting of details from the larger composition into which they are inserted. This technique has a good many possibilities, but it has not as yet been developed in the manner that it deserves.
3. Valerian Borowczyk's masterpiece, *Goto, l'île d'amour*, for the time being represents the ultimate application of this notion and is also a fine instance of the use of a "complex dialectic" (such as will be discussed in the following chapter).
4. It is obvious that breaks and contrasts in style have been attempted in a much freer way in color films than they have ever been in black-and-white (as in Antonioni's *Red Desert* and Resnais's *Muriel*).
5. Alternations between color and black-and-white sequences for purely narrative purposes (as in *Stairway to Heaven* or *Bonjour Tristesse*) have been disregarded.
6. André Hodeir, however, has proposed a rather fascinating use for reverse motion. A sequence might be shown with all the images in normal forward motion and then be repeated with the images in reverse motion (with perhaps a different sound track as well), with the series of images in each case having a perfectly understandable though completely different meaning.
7. See Chapter 10.
8. We should not overlook the greatest pioneer in this area, Dziga Vertov, who juxtaposes "live" images with "staged" ones in a surprisingly modern way in his *Man with a Movie Camera*.
9. *Formally* the same, that is. It should be made clear that, when referring to a

parameter's structural function, I am not overlooking the fact that the parameter performs other functions as well within the complex object that a film represents.

10. One that Jean Epstein had advocated and experimented with as early as 1927 in *La Glace à trois faces*, his first film to embody his belief that "there are no stories, there never have been any stories, there are only events with neither head nor tail, with neither beginning nor end."

11. This particular parameter has an obvious corollary involving the length of time that elapses between a movement into or out of frame and a shot change. These intervals, as we have seen, play a very important role in Bresson's work.

5

Absence of Dialectic
and Complex Dialectics

The preceding chapter drew up a kind of inventory of the many simple dialectics that may be detected in the formal strategies of a given film. Before going on to examine some examples of the complex structures that can result from the more or less deliberate and carefully planned combination of several simple structures, a long parenthesis is in order. At least one of the conclusions that can be drawn from the brief analysis in the preceding chapter is that any film contains dialectical structures, if only because there is bound to be some degree of contrast between sequences (however unpronounced) and some sort of interaction between the shot changes within a given sequence (however banal). This is not to say that there are more than a handful of films in which these "dialectics" are used in any systematic way, and films in which there is any real organic coordination between them are even rarer. In most cases, these dialectics merely exist in what might be termed their crude natural state, as simple unorganized alternations. These alternations nevertheless are embryonic structures, so to speak, and the fact that they exist is welcome confirmation that the ideas set forth in this book, and above all the hopes expressed for future developments in cinema, are not mere speculation but, rather, conclusions that can be drawn from *current film practice.*

On a number of occasions in the history of cinema, there have been attempts to abolish all formal dialectics at the level of *découpage* and use only what I might call a "dialectic of images." Many of these experiments have been very interesting; one of the most recent of them, Jean-Daniel Pollet's *Méditerranée*,[1] is also one of the most radical, for it is a film with no "matches" whatsoever. It consists, in other words, of juxtaposed recurrent shots that have no connection between them other than their relationship (with one exception) to the *mare nostrum*—statues, landscapes, still-lifes . . . as well as a similarly recurring shot of a girl on an operating table —the film-maker hoping that the order in which the individual shots follow one another on the screen will awaken some kind of poetic echo or resonance in the viewer's mind that will somehow evoke the ineffable feelings, the *je ne sais quoi* that he himself doubtless experienced while viewing these same juxtapositions of images. This approach bears a certain resemblance to the "montage of attractions" advocated by the young Eisenstein, a conception of editing that, it might be added, the Russian master subsequently repudiated once he realized that film form essentially depends on a dialectical opposition between a continuity and a discontinuity. There are indeed elements of a dialectic in *Méditerranée*. A spoken commentary and a musical score accompany this series of unfolding images. However, just as the juxtaposition of images obeys a kind of total empiricism, a blind faith that *something* will always result, so the relationship between images and commentary is completely arbitrary, as if the film-maker had been content to let commentary and images develop independently, confident that they would "go well together." This is not to say that secret affinities between the images and the commentary do not exist, for undoubtedly they do. And surely we should not deprecate a film simply because it is "obscure." Film has long since gone past the stage where simple narrative statements are sufficient. Nonetheless, if the space-time of both commentary and images is to be something more than the mere setting of two continuities seemingly blissfully unaware of each other's existence side by side

with no dialectical or any other kind of structure being thereby created, their actual meeting points, the moments at which the two
continuities converge, must not be completely fortuitous (film form
having also gone beyond the Surrealist aesthetic that found transcendent meaning in such events as the "chance encounter of a
sewing machine and an umbrella on a dissecting table"), and the
relationship between image and commentary must not be indecipher-
able, for obscurity of meaning does not necessarily imply an "illegible" structure. In fact, it may even be maintained that the more
hidden the meaning of a work is, the more apparent the principles
of structural tension underlying it should be. The main element
absent in *Méditerranée* is precisely that *tension*, without which no
work of art will seem to be a deliberate creation rather than pure
happenstance.

What is missing, in short, is an *organized interaction*: Only the
encounter between the separate formal elements appears to have
been planned, for the actual *forms* of this encounter seem gratuitous.
A rather deliberate attempt at structuring this succession of shots
had admittedly been made, for they are very few in number and have
been constantly repeated for *different durations* of time. Whether
concerted or not, this may represent something of an attempt to
apply principles similar to those of serial music, whereby the entire
work is based on the constant permutations of a very small number
of formal objects (a series or tone row of twelve tones in different
registers, a certain group of intervals, a certain range of tone qualities, and so on), these permutations bearing principally on the order
of occurrence and on the relative duration of these various elements.

I must, however, insist once again on the limits inherent in an
imitative approach of this sort. A musical tone is a basic element
and there are only twelve of them, or so the chromatic approach to
serial music would have it. The restricted nature of the basic musical
material in twelve-tone compositions is therefore an organic fact. To
limit the range of basic film material in a similar way is a very arbitrary decision in my view. Moreover, each musical tone is unique;
therefore, when tones are combined into a new formal entity, the
result is something a good deal more autonomous relative to the
initial components than is the case when two rather haphazardly
chosen shots are spliced together. Two successive sounds always have

a *vertical* relationship, since the ear situates them on a chromatic scale, as well as a *horizontal* relationship in time, this twofold relationship constituting only one of many dialectical dimensions of musical discourse. Musical parameters are so tightly interwoven that even very simple material can yield extremely rich developments, whereas, in film, limiting the material necessarily limits what can result. The images in *Méditerranée* are linked only horizontally in time. They are more or less long, more or less short, and reappear with this or that frequency. But there is no vertical link between them, since they have been purposely chosen because of their mere disparity. Those vertical relationships between shots provided in part in cinema by the forms of spatial and temporal articulations and by plastic relationships created through editing are entirely absent here. The lack of tension, the feeling of monotony, we experience watching *Méditerranée* unfold—despite the beauty of certain shots, of the narration, and even of the music, in and of themselves—stems from this fact.

It might seem rather strange to have lingered for so long on a film that seems to have taken the wrong track. This mistaken approach teaches us an important lesson, however. Film form,[2] it would appear, simply cannot exist without some kind of underlying dialectic; the mere linear alternation of disparate images does not suffice to create a film. Interestingly enough, Pollet's subsequent film, *Le Horla*, based on the Maupassant tale, seemed to evince the maker's awareness of this fact, at the same time as it was a development of the discontinuity principle of *Méditerranée*.

Le Horla is also based on using a minimum amount of material, repeating shots for constantly varying durations, but here the play of permutations operates in conjunction with another simultaneously unfolding continuity, a voice-over narration that establishes a sort of standard of temporal measurement. Each image can be situated more or less precisely relative to the time established by the narration, and the viewer is thus aware of jumps in time and space. These transitions almost automatically create tensions and rhythms that link the film's separate components together in a single formal structure. When repeated a second time, the shot of someone walking down a corridor strikes the viewer as both the "same" shot as before and a "new" shot, because it now occupies a different position in narrative time. In *Méditerranée*, by contrast, the voice-over established no temporal structure of its own, and therefore it seems to the viewer that he is merely seeing the same shot over and over, *ad nauseam*, and variations in the duration of shots seem to be a mere intellectual exercise on the part of the film-maker. In other words, the repetitions of shots in *Le Horla* move the film forward and strengthen its unity, whereas in *Méditerranée* they cause the film simply to mark time or to fall into meaningless bits and snippets. This does not mean that only a conventional narrative can provide a valid framework. In *Le Horla*, the contrast between the old-fashioned style of narration (Maupassant's text) and the daring with which it is visually developed is in fact quite disconcerting. One can very easily conceive of other possible forms of relationship between an image and a verbal text, but these must necessarily be *temporal*. The important point to be made about *Le Horla* is that the relationship established between the various elements is structural and organic. The film's component elements are not simply set side by side and end to end in the mistaken belief that the juxtaposition of several "beautiful" elements will always be more beautiful than any one of them taken separately, which seems to us to be the notion underlying *Méditerranée*.

This radical disjunction of word and image constitutes a dialectical principle often followed in film. In *Rope*, Hitchcock makes use of it to create a particularly tense feeling of suspense as the camera lingers for long moments on a housemaid methodically clearing the top of the chest in which the dead body has been hidden; at the same time, a long voice-off conversation, very relevant to the drama at hand, but completely unrelated to the visual image, is taking place between several of the characters.

The sequence in the Institute of Semantics in Godard's *Alphaville* unfolds according to similar principles, and the complexity and the pronounced dissimilarity between the two component elements (Alpha's speech off screen and the flashlights darting around in the dark) is such that the film must be seen several times before the scene can be grasped in its entirety. Jerzy Skolimowski uses this same technique much more systematically, and his first two films are based almost entirely on the pronounced sense of disorientation that results from this sort of radical disjunction. Another film, however,

Michelangelo Antonioni's *Cronaca di un amore*, the whole structure of which hinges on a similar dissociation of sound and image, represents an almost unparalleled achievement, an accomplishment so successful that this masterpiece should be considered a perfect example of its kind and analyzed in detail.

The film is proof of a firm bias (in the nobler sense of that word) in favor of stripping the image of any sort of narrative function. From the point of view of "story-telling," *practically nothing ever occurs on the screen.* But, even though *Cronaca di un amore* is not exactly an "action film," neither is it a film that "has no plot," for the narrative line deals with two violent deaths (one a murder by "omission"), machinations aimed at a second murder, and an investigation by a private detective. Clara and Guido cause the death of Guido's fiancée, an obstacle to their love, by doing nothing to prevent her from falling down an elevator shaft. However, her demise causes the two lovers to have a falling-out. A few years later a wealthy Milanese industrialist whom Clara has married solely for his money begins to brood about his wife's past, and has a private detective agency investigate it. This investigation indirectly results in the reunion of the two lovers; their love is rekindled, and they soon get around to plotting the husband's death. The detective learns that they have become lovers again and informs the husband. Stunned by this revelation, the husband proceeds to kill himself at the wheel of his car just a few miles before he reaches the bridge where Guido is lying in wait to murder him. Once again a death that the two lovers have ardently wished for, but that they cannot be accused of causing, separates them.

This narrative symmetry could easily have resulted in a coincidence-packed melodrama of the worst Hollywood sort (as the pastiche Bardem made on the same subject amply proves). Antonioni, however, has constructed one of the most perfectly and completely structured films in the entire history of cinema out of this narrative material, essentially through the disjunction of spoken word and image that we have referred to.

During the golden age of film theater (the 1930's), films in which the essential action occurred in verbal rather than visual form, films that would be totally incomprehensible were the sound to be turned off, were naturally quite common. The pendulum had simply swung

back, so to speak, for during the heyday of the silent film the ultimate aim had been to create essentially a *visual* narrative line, reducing the number of interposed titles to a strict minimum. The talkies
of the 1930's—and how talkative they were!—were based on love
stories and comedies of manners, narrative material well suited to
this form of filmed commercial theater, and the entire action could
very easily be staged within a single bedroom or living room, for the
spoken word was the action. The microphone and to a meager extent
the camera (for, if the visuals were completely eliminated, the film
would still be quite understandable) were above all *narrative* tools
(the remarks on "the zero point of cinematic style" in Chapter 1
being quite relevant here).

In *Cronaca di un amore*, however, something altogether different
occurs. The spoken word is no longer the action. Rather, it is a narrative vehicle that *describes* all of the action that has already occurred or will (perhaps) occur. One of the film's basic structures, in
fact, consists of the dialectical interaction between the spoken descriptions unfolding on the screen and the past or future actions to
which they refer.

Thus, as the film begins, the head of the detective agency *tells*
one of his investigators about the husband's suspicions; several wit-
nesses *tell* the detective about Clara's childhood and adolescence; an
old friend of the lovers *tells* Guido (by letter) about the detective's
visit to her; Guido *tells* Clara what their friend has told him, and so
on. *Cronaca di un amore* thus essentially consists of a long series of
recounted facts and intentions expressed verbally, and the rare sequences, usually arguments or love scenes, in which the spoken word
becomes genuine action, as in yesterday's film theater, constitute
exceptional poles in the film.

Whether the spoken word is a narrative vehicle or the basic action,
the result in either case is that the *complete freedom of the camera
is restored*. Rather than attempting to reproduce theatrical space, as
the American directors of the 1930's endeavored to do, or performing
perfectly gratuitous arabesques around an otherwise absolutely banal
theatricality, as Aldrich does in *The Big Knife*, Antonioni creates a
relationship between his characters as they speak and his camera as it
records them speaking, which can perhaps best be described as a
ballet. It is a ballet, moreover, of an unprecedented complexity and

The Birds

a

b, c

La Notte

a   Giovanni (Marcello Mastroianni) has vanished down the hallway
    leaving this protracted empty frame.

b, c   Cut to a new frame of indeterminate scale
       (despite the push–button clue, undetectable at a glance).

La Notte

a   Giovanni (Marcello Mastroianni) glances out of the
all but invisible window.

b   Cut to . . . what he sees?

c   Moreau's entrance determines both scale
and probable "distance" of scene.

a

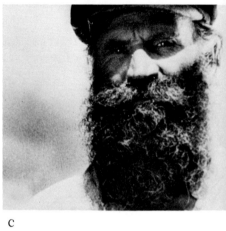

c

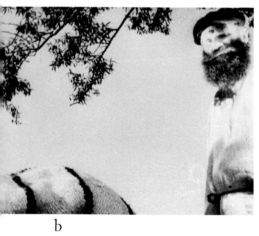

b

d

Bezhin Meadow

The sequence is complete,
as it appears in the posthumous
version of the film, except
for two titles, a repeated
close-up, and a cutaway
shot of the horses.

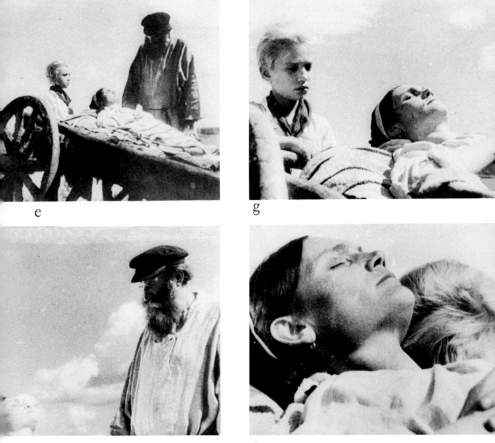

e

g

f

h

i

k

j

l

La Notte

a   The "nymphomaniac,"
having dragged Giovanni
(Marcello Mastroianni)
into her room, kicks
the door shut . . .

c   The rebound . . .

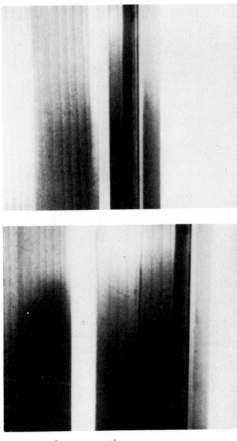

b   The lock fails to catch
and the door rebounds.

d   . . . continues . . .

e

h

f

g

La Notte (continued)

e ... until the girl enters
the frame again,
shutting the door
definitely.

f She slides along
the wall ...

g ... the camera
pans with her to h.

rigor. In Chapter 2, we have already seen how the space defined by the very prolonged shots of this film is organized internally through movements into and out of frame, how fluctuations in the suggested extent of off-screen space are determined by off-screen glances, and so on. What is particularly important to emphasize at this point, however, is that in *Cronaca di un amore* the camera movement neither humbly follows the "natural" movements of the actors, as in academically transparent cinema, nor weaves the arbitrary and frenetic arabesques around the actors' movements characteristic of the films of a Max Ophuls or an Alexandre Astruc. Rather, the manner in which both the camera and the actors move is equally stylized, with each of these two sets of movements determining the possibilities of the other. Thus the similarity to a ballet: The camera at every moment executes something equivalent to a dance step, with not only the actors as partners in the choreography but the shadows they cast as well. Di Venanzo's admirable lighting and Piero di Filipone's sets are in fact set up in such a way that there is only a single, relatively dark shadow for each actor, the image contrast otherwise remaining quite low. Of course, the ballet is not so much between the camera and the actors as between the actors and the evolving spatial area as defined by the camera: the field, or rather its two-dimensional projection, the frame. The dynamic progression of this ballet depends on constant changes in image composition through the use of every conceivable technique, by reframing, by having extras move through frame, and above all by movements into and out of frame and by changes in shot size within the shot. This constant recomposition of the film's space is its essential plastic characteristic.

Another important element in the film's underlying rhythm is the continual alternation between short (usually single-shot) sequences making maximum use of off-screen space (as when the detective is in the newspaper office or when he meets with his colleague in the police force) and longer sequences, involving two or three shots (the sequence in the night club, the film's key scene, being singularly privileged in that it extends over some ten or more shots). The film's only weakness lies in the manner in which the shot changes function. Because of the length of many of the shots, the fact that cuts from one shot to the next are disruptive breaks is very obvious

and consequently they should logically have some extremely important function to fulfill. In actual fact, however, the transitions are
often quite awkward and serve no purpose. One often feels that cuts
occur simply because the director has run out of dolly tracks—or of
imagination. The fact that there are almost no abridgements within
sequences, except for those of a very banal sort (such as transitions
from interiors to exteriors), is especially noticeable. It is an understandable approach, but one that makes striking cuts perhaps much
harder to come by. There are, however, a few remarkably successful
shot changes, due nearly every time to some break in spatial continuity. In the first of two hotel rooms where the lovers meet, a very
prolonged shot during which, among other things, Clara looks for a
misplaced earring is followed by an empty frame showing a corner
of the bed. Clara then crawls into frame to pick up the earring that
Guido has just thrown on the bed; this justification for the shot is
not provided, however, until several seconds after the transition has
occurred, thereby making the break in spatial continuity all the more
emphatic. In a later scene during which the lovers take refuge on a
staircase, we follow their ascent in a series of long crane shots, and,
just as we hear the loud off-screen sound of an elevator door slam-
ming shut, the lovers break off their argument (they are already talking about murdering the husband) and lean over the railing, sharing
the same painful memory of Guido's fiancée falling to her death
down the elevator shaft. The next shot shows the elevator approaching the camera from a very pronounced downward angle. The shot is
invariably experienced by the viewer as a "subjective" shot, as something the lovers see. Nevertheless, when a tilt, begun as the elevator
started upward, brings the camera back to a horizontal position, we
realize that it is actually on the other side of the elevator shaft, and
that the lovers still looking over the railing are actually facing us and
quite a distance away. In both cases, a "retroactive" match of the
kind described in the first chapter is involved, a technique that I feel
is one of the many possible ways in which a shot change can be
brought forcibly to our attention and its essential nature as a break
revealed, a fact of which Antonioni, in spite of my criticism, is a
good deal more aware than most film-makers.[3]

   This scene also brings us face to face with an essential problem inherent in any view of film form as a dialectical interaction: Because

of this radical disjunction between images (here treated as an almost abstract ballet) and spoken words (here treated as the sole narrative vehicle), how can the two components be interrelated?

To have maintained this separation between sound and image throughout, shooting each sequence with this disjunction alone in mind (with an image ballet on the one hand and a word narrative on the other, as is the case in the admirable sequence in the empty regatta basin), would have been to reject the possibility of an essential structural unity in the form of a continual and alternating series of divergences and convergences between sound and image, a dialectical rhythm that sometimes joins and sometimes separates what used to be called form and content. The transition between shots in the elevator shaft as described above provides an example of how this dialectical interaction functions. We are visually reminded of the lovers' thoughts and words for the few seconds during which the shot appears to be subjective (even though such subjective shots are extremely rare in this film). The moment we realize our "mistake," we are once again "outside" the characters' minds, and image and word move apart again. The great number of ways in which narrative and image are related in *Cronaca* is remarkable. (The "symbolic" method just alluded to occurs only once.) When the maid, present during the fatal elevator accident, recounts her version of the death scene, only on one occasion do her present actions coincide with her past actions: Having gone off to put her shopping basket away, she then runs back to the landing where the detective awaits her, simultaneously recounting how she had run toward the elevator after her young mistress had fallen down the shaft. (There is a similar device in *"Tentato suicidio,"* the sketch Antonioni contributed to the group film *Amore in città.*) The violence below the surface erupts on screen only four times: when Guido slaps Clara at the nightclub, at their first tryst in a cheap hotel room, on the bridge, and when Clara pretends to strangle Guido in a second hotel-room scene. These four moments are key points in the film as well. The accident in which the husband dies occurs as a very distant sound followed by a tiny glimmer of light on the horizon. Because of its marvelous understatement, this device permits Antonioni to respect the essential principle underlying the entire film (the elimination of all on-screen action), and at the same time it fulfills the need to highlight this particular moment by "showing" it rather than recounting it. A few shots later, the only "realistic" (in the sense of "repugnant") image in the film occurs, the one occasion on which Antonioni violates his principle of extreme and elegant stylization, and also a particularly dramatic moment of convergence between story and image: a close-up of the husband's dead body.

In the films Antonioni has made subsequently (*Cronaca di un amore* was his first feature-length work), he has unfortunately been excessively preoccupied with problems of content and, with the exception of *La Notte* and *L'Éclisse*, has dealt only incidentally with structural problems. He is obviously extremely conscious of these latter, but at the same time he seems wary, and even suspicious, of them. In *Cronaca di un amore*, however, he attempted to deal with a whole range of basic problems, ones that should be of utmost concern to every contemporary film-maker, and even if he was not able to solve all of them, the film represents an absolute turning point in the history of cinema.

*   *   *

Although little attention was paid it for a number of years, *Cronaca di un amore* is almost universally hailed as a masterpiece today, while another work that seems to me to be the second turning point in the history of cinema in the last twenty years remains almost entirely unknown to film-lovers and even to most young film critics.

Marcel Hanoun's *Une Simple histoire* was coproduced by the French national television network and the director in 1958–59. The film was shot in 16 mm on a very low budget. Hanoun quite literally made the film all by himself. *Une Simple histoire* nonetheless is as far removed as possible from the kind of improvised reportage that might reasonably have been expected considering the shooting conditions and subject of the film. The "plot," inspired by an item on the back page of a newspaper, has a bare, spare pathos reminiscent of one of Cesare Zavattini's classic film synopses: A woman, in all likelihood an unwed mother, arrives in Paris with her child, a little girl six or seven years old. She has only a hundred francs in her purse and has come to the city to look for work. Although she is taken in at first by a friend who lives on the outskirts of the city, she is soon forced to move from one dreary hotel to another, when her friend, fearing that the woman's presence in her house may inconvenience her lover, asks her to leave. A futile search for work follows, and she also has difficulty finding a room or keeping one more than a few days because she has a child, a hard time finding someone to care for her little girl while she looks for a job, and many other vicissitudes. Finally, after a certain number of days have gone by, her money is all gone, and she and the child are forced to spend the night in a vacant lot but are taken in the next morning by a kind woman who lives in a low-income housing project across the street. Such is the story, indeed a very simple one. Yet, starting from this basic skeleton, Hanoun constructs the most elaborate, most rigorously controlled formal structure of any feature film thus far made. In my opinion, Hanoun has created one of the few genuine masterpieces in the entire history of cinema.

The narrative line, as briefly described above, actually pivots around a single very important break, in the form of a flashback, which occurs some ten minutes into the film. At the beginning of the film the kind lady looks out of her window, sees that a woman and child have spent the night outdoors, and goes down to take them in. Later, alone in the lady's apartment with the little girl, Sylvie, the woman recalls everything that has happened to her since she has come to Paris. From that moment on the story is such as I have described it, right up until the night spent in the vacant lot. In addition, however, the film closes in a remarkable and strikingly original way: The circle is never fully completed, for we never return to the present; the flashback is left open, so to speak.

The entire film, including all the action prior to the flashback, is accompanied (although, as we shall see, "accompanied" is much too weak a term) by an off-screen commentary, spoken by the woman, which constitutes the basic structural feature of the film. To an inattentive viewer, the woman's running commentary appears to be merely redundant, and, during the film's brief run in two Paris art houses, her off-screen narration was greeted by continuous howls of laughter on the part of the audience. This is simply because it nearly always violates a cardinal rule, one discussed in any elementary manual on "how to make a perfect film": It describes what is on the screen before the viewer and repeats what has already been said in "synchronous" sound (an admittedly inaccurate term as the film was of course entirely post-synchronized). But if this is all the viewer sees in the commentary he is indeed inattentive, for anyone who pays closer attention soon notices that it functions in an altogether different manner, that its relationship to both the visual images and the spoken dialogue is constantly shifting in an extraordinary and extremely complex way throughout the entire film, in accord with a principle of variation fully deserving the term *dialectical,* which has been used perhaps a bit too loosely elsewhere in these pages. I shall now endeavor to define the poles between which the parameters of this commentary evolve.

First of all, with only two notable exceptions, the commentary functions as a simple statement of fact. The woman describes what is happening to her, what she has seen or what she has been told (even mentioning the fact that there have been times when she has said nothing or been told nothing), or (much less frequently) what she has thought or felt. On only one occasion do her remarks take the form of a complaint or rebelliousness, and even in this case they are presented as if they were just another statement of fact. Toward the end of the film, unable to sleep, she discovers in a drawer in her hotel room a magazine of the *True Confessions* variety with the story told in photos, and describes its contents (off screen) in more or less the following words: "Everyone in it was very good-looking, they drove sports cars, they didn't have to work, and drank whisky all day long." This provides a first example of Hanoun's amazing sense of a "privileged moment," with another occurring on the one occasion when the woman refers to what her life was like prior to the tribulations she is now undergoing: "I thought of going back to Lille; my father might have taken me back, but my stepmother would have made it rough for me."

Let us now examine the structural relationships between the commentary and the spoken dialogue. As it endlessly repeats what has already been said, the commentary alternates between a direct and an indirect style of narration, either quoting words already spoken on screen with the quotation marks understood or simply summarizing what has previously been said. Whenever there is an actual quotation, it is at times perfectly accurate and at other times inaccurate, whether because of inversions, substitutions of one word for another, or omissions of certain words, or a mixture of these. When a summary occurs, it may contain a quotation (either exact or inexact) or be simply a précis of the previous dialogue that may or may not be accurate, for the order of ideas expressed may be changed or there may be omissions. What gives this interaction its relief, however, is the varying time intervals between the off-screen commentary and the actual on-screen dialogue. The voice-over can completely precede the phrase spoken on screen or completely follow it (and at relatively longer or shorter intervals as well, naturally), these two possibilities constituting the outer limit of a vast range of overlappings between narration and dialogue, going so far as to include their exact congruence, when a phrase of dialogue and a phrase of the narration are precisely equal in length, although not necessarily identical in wording. Consequently it very often happens that the meaning of a given phrase can be grasped only by listening to both of the overlapping tracks simultaneously, key words emerging out of the more jumbled, incomprehensible portions to complete the meaning of what was heard during other more clearly understandable portions. I believe I am safe in saying that the same "pattern" of the two elements never recurs, for on no occasion are the disparities in time and wording exactly similar, and the "reading" of each new group is thus a different adventure. At times a phrase starts simultaneously on both tracks but ends on two different words or at two different points in time; conversely, the two tracks may start out of phase and end on the same word or at the same time. When to these many variables, we add the range of relationships between sound levels that Hanoun has created in the sound mix, extending from a perfect balance of the volume of the two tracks to the total suppression of the "synchronous" spoken words, we have some small idea of the vast realm of possibilities open to Hanoun, and he has resolutely attempted to exhaustively exploit them.

As I have already said, the commentary not only describes the words and gestures of individual characters and the objective facts but also allows the woman to express her thoughts and feelings. In this case, however, what may be described as a "structuring by elimination" comes into play, an altogether remarkable device both because of its formal and its poetic effect.[4] As the woman's situation worsens, she increasingly shrinks from revealing her thoughts or her feelings (having shown these latter only three or four times previously anyway). Her voice-over remarks become flatter and more dully matter-of-fact and even include a line whose overwhelming banality indicates how severe the alienation this woman is undergoing is and thus constitutes the crowning moment of the film. As she stops near a railing on one of the city's outer boulevards, she says in voice-over: "I walked by an underpass. Cars were going in one end and coming out the other." The scene in the vacant lot follows, a sort of pathetic coda during which we hear her "inner monologue" again, very briefly: "And then I no longer remember . . . I found myself in a vacant lot . . . I bundled Sylvie up in my raincoat . . . she fell asleep . . . I did too . . . I woke up with a start . . . I was afraid . . . I was cold [a very long close-up of the woman staring off into space follows, and then a long shot of the housing development, the final image in the film] . . . lights were still on in some of the windows."

Successfully describing the dialectical interaction between commentary and image in *Une Simple histoire* involves examining both the film's visual structure and its temporal dialectics. A close reading of the scenario would no doubt allow us to determine how many days pass between the woman's arrival in Paris and the morning when she is taken in by the charitable lady. The passage of narrative time, however, is not made "palpable" through the actual succession of days and nights on the screen, but rather through the way in which the woman's hundred francs dwindle away, for she is shown again and again anxiously counting and recounting her money. Using this concrete device to make us acutely aware of the passage of time, Hanoun's *découpage* employs throughout an amazing variety of temporal ellipses within the time flow thus established. Regardless of whether or not it preserves spatial continuity, a shot transition can abridge any amount of time ranging from a few seconds to twenty-four hours or more. Hanoun is the first modern film-maker to my knowledge to have systematically abridged time through changes of scale along the same camera angle.[5] So as to make the constant variations in the extent of time abridged both apparent and *aesthetically functional*, Hanoun naturally incorporates the voice-over commentary into his system of ellipses. The simple indication of the actual extent of time abridged is not all that is involved (although that too sometimes occurs, as when an admirable match along one camera angle indicates the passage of a whole night through a very minor change between the scales of two successive close-ups, each showing the woman in bed but each lit differently, with the second of these followed by the woman saying: "I woke up in the morning. It was the overly bright sun that woke me . . .". Hanoun uses the voice-over mainly to create some sense of what transpires in the time span abridged in these very abrupt elisions (there is not a single dissolve in the film and very few fades). At one point, a shot taken in the hotel room is followed by a long shot out in the street. The woman is shown holding her child by the hand and bending down to pick up a croissant lying on the sidewalk, as the commentary says: "I bought a croissant for Sylvie . . . she didn't want it and threw it away . . ." Yet, before the sentence ends, she has offered the croissant to a bum who staggers by. And the remaining portion of the scene is recounted with a very noticeable lag not only between verbal text and visual image but also between the moment when we grasp what is going on and the moment when the woman describes the scene in the voice-over, one of many forms of possible interaction between narration and image. The woman never uses the word "bum": He is, in her words, a "man" passing by, and only at the very end of the scene does she rather delicately add that "he had been drinking" although from the moment he appeared on the screen it has been obvious to the viewer that he is dead drunk.

Another scene provides some indication of how complex the interaction between the forms of temporal contraction and the voice-over can become. Having seen an ad in the paper with the address of a company that is hiring people, the woman and child make their way down to the *Métro*. In the next shot, the woman walks past a street sign, exits, and the screen remains empty. The voice-over says, "I finally found the street." An establishing shot of the inside of a café follows. Sylvie is seated in the foreground with her back to the camera, and the voice-over continues, "I had asked someone to take care of Sylvie, but even so the job had been taken by the time I got there." At this point, the woman walks into frame and sits down facing Sylvie and the camera. In a matching medium shot from the same camera angle, the woman lifts her head and looks toward the camera. "I ordered a cup of chocolate," the commentary continues. There then follows a new shot, still from the same angle, as she drinks her chocolate in close-up. "Sylvie had gone outside without my noticing [she lifts her head toward the camera], but the waitress saw her and brought her back inside." A new shot from the same angle takes us back to the initial composition. Sylvie is once again (or still?) sitting facing her mother with the waitress already exiting from frame. In this extremely complicated scene, the narration not only suggests the action taking place in the span of time omitted between shots (resulting in this case in the complete elimination of all dialogue in the scene, all the supposed lines having been spoken in the intervals between shots) but also suggests events taking place in a kind of no-man's land, for they might be construed as occurring either off screen or during some portion of abridged time. *Une Simple histoire* abounds in complex structures of this sort, never before used by any film-maker.

Other more "incidental" structures, finally, are grafted onto these overarching dialectical movements, which play the primary role in determining the film's formal structure as a whole. These incidental structures are based on the woman's various encounters, such as her different confrontations with hotel-keepers and others (though we never actually see the people she asks for jobs). The most interesting of these structures appears to me to be the one centered on her search for food. On five separate occasions, the voice-over speaks of the purchase of either milk or some kind of canned goods, yet we never witness the actual buying or consuming of any of these items, only their preparation on a gas burner in hotel rooms. This preparation of food, which becomes one of the obsessive themes in the film, is prefigured before the flashback by a very brief dream the woman has as she dozes off in her chair in the lady's apartment: A gas burner sits in the middle of a vacant lot and the woman dances happily around it heating up some milk as the birds sing and the sun shines brightly. On the last day, however, just before the woman vacates her last hotel room, we finally witness the purchase and consumption, though not the actual preparation, of food. This constitutes a kind of "negative reversal" of the structure as so often repeated previously. The formally crucial moment this reversal in structure represents is followed by a similar one. While buying a croissant for Sylvie (the third one to appear in the film, the first having been given to the child by a kind-hearted waitress), the woman does something foolish with the little money she has left—she buys her daughter a little surprise-package, resulting in the only line in the entire film spoken by Sylvie. "It's ugly," she says, as she throws away the favor she found in the paper cornucopia.

Besides these patterns with variations repeated all through the film, there are a number of formal devices that occur only very rarely, but that are structurally linked through their complete "unreality" in an otherwise "realistic" context. The dream described above is the first example. A day spent searching for work is depicted by a long single close-up of the woman looking into the camera, raising and lowering her eyes as a montage of factory noises indicates the compression of time. In the shot immediately following, another "magical" device occurs, in the form of another temporal ellipsis. The woman exits from a building and then from frame, leaving the screen empty, as the voice-over says that at one place they told her to return the next day. She then exits from the building and from frame once again with no intervening change of shot. "But the next day there was nothing," the commentary says. (The fact that two "magical" devices are used in immediate succession in itself constitutes a form of emphasis.) Later she leaves her hotel at night and gets lost in the surrounding streets. Her wanderings are indicated by her crossing the screen twice, first from right to left, then from left to right, against the same perfectly abstract black background. Near the end of the film, finally, when she has run out of money and is evicted from her last hotel room, she goes to a railway embankment and stares down at some train tracks visible through an iron fence in a series of shots and reverse shots. "I passed by some railroad tracks," the commentary says. The sound of an approaching train grows louder and louder, yet when the reverse angle shows the tracks, they are rusted and overgrown with grass. The sound of the train then grows louder still, so loud in fact that the rest of the voice-over is nearly inaudible. "But they must not have been used for a long time," her voice then adds.

Although I feel that I have succeeded in describing the film's structural complexity, I am not so certain that I have accounted for the qualities that make *Une Simple histoire* a masterpiece. Although the poetic force of such scenes as those in the café and overlooking the railroad tracks seems evident even when described in simple technical terms, there is almost no way to describe the astonishing performance of Micheline Bezançon, an actress as unjustly neglected today as the film itself; nor does there seem to be any way to give the reader any idea of the extraordinary beauty of her delivery of a text that on paper might seem flat and even simple-minded.

"Attentive viewers" who do not like the film (and generally those who find it not to their taste scoff at it or hate it with a passion) usually object to the subject, which they find puerile, sentimental, saccharine, or trivial. When it comes to judging a truly cinematic work, that is to say a work multiple in dimension and formally exhaustive in treatment, to take issue with the subject is to commit a great error. After all, are not the subjects of *Crime and Punishment* and *Macbeth* just as trivial when reduced to their bare outlines? The manner in which the subject is formally developed is what makes them masterpieces; and the same is true of *Une Simple histoire*.

The film ought to be given wider distribution. Surely in each generation of film-makers, there are two or three minds capable of grasping its enormous, indeed incalculable significance (as did Jacques Becker, who saw it while in the process of filming his own masterpiece, *Le Trou*). Hanoun's absolutely rigorous attitude vis-à-vis the material he was treating is exemplary, and material here means the sum total of faces, words, gestures, sounds, images, shot and scale changes, and so on, a whole in which every element is, a priori, absolutely equal in importance and in which *everything* plays a functional role in the plastic organization of the film. The organization he thus achieves is admittedly empirical, but in the last analysis only an empirical organization can attain in film that complete organic articulation that thus far in the history of cinema only Marcel Hanoun has achieved with his "Simple Story."[6]

Notes

1. Although practically never shown publicly, even in Paris, this film was taken up at one point by radical French literary and film critics (especially those involved with the magazines *Tel Quel* and *Cinéthique*) who considered it a fundamental break with bourgeois representational film-making. I have decided to keep this somewhat polemical passage not so much on account of its polemical character, but because I feel it tackles a fundamental miscon-

ception, one that has been cropping up in much recent "advanced" European film-making (cf. in particular *Fata Morgana* by Werner Herzog).

2. Existing in this embryonic state in almost any commercial film.

3. The special importance assumed by the cut when it occurs within a context otherwise characterized by prolonged shots is quite apparent in the work of Kenji Mizoguchi, the director who has unquestionably used the plastic potential *within* each individual shot to the greatest advantage. In most of his films, however—*The Love of Actress Sumako* (1947) is a notable exception— he seems to pay almost no attention to the transitions *between* shots. In *The Life of O'Haru*, his masterpiece, only some five or six transitions seem to make any functional use at all of the privileged position they occupy, terminating as they do very long shots. Preoccupied with the skillful reframings at which he excels, Mizoguchi simply ends a shot when there is nothing more he feels he can do with it, continuing on to the next shot just as one might turn the pages of a picture book. The important thing to be pointed out here, however, is that the more prolonged the shot is, the more apparent this quite shocking neglect becomes. This serves to underline a basic fact: the longer the shot, the more important the manner in which the film-maker cuts to the next shot.

4. Another formal approach not without analogies to twelve-tone music.

5. A technique, however, that the great pioneer film-maker Léonce Perret had thought up as early as 1912!

6. Today I have to admit that this is something of an exaggeration. For although I still feel that few directors have achieved what Hanoun did achieve, I would now add one or two other films here, in particular, Dreyer's *Vampyr*, a film that at the time of writing I scarcely knew.

6

On the Structural Use of Sound

The fundamental dialectic in film, the one that at least empirically seems to contain every other, is that contrasting and joining sound with image. The *necessary* interrelationship of sound and image today appears to be definitely established fact, as even the most doubting critic must concede once he has examined the history of film. From the very beginnings of our art, starting with Méliès's showings of his films in the basement of a Paris café, audiences and film-makers alike felt the need for some sort of sound (that is, musical) background for these images whose *silence* was unbearable,[1] despite the fact that it was this very silence that was the source of a great dramatic art now unfortunately lost.[2]

Robert Bresson, commenting on his own film practice, has made some rather revealing and pertinent remarks on the dichotomy of sound and image.[3] According to this film-maker, sound, because of its greater realism, is infinitely more evocative than an image, which is essentially only a stylization of visual reality. "A sound always evokes an image; an image never evokes a sound," Bresson contends, and he then goes on to state, with just a touch of false naïveté, that he replaces an image with a sound whenever possible, thus remaining completely faithful to the principle of maximum bareness and spareness underlying his creative method.

But is this the real essence of the problem of the relationship between sound and image? Aside from the fact that Bresson's second tenet does not really seem to follow from the first, I am not entirely certain that sound is as realistic as all that, although it certainly can be. Gregory Markopoulos's film *Twice a Man*, for instance, is preceded by some five minutes of sound effects that half the audience is apt to describe as falling rain and the other half as a crowd applauding. Obviously the image could help us decide, but as it happens the screen is blacked out, so that the sound in effect occurs off screen and is therefore precisely the sort of sound Bresson maintains can replace an image. As this example indicates, the ease with which a sound can be "deciphered" can vary as much as the ease with which the image can be "read." An extreme auditory "close-up" of a drop of water dripping into a sink is as difficult to recognize for what it really is as an extreme visual close-up of the joint of a woman's thumb (see *Geography of the Body* by Willard Maas). Any sound engineer can tell us how difficult it is to make certain sounds seem "natural," particularly if they occur off screen—that is to say, without the explanatory support furnished by the image. Bresson himself always uses easily identifiable off-screen sounds such as footsteps and creaking doors, thereby considerably limiting his sound palette. And Bresson's contention notwithstanding, a face or landscape filmed without extraneous "effects," although always a stylization of reality, as we are aware *after the fact*, will seem just as "realistic" as a door we merely hear creaking on the sound track. The evocatory effect of sound seems to me to relate more to the powers of suggestion inherent in off-screen space in everything relating to it: An off-screen glance is just as evocative. There does not seem to me to be anything *inherently* evocative in the nature of sound, even if off-screen space is obviously frequently brought to life through the sound track.

It seems that the essential nature of the relationship between sound and image is due not to the difference between them, but rather to the similarity between them. A previous chapter described how a camera's nonselectivity contrasts with the natural process of selection of the human eye, and the consequence to be deduced from this fact: the need to consider each composition as a totality. There is a similar difference between the way the human ear hears and the

way a microphone records. As an example, we might use a conversation taking place inside a moving car. In a real-life situation such as
this, it is usually quite easy to ignore any sounds that might interfere
with our comprehension (the noise of the motor, the wind, the
radio, and so on) and grasp what our fellow passengers are saying
despite such sounds. A microphone recording the same conversation
under the same conditions could not distinguish between the different sounds, however, and would jumble them all together;[4] and
the sounds emerging from the single source of the loud-speaker in
the theater would all be equally "present," much as a camera reduces
the three-dimensionality of real space to the two-dimensionality of
screen space.

Just as a game in progress on a pinball machine cannot be filmed
in a comprehensible manner without somehow toning down the surface reflections on the glass above, so too the possibilities of recording a comprehensible conversation in a car are rather slight. For such
a conversation to be understandable, background noises and dialogue
must be recorded separately and their relative levels determined
during the sound mix.[5]

Because of the "equal presence" of all the sound components of a
film as they are channeled through the "funnel" of the loud-speaker
in the theater, an over-all "musical "orchestration of all the distinct
elements of the sound track seems to be imperative, in somewhat the
same manner that the way in which a visual image is perceived demands that constant attention be paid to the total visual composition.

As has already been indicated in Chapter 4, there are certain dialectical possibilities inherent in the very nature of the sound track,
not unlike the "photographic" dialectics already discussed. I shall
now attempt to draw up a list of these.

The example of the car presupposes the existence of at least two
different kinds of *auditory material*, "live" or "synchronous" sound
on the one hand and recomposed sound produced by a mix—two
types of sound that unquestionably provide the two poles of a dialectic similar to those dialectics of materials already discussed in reference to the visual image and bearing a great resemblance to one of
them in particular. This sound dialectic would normally occur in
conjunction with the dialectical alternation of "live" and "staged"

shots and reinforce it. In actual practice, however, "improvised" shots are often completely post-synchronized ("dubbed") in a sound studio, whereas carefully staged shots are often accompanied by background sounds recorded live. Generally, it is a question of mere convenience: The director simply chooses the handiest means available to make the scenes being filmed as "lifelike" and as comprehensible as possible. Nonetheless, a complex interaction among these four poles is quite conceivable, and it might well become an essential underlying pattern for a new kind of film (I shall discuss this possibility in more detail in Chapter 7, when I take up the subject of the manipulation of chance). Even now, alternations between live and reconstituted sound occurring in conjunction with the corresponding visual alternations provide certain television programs with a very simple yet very effective structural framework. A transition from the noiseless environment of a sound stage or sound studio to the chaotic bustle of life in a shot taken in the street enormously enhances the viewer's awareness of the sudden break implicit in such a transition. This break, moreover, is experienced in an infinitely more *physical* manner than would have been the case had one carefully controlled shot been followed by one only a little less carefully controlled, if only because of the sudden tremendous increase in both the area and the indeterminacy of the off-screen space. The ambient silence a studio provides is one of the principles underlying studio recording, in fact; sounds are then introduced into it in such a way as to make our awareness of off-screen space as clear and simple as possible; and the greater or lesser differentiation of off-screen space provides another possible way of interrelating the various dialectics.

Another essential sound parameter results from the *apparent microphone distance*. A number of very complex auditory phenomena, the most important being resonance or "echo," are what determine the apparent distance between the recording microphone and the sound source (or more accurately, between this source and the theater loud-speaker, usually located just behind the screen). Structural interactions between auditory and visual space can be created rather easily through the use of this parameter, and significant but isolated attempts to do so exist in the contemporary film. (The very fact that such attempts are relatively rare provides yet another proof of

my contention that sound experimentation is at least ten years behind other areas of investigation of the formal possibilities of film;
the reasons for this will be examined at the end of this chapter.)

The long shots of a couple walking on the beach and talking to
each other in a sound close-up in Agnès Varda's *La Pointe courte*
provide perhaps a rather rudimentary example of the manner in
which a sound "presence" can counterpoint a visual one. Orson
Welles in his *Othello*, however, by emphasizing and even exaggerat-
ing the congruency of auditory presence and visual presence, has
creatively demonstrated the dynamic possibilities inherent in juxtapositions of extreme close-ups and long shots. Extreme close-ups are
associated with an extremely intimate sound "presence," the long
shots with an exaggerated booming echo, and the sharp contrast between them serves as one of the elements of the deliberately jerky
découpage of this film, already mentioned in Chapter 3.

Another form of interaction between visual space and sound
presence perhaps even richer in potential can be found in Mizoguchi's *The Crucified Lovers*, a film that even today remains at the
very forefront of experimentation in the relations of sound and
image. Toward the end of the film, prior to the lovers' final cap-
ture, when Sessame's brother steals off to get the police, the silence
that attends his slipping away into the distance is suddenly interrupted by a musical motif played fortissimo, percussively, on the
zither-like *samisen* in extreme sound close-up. The contrast between
the remoteness of the visual "subject" and the close proximity of the
sound "subject" produces an extremely startling effect; it is almost
as if a new character had suddenly appeared in the shot in an extreme visual close-up, although it is precisely the absence of any new
visual presence in the area close to the camera and the resulting *surprise*[6] that makes this moment such a dramatically tense one.

It will be noticed that, concerning the modes of interaction between the various sound materials as well as those between auditory
and visual space, I make no distinction between music, dialogue,
and sound effects. These two types of dialectical interaction can in
fact involve any sort of sound. Shared as it is by a small but growing
minority of film-makers these days, this attitude brings the ultimate
aim of contemporary experiments in the use of sound a step closer
to realization: the creation, that is, of a coherent, organically struc-

tured sound track in which the forms of interaction between sound and image will be closely tied to other interactions between the three basic types of film sounds: dialogue; music; and sound effects, whether identifiable or not. Mizoguchi's[7] *The Crucified Lovers* is a pioneer effort in this direction as well. The particular quality of Japanese music (to be discussed further below) with its predominance of abrupt percussive sounds and its eminently "graphic" structures obviously made it easier to create some form of interaction between sound effects and music. Yet, even granting the advantage Japanese music confers, Mizoguchi's sound track is a unique achievement in the history of cinema. In a scene in which the hero hides in an attic, a succession of sounds with a distinct rhythm of their own created by the wooden bowls from which the hero has been eating, then by a ladder banging against the wall, provide the first notes (of somewhat indeterminate pitch) in a musically orchestrated structure that goes on to incorporate instruments with tone qualities similar to those of these "natural" sound effects. Another musical passage ends on a "note" that in fact is the sound of a door closing in frame. Aside from the organic, dialectical link established in this way between "functional" sound effects and music, the very fact that the sound effects are synchronous with a visual image results in other interactions, this time between the images and the entire sound tissue of the film, which at times shifts without a break from an off-screen to an on-screen "presence."

Another possible relationship between sound, particularly music, and image (a dialectical relationship in so far as it periodically draws sound and image together) involves the creation of an *analogy* between them. A scene of struggle in a bamboo thicket is accompanied by a brief flurry of sounds made on instruments similar to wood-blocks that are strongly suggestive of the sounds that might result were one to tap on the bamboo stalks filling the screen. It is difficult to conceive of this approach ever leading to any very substantial developments, yet Eisenstein considered this a very important form of interaction (as exemplified in the coronation scene in *Ivan the Terrible*, where the close-up of the imperial globe is accompanied by an extremely low and resonant bass note), just as he attributed great importance to all other forms of analogy between sound and image, as his analysis of Prokofiev's score of *Alexander Nevsky* indicates.

Let us now return to a possibility suggested above, that of integrating sound effects and music into a single sound texture. Obviously dialogue, the third form of sound, can also play a role in creating such a relationship. Once again, there is no doubt that Japanese theatrical diction, with its shrieking, panting, rumbling sounds constituting a tonal range similar to that of Schoenbergian *Sprachgesang*, is particularly capable of organically interacting with other forms of sound so as to create a single complex sound texture. Mizoguchi (in *The Crucified Lovers* and other films) and Kurosawa (notably in *The Lower Depths* and *The Hidden Fortress*) have explored some of the possibilities of "musically" orchestrating dialogue, if not specifically incorporating them into the over-all sound complex. Yet it is Joseph von Sternberg, approaching the Japanese language "from the outside" (the dialogue in *The Saga of Anatahan* is not supposed to be comprehensible to the audience), who most consciously exploited the resources of that language, sometimes closely coupled with stylized sound effects, to create purely auditory patterns.

Nonetheless the most interesting attempt to treat dialogue as both the vehicle for the dramatic action and musically organized sound is Abraham Polonsky's "film maudit," *Force of Evil*. Here the entire dialogue takes the form of alliterations, dissonant rhymes, and rhythmical effects of every sort, even at times serving as a sort of "relay" for the sound effects, as when knocks on a door repeat the rhythm and timbre of the preceding line of dialogue.

In the examples thus far cited, sound effects, even when treated in close dialectical association with music or dialogue, have in each case been related in some manner either to an event seen on screen or or to an off-screen event linked in some way to the action and playing some role in it (as the sea-shell curtains in *Anatahan* or the knocks on the door in *Force of Evil* do). Certain sound technicians, however, have explored the possibility of treating sound effects much more freely, giving them the role the musical score purportedly plays in most films that have one. The person in France to have most systematically experimented with this approach is Michel Fano, a composer turned sound engineer and then film-maker, but whose attention is primarily directed toward what his Brazilian counterparts refer to as "audioplastics"—that is, with the conception and technical execution of the entire sound complex, during not only the editing but also the actual shooting as well, in so far as preconceived sound structures can determine certain visual components. Michel Fano's most interesting work has been in collaboration with Alain Robbe-Grillet, whose films represent the most exhaustive and thoroughgoing attempts I know of to organize musically off-screen sound. Mizoguchi, as we have seen, created a sound texture in which visually identifiable on-screen sounds synchronous with the image were intimately associated with musical elements (occurring by definition, off screen), these two sound parameters being linked through similarities in tone quality as well. Although among the first to realize the importance of the use of sound in *The Crucified Lovers*, Michel Fano nonetheless proceeds in an altogether different manner. He often starts with a visual element (the garage or the harbor in *L'Immortelle*, for instance) and then progressively incorporates off-screen sounds into the sound track, organizing them into "musical" structures—hammer blows supposedly coming from the garage, a concert of sirens from the ships in the harbor—thereby contrasting a highly articulated and "graphic" off-screen auditory space with the plastic and dynamic organization of the images.

This extreme stylization of off-screen sound (in which synchronous elements can function as rhythmical punctuation—the pneumatic train doors and the hardware store chimes in *Trans-Europ-Express* are two notable examples) is achieved through the organization of real-life sounds (usually left just as they are or tinkered with only a little bit) into structures that, if not exactly serial (the sounds involved often being of indeterminate pitch and in any case untempered), nevertheless are quite similar to the strategies of contemporary music.

Fano thus far has not included all three types of sound (sound effects, music, and dialogue) as components, nor has he established the constant "relays" with the image that are needed if the full *dialectical* implications of this type of organization of sound are ever to be realized. This would obviously require the total collaboration of film-maker and sound engineer throughout every stage of the conception and execution of a film.[8] A first step has nonetheless been taken, and there is no reason why a film-maker should not some day be able to create a vast dialectical interaction between sound and image by applying, among others, the principles of serial organization to his *découpage*, exploiting, on the one hand, the various temporal and spatial dialectics we have outlined, and, on the other, the possible forms of combining the three types of sound and integrating the resulting auditory configurations with the film's over-all plastic conception.

Fano is not altogether alone in his research in this direction. When Jacques Rivette asked Jean-Claude Éloy to create the sound effects and music for *The Nun*, he indicated his interest in this kind of experimentation. And a group of young Brazilians, working notably with Pereira dos Santos on his *Vidas secas*, have shown talent and sensitivity to the plastic organization of sounds motivated by the image (as particularly demonstrated by the incredible beauty of the prolonged creaking of a cartwheel that serves as a "musical" accompaniment to the credit sequence in this film).

The accomplishments of these young Brazilians, however, also reflect the desire on the part of a large number of film-makers to eliminate entirely any sort of traditional music score, believing as they do that more or less structured sound effects,[9] possibly combined with musical themes drawn from our classical musical heritage (as, for example, the use of fragments from *La Traviata* in *Trans-Europ-Express* or motifs from Beethoven's quartets in *Une Femme mariée*) can and should replace what in their eyes is a totally discredited convention. In view of the very bad uses to which musical scores have been put in the sound film, this attitude can easily be defended. Nevertheless, to reject categorically the possibility of complete auditory stylization that music provides is to deprive oneself somewhat arbitrarily of a raw material that, when properly approached, can lead to an undeniable enrichment of a film. Without its musical score, *The Crucified Lovers*, for instance, would be a rather minor work. For, no matter how moving Chikamatsu's story is, the film is far from the plastic equal of *Sansho the Bailiff* or *The Life of O'Haru*; it is the score and the sound effects that make the film into a near masterpiece.

Films about which the same can be said are few in number, as there are few works of cinema in which music is an organic and integral part of the over-all formal texture. As I have already indicated, Japanese classical music seems particularly amenable to this sort of integration.[10] It would appear that this is due to the extremely flexible, supple, "open" quality of this music (which is not subject to the "tyranny of the bar-line" as Western music is and above all is not restricted to tonal structures) that makes it infinitely more adaptable to the eminently nonmeasurable rhythms of film "action" and film editing. Japanese music, however hieratic, seems to have a freer flow, an empirical quality closer to that of the film image. Moreover, as was mentioned in the discussion of *The Crucified Lovers*, a large number of the timbres found in Japanese music are similar to everyday sounds, thus making the organic interaction of sound effects and music suggested here easier to achieve.

What might a Western film-maker conclude from these observations? The generalized use of Japanese music in its pure state is obviously not possible in Western cinema. One revealing fact, however, might be pointed out here: Japanese music was not really accessible to the Western ear until after the introduction of atonal music; young serial composers see profound affinities between their work and classical Japanese music, as would not have been the case with any Western musician before Debussy.

Serial music, then, the most "open" form in the history of Western music, with its unprecedented rhythmical freedom and its use of timbres that classical musicians considered vulgar noises, seems uniquely suited to organic, dialectical integration of music with sound effects, as well as with the filmed image, whereas traditional tonal music with its predetermined forms, its strong tonal polarities, and its range of relatively homogeneous tone colors can provide only an autonomous continuity existing *alongside* that of the images, merely running parallel to the dialogue and sound effects or accompanying the images with a musical synchronicity of the sort found in animated cartoons.[11] Serial music, on the other hand, provides the most open form conceivable. In its interstices, every form of sound has a natural place, and it can provide an ideal complement to the "irrational" quality of the concrete image as such as well as to the more rational structures created by the *découpage*. Serial composers starting with Webern were, moreover, the first to consider silence as an essential musical component. After a long period during which the talking picture with a musical score seems to have been haunted by the terror, or perhaps the memory, of silence, young film-makers have at last begun to be aware of the dialectical role silence can play relative to sound. These film-makers have even suc-

ceeded in making a subtle yet basic distinction between the different
"colors" of silence (a complete dead space on the sound track, studio
silence, silence in the country, and so forth), thus glimpsing some
of the structural roles such silences can play (as is particularly evident in *Deux ou trois choses que je sais d'elle*).

The reader will rightly feel that this chapter is more sketchy than
some of the others. This is largely because it was written ten years
too early, for, as has already been said, the evolution of film sound
lags far behind that of the film image. Even in the most "advanced"
contemporary films (*Une Simple histoire, Last Year at Marienbad,
Nicht Versöhnt, Persona,* and others), sound plays the role of a
"poor relation" of the image: From the standpoint of its inherent
possibilities, it participates in the experimental search for new forms
only in the most minimal sort of way. The few experimenters who
could remedy this situation have thus far not been given the means
with which to do so. To organize successfully and totally a sound
track both internally and relative to the image, to create a total
sound texture and bring every one of its components under control
(by manufacturing street sounds from discrete real sounds, for instance), the amount of money budgeted for sound in an ordinary
film project would have to be doubled. That subtleties of this sort
should seem rather pointless to those who finance films is more or
less to be expected, and thus the immediate future looks bleak. But
one can always hope that the qualified experimenters will some day
find the means with which to carry out successfully the formal research that is crucial if cinema is ever to realize fully its inherent
potential in this area.

Notes

1. It is usually maintained that this silence was unbearable only because it
allowed the noise of the projector to be heard. This silence, however, is no
less painful in situations where the projector noise cannot be heard, as is the
case at the Cinémathèque Française. Fritz Lang's *Mabuse* made a much
greater impression on all of us when we were finally able to see it with a
musical accompaniment like that provided in the days of silent film. Admittedly the music in this case is little more than sound background; nevertheless, it provides a time scale against which the "rhythms" of the *découpage*
become far more concrete.

2. Garrel's completely silent film *Le Révélateur*, as well as many "new American" films, seem to indicate that this is not entirely true.

3. In a program in the *Cinéastes de notre temps* series, directed by François Weyergans.

4. Under certain conditions directional—that is, selective—microphones can remedy this, but this fact does not invalidate the present argument, at least in so far as human perception is concerned; especially when the peculiar and rather bad quality of the sound thus obtained results in merely another stylization, a phenomenon comparable to what happens to a voice heard over the telephone.

5. Godard, who is quite interested in sound interference of this sort, often records similar scenes in synchronous sound (or recreates the same effect in a studio), doubtless to make us aware of the effort our ear must make to understand whatever message is being transmitted.

6. See Chapter 8.

7. A certain amount of similar experimentation can be found, although in far less systematic form, in some of Mizoguchi's other films, notably in *Story of the Late Chrysanthemums*, *The Life of O'Haru*, and *Sansho the Bailiff*.

8. Just before the French edition went to press, I saw *L'Homme qui ment* (*The Man Who Lies*), the admirable outcome of all the experiments Fano had undertaken previously, a film in which the three types of sound are integrated in an almost flawless manner, although their integration with the image and the film's *découpage* is perhaps a bit too episodic. And of course we must now add Fano's own film on animals, *Le Territoire des autres*, his most important experiment to date.

9. The opposite procedure, in which musical and paramusical elements replace certain sound effects, resulting in a form of dialectics of materials, often explored when sound was first introduced (notably in Boris Barnett's *Okraina*, the first feature film to have a sound track based on artificial sounds, obtained by filming geometrical patterns directly on the optical track) and by Sternberg in his *Saga of Anatahan*, has apparently been temporarily abandoned, except for its use in purely experimental films. This dialectic nevertheless is rich in possibilities, and it will surely soon be explored again.

10. Aside from the Mizoguchi films already mentioned, other films in which this integration is partially achieved are Kon Ichikawa's *Enjo* and Ishida's *Fallen Flowers*, (1939).

11. The exceptions to this seeming general rule are few and far between. One of the most noteworthy is Giovanni Fuco's score for *Cronaca di un amore*, where the use of two instruments with strongly contrasting tone qualities (a saxophone and a piano, usually used separately), of a musical style closely associated with the film's *découpage* and even with the dialogue, and of a quite subtle musical development in which the themes consist of little more than recurring musical intervals creates a "graphic" relationship between music and film; the score in fact is one of the principal elements contributing to the film's unity.

III

Perturbing Factors

7

Chance and Its Functions

The concept of sheer chance is a very fashionable one in contemporary art, and, like every fashion, there is a very serious concern underlying it. This particular fashion sheds considerable light on one striking trend in current aesthetic theory: the many ways in which, in the West, the traditional integrity of the work of art is being challenged, and the manner in which the artist's heretofore inviolate, demiurgic role is being questioned. These explorations also extend beyond these avant-garde concerns, however, for they reflect a very widespread, although confused, impatience with the solidly established tradition of the "closed" as against the "open" work of art.

What might the terms "chance" and "open work" mean in film? In literature, theater, painting, dance, and above all music, these terms have meant, among other things, the sudden intrusion of more or less "natural" contingencies into the totally artificial world of the work of art, in which *in principle* they are completely out of place. This phenomenon occurs in cinema as well, although in an altogether different form, as we shall see further on.

At this point I shall undertake a brief survey of the use of chance in another art, music, not because I am persuaded that such techniques should be directly employed in film, but rather simply to examine what the general nature of chance in art might be, and what possible pattern of interferences there may be between the contingent and the determined. I have chosen to refer to chance in music rather than in painting, literature, or dance because music lends itself most readily to an examination of the problem in abstract terms, thus clearing the way for a more concrete application of these ideas to film later in this chapter. Moreover, it is composers who have been the most deeply concerned with this problem and explored it the most systematically.

It is often said that young composers of the contemporary school are endeavoring to introduce random elements into their music, but in actual fact this is merely one of many possible aleatory techniques, and what is more, it appears to be the most dubious, or, if the reader prefers, the most radical of any currently being employed in their art. Those giving themselves over to experiments of this sort are divided into two groups, which occasionally overlap. There are those, first, who introduce into the work as it is being performed a contingent world completely beyond both the composer's and the performer's control, its relationship to the work consequently being totally fortuitous. John Cage and his "prepared piano" provide an example: He places on the piano strings various loose objects, which move about during the performance, thus distorting the tonalities of the instrument in an absolutely unpredictable manner; some of his young German disciples provoke audience reactions, which are then "incorporated" into the work being performed, somewhat in the manner of a happening. As I have said, this constitutes the most radical approach to the aleatoric, the joyful and lucid abandonment by the composer of a portion of his conscious control over the work.

This temptation, however, to "let go of the reins," to relinquish control, is also felt by other composers, with one crucial difference: They prefer to see the breath of sheer chance—that is to say, of the purely accidental—pass over their work *before* it is placed before the public. Cage has composed music by flipping a coin ("Music of Changes"), and a few contemporary composers, the best known in France being Ianis Xenakis, have gone so far as to entrust certain decisions regarding composition to computers. We are obviously confronted here with the notorious notion of "controlled chance"—one that can conceal a good deal of confused thinking. When a listener asked Xenakis whether he deliberately tampered with the results he obtained from his computers, the composer is reported to have replied, "Yes, for aesthetic reasons."(!)

However, any film-maker, in particular, can attest to the fascination experienced by a creative artist when he contemplates and "displays" objects or materials that he himself has not created and that strike him as being all the more beautiful simply because they are not a product of his talent (that is, Man, the Artist, is not their Creator). One thinks here of Marcel Duchamp's "ready-mades." He can also attest to the even greater satisfaction the artist experiences when he *reworks* materials and objects of this kind, deliberately integrating them with others of his own creation, reincorporating them into a closed work—in short, snatching them from the slag heap of the accidental where they originated and preserving throughout the unique originality of these materials fallen from another world, as in Schwitters's collages.

However, the forms in which chance predominantly occurs in contemporary music, mainly because they are the forms the aleatoric takes in the works of the most respected composers, has nothing at all to do with the random. These types of chance enter into the elaboration of "open" works—ones, that is, capable of assuming a multiplicity of forms, either through the sharing of creative responsibilities (as in improvisation within predetermined limits) or through the incorporation of "alternatives" in the work (works with a variable rather than a fixed mode of performance, with interchangeable movements, and so on), or, more frequently, through a combination of both approaches.

On several occasions, I have established parallels between the potential structures of film and those currently being effectively employed in serial music. In almost every instance, anticipating possible objections, I was careful to state that analogies of this sort were valid only to a limited degree and emphasized that they should not be taken literally. It is in dealing with the problem of the aleatoric, I feel, that I will be best able to distinguish between the absolutely abstract world of music and the simultaneously abstract and concrete world of film, a distinction that should be kept in mind whenever any parallel between the two arts is suggested. Of the two different forms in which the aleatoric can occur, the first (its direct intervention in a work, whether controlled or uncontrolled) seems the more "organically relevant" to film, whereas the second (its use in the creation of works with multiple modes of performance) seems to be the more relevant to music. The formal strategy involved in creating a work with multiple itineraries, regardless of whether or not the soloists are given any initiative, is a logical extension of the serial approach in general and, through it, of the entire history of Western music. No basic historical continuity is destroyed by it, while the deliberate introduction into music of completely random elements, coming from outside the sound-proof concert halls and other places where music traditionally has sought refuge, unquestionably constitutes an act of *subversion* against the very foundations of music as an art, or at least what would still appear even today to be its very foundations. The random, at least in our sense of the term, is a foreign body forcibly introduced into music.[1]

In film, however, precisely the contrary is true. Here the very idea of an open work is the "foreign body," if only because of the small number of film-makers actually advocating it. That this number should be so small might seem to be due to the technical problems involved, an explanation that is not altogether false, though these problems are not insurmountable ones and do not affect the basic point at issue at all. Several films have been projected simultaneously on the same screen or on two adjacent ones, but attempts such as these are merely frivolous, a kind of deliberate reductio ad absurdum. A more serious experiment might take the form of creating a film with multiple interchangeable facets, using differently edited versions of the same material, for instance, or perhaps by filming works with multiple itineraries on videotape, incorporating some sort of technical improvisation while they are being made. If such experiments have in fact been undertaken, they have thus far had no major repercussions. A film's integrity appears for the moment to be as fundamental to a definition of cinema as music's need to be sheltered from the random sounds of life has always been. After some ten centuries of closed works, this conception may have exhausted its seminal potentialities as far as music is concerned. The very notion of the film as a work of art, by contrast, goes back only a few decades, and it would thus be quite surprising if the time had already come to challenge this concept, simply to keep up with older and more hallowed arts, to provide oneself as it were with an as yet undeserved patent of nobility. And this is all the more true when prospects for a new type of film similar to that outlined here are just now beginning to come into view. Admittedly the sort of work we suggest will still be a closed form, but it will be one of a complexity and richness unprecedented in the entire history of art.

On the other hand, while chance per se constitutes an intrusion into the world of music,[2] the aleatory is quite at home in film and always has been. Since the very earliest days of cinema film-makers have had to put up with chance, willy-nilly. At the beginning, films were almost totally at its mercy. Lumière set his camera up on the station platform at La Ciotat and waited for the train to pull in. When it came in sight it was he who decided when to crank away behind the camera, but chance remained in complete control of the *mise-en-scène*. The bulk of the film's action consisted of *unpredictable* gestures and movements of passengers getting off the train and people waiting for them on the platform. Nevertheless, even as early as this film, one of the first ever made, Lumière had already begun that *struggle against the accidental* that was to characterize nearly all film-making for the next sixty years. The very fact that he chose to set up his camera in one spot rather than another enabled Lumière to predetermine successfully the plastic behavior of *one* of the elements in his composition, the train itself, an entirely predictable element. Both literally and figuratively, he thus established a *frame*, thereby delimiting the area in which the unpredictable remainder of the action would occur. Seeing beyond the purely negative attitude toward the accidental, and the ruthless struggle to eliminate it, Lumière had taken a first step toward its *control*. This is an idea we will come back to later. At the same time, Lumière filmed events that were completely under his control, as in *L'Arroseur arrosé* and other such films—a huge step "forward" in which the accidental is kept outside the frame as much as possible, relegated to some vague and remote off-screen space from which it will only occasionally and timidly re-emerge, until its rehabilitation some sixty years later. Lumière's films such as these were, in short, the beginning of *mise-en-scène*.

The battle against the accidental was not won immediately—chance had to be overcome in all its manifestations, and in certain cases only technical progress could successfully bring the contingent under control. In any case, the film studio gradually became the refuge of an art seeking to escape the accidental, for it furnished an environment in which everything could be more and more perfectly controlled, thanks to increasingly refined techniques. Efforts in this direction eventually led directors to adopt the British independent frame, confining both actors and technicians within the strait jacket of the *storyboard*, and (in the United States especially) to replace actual location shooting with more and more elaborate special effects (mats, background plates, Dunnings, traveling mats, and other techniques allowing actors and background to be filmed separately), making it almost entirely unnecessary ever to venture outside a studio where random intrusions can often only be prevented through the expenditure of enormous sums of money. It is worth noting that this overcoming, or rather *banishing*, of the accidental developed hand in hand with the progressive enthronement of that "zero point of cinematic style," which, as stated earlier, was aimed principally at rendering technique invisible but also at eliminating any "defects" resulting from chance intrusions of any sort. As we shall soon see, it is not altogether an accident that the rediscovery of the contingent and the renewed rejection of that "zero point of cinematic style" should have occurred at almost the same moment in the history of cinema.

I have perhaps created the false impression that I believe that every film-maker from Lumière on is a rabid enemy of chance, that all film-makers yield to the intrusions of the accidental only against their will. Although it is true that the most creative function of chance has only been understood very recently through the work of film-makers such as Godard and Rouch, some directors of exceptional insight had nonetheless already anticipated the function chance might fulfill in the realm of film syntax. At least as early as 1920, a number of directors made no attempt to prevent the intrusion of chance. On the contrary, they were quite willing largely to subordinate their camera to the aleatory world they referred to as "reality." This group was of course the first generation of great documentary film-makers: Dziga Vertov, Joris Ivens, Walther Ruttman, Alberto Cavalcanti, and others. It would never have occurred to them however to refer to *L'Entrée d'un train en gare de la Ciotat* as an aleatory film, nor would it to the contemporary "leftist" historian of cinema: To both, it is simply the first film to "bear witness." In part, this is a matter of vocabulary, but it is chiefly a value judgment. When there is a revolution to carry out in the Soviet Union or bring about in other countries, one can hardly allow oneself to dwell at length on the aesthetic implications of permanently capturing the unpredictable on film, of transforming chance into an aesthetic object. If one shares this ethical bias, films have a precise function, a social function: They should be windows open on the world, and so on. However, when we see the astounding stylistic experimentation being carried out in a propaganda film such as Dziga Vertov's *Enthusiasm*, we have a sneaking suspicion that despite possible misgivings he has been unable to resist the aesthete's fascination for creative new techniques of his own devising.[3]

This attraction is quite normal, for Vertov was above all else an editor, as, to a lesser extent, were all the great creators of the Soviet silent film. In the peace and quiet of the cutting room, the editor has always been the first to reflect on the extraordinary variety of material that the world of chance, once captured on film, provides him and the creative power of his scissors. Even in the case of the most meticulously "staged" films, the editor will soon notice that minor accidents completely beyond the control of the director, who was not able even to see them during the shooting, have given him an opportunity to create a very strong articulation between two shots.

Having become aware of this, certain film-makers began to approach the shooting, particularly of action scenes, from an entirely different perspective. Through the proper choice of lenses and camera setups, the film-maker would simply demarcate a framed area inside which events were permitted to unfold in only a partly controllable manner, so that the film result would consist of something known beforehand to include thousands of "valences," such a large number of possible "interesting" matches that restructuring the action through the editing would become the film-maker's essential task, the stage in the creative process in which he could truly exercise his will, with a freedom that depended largely on the range of possibilities he had left open during the shooting stage. As early as *Strike*, Eisenstein shot the sequence with the firehoses from very carefully chosen camera angles, which, although they did not give him control over the actual details of composition (seemingly impossible in a scene involving so many imponderable factors), nonetheless would later afford him innumerable possible matches between the images thus deliberately "provoked" (through reversals in the angles of the water spouts, crowd movements in opposite directions, and so on). Conceivably, this same activity could have been meticulously staged shot by shot, but in such a case not only would the participants' acting have appeared less dramatic, but the editing in particular would have been infinitely less flexible and rewarding to the eye. In such a situation, the accidental in fact provides far more subtle and more complex cutting possibilities than any film-maker can foresee (or could at that time at any rate). In the scene in *October* where the buxom bourgeois women in their rustling laces poke out the young sailor's eyes with the tips of their umbrellas, Eisenstein brings the camera right up to the action and follows it very closely, aware that, in addition to the intrinsic beauty of the shots thus obtained, this kaleidoscopic flurry of dancing silhouettes, whirling cloth, and dripping blood will result in a cascade of images, visible in all their detail only in the developed film, for the cameraman himself will not even have seen them as he views the action through his small eyepiece (a feather boa visible on screen for a few fractions of a second, a flare frame only a few inches long), aware that these "accidents" will later afford him the possibility of cutting to another shot in a visually interesting way at almost any frame. Having all but entirely relinquished control during the shooting and thus left certain of his prerogatives in the hands of chance, the film-maker regained the control he had surrendered a hundred-fold in the editing; he had ensnared chance, so to speak. The accidental had been given free rein and yielded everything it could as the actors performed more or less spontaneously and the camera froze it all into a succession of minute frames, sixteen to the second. The film-maker could then proceed to *choose* among many possible matches, and it was precisely this great number of possibilities that, in the final analysis, allowed him to dominate chance rather than be dominated by it (as would have been the case if, for example, this scene had been filmed in a single unedited shot).

All this might seem to be belaboring the obvious: Film, it may be objected, has always involved a series of compromises between the accidental and the deliberately controlled. True enough. Yet it is also, and mainly, a matter of degree—and of a director's basic approach. There are those, as we have pointed out, who have always done their utmost to eliminate random elements, and a great number of others who have paid some tribute to chance, although not all of these have done so in the same spirit. There are those who only apparently allowed it to play a part, their principle concern being to banish the genuinely contingent and replace it with a *semblance* of sheer chance. This practice is particularly characteristic of the group of British directors whose films for the General Post Office Film Unit gives us apparently spontaneous scenes; these scenes are not exactly recreations, professionally acted on sets (the settings and people were "real"), but the mail sorters on the Glasgow train (*Night-Mail*) who were playing their everyday roles for the camera did so in carefully lit, carefully planned situations. A second group, including a majority of Hollywood directors, compromise with chance in a completely pragmatic and even opportunistic way. They learned from the Russian film-makers that violent action or "mob scenes" turned out best if shot according to the "probabilistic method," and followed their example.

The Americans' hardheaded practicality also led them, however, to employ a similar approach in situations where it does not "pay off" nearly as well. They developed the stereotyped shot and reverse shot method of shooting (with each scene filmed several times from several different angles and distances), which seemed to give them more freedom in the cutting stage, for it allowed them to choose the shot best setting off the *acting*. This approach, nonetheless, resulted in a limited range of *plastic* possibilities during editing, for it eliminated almost all the formal relationships of possible interest in such scenes, which would have been better served had the shots been set up and filmed in a more complex fashion, since it is always possible to cope with acting problems through multiple takes. The "zero point of cinematic style" conditioned their limited view of chance. A whole cinematic tradition, in fact, pretends to favor intrusions of the accidental, but this tradition does not view chance as a totality of events of every possible kind, whether dramatically expressive or simply plastic, capable of being captured and fixed on film, but rather as having almost entirely to do with the performance of the actors. The American shot and reverse shot technique was, and essentially remains, a method conceived as a way of enveloping the actors from every side, establishing a formal composition of a minimum complexity within which they may be fairly spontaneous, and even go so far as to completely improvise (it was probably the Marx brothers who have derived the most advantage from the freedom this shooting method offers).

For almost thirty years, then, the problem of the degree of control over the image captured on film was posed exclusively in terms of its expressive "content," in terms of the actor and the dialogue—director X perhaps allowing his actors to improvise somewhat, director Y perhaps preferring to shoot scenes with actors in the street with concealed cameras to make them appear more lifelike.[4] The Eisensteinian notion that the aleatory could actually affect form as well as content does not appear to have interested anyone in feature film-making based on fictional subjects except Eisenstein himself. Even in his sound films, seemingly less experimental in form than his silent films, whenever he confronted material the least bit beyond his control, Eisenstein devoted himself to creating a second very extensive cinematic material out of this "real" raw material. He used every possible angle and camera-subject distance when filming the chance fragment, with only a general idea in his mind of how these angles and shot sizes would interact together, the actual articulations between shots being determined to a large extent by the thousand and one "accidents" detectable only on the editing table.[5]

Outside of fiction film-making, this approach was adopted by numerous Scandinavian and English-speaking documentary film-makers who soon realized that the more or less uncontrollable reality that interested them could best be approached in this manner. But their attitude came closer to a newsreel editor's in so far as during the actual shooting they were nowhere close to having as clear a conception of how the footage would eventually be edited as the Russian master had. They therefore found themselves confronted in the editing room with material that had been insufficiently "preconditioned" (as also occurred in the case of almost every director who attempted to adopt Eisenstein's method when filming their "action" scenes). Perhaps this is why the films that resulted so often have a gratuitous air about them, rather complex structures at times having been grafted onto formal and/or ideational statements that were singularly undistinguished. In Eisenstein's work on the other hand, the poetry of structures is an essential part of the film's statement, particularly in those sequences in which controlled chance occurs in some form or other, sequences in which visual texture and statement seem to emerge simultaneously (in the famous Odessa steps sequence, in particular). Eisenstein of course worked only with material that he could at least partially control. Some form of partial control is even an essential feature of his method, and the creator of *Ivan the Terrible* can scarcely be imagined going out into the streets camera in hand. The parallel here established between Eisenstein and the documentary film-makers of the 1930's might thus appear to be somewhat unjustified and even unfair to these latter (who in fact made some quite respectable films), but the fact remains that documentary film-makers are almost the only Western directors to have been influenced (for good or ill) by Eisenstein and the other great Russians[6] as well as being almost the only ones who have claimed to be disciples of his. Directors of the fiction film had to undergo a good many other shocks—including television—before they were to become at all aware that a great many positive advantages could result from something every film-maker discovers early in his career: that *film material is always refractory to some degree.*

Over the last fifty years or so, film directors essentially attempted to eliminate, as much as possible, any intrusion of mere chance, of the contingencies of everyday reality. Only relatively recently has anyone become interested in aiming a camera at this uncontrollable world, not only for sociopolitical and informational purposes but also with the awareness that, out of this confrontation between camera and contingent reality, new forms and new structures could result, either by further developing, through editing, material filmed in such a way as to respect its profoundly *accidental* nature (something the old school of documentary film-makers never succeeded in doing) or, even more importantly, by incorporating chance material into other completely preplanned material. This is clearly the same sort of a dialectical interaction between different types of material (such as practiced by Godard) that is described in Chapter 4, although it is seen here from a slightly different perspective.

One of the most important insights to have come from television was the realization that the camera's relationship to this imperfectly controllable, "spontaneous" chance reality was not necessarily that of a spectator: The camera could also participate in a reciprocal exchange. This discovery was the source of *cinéma vérité* in all its manifestations and, in general, of a whole new world of narrative forms involving shifts in the role of the camera (from actual participant to passive spectator, from a mere "provocateur" of events to active dictator of them, and so on) as a formal and structural device, as the very basis of film discourse.

Shirley Clarke's film based on the play *The Connection* provides a *simulation* of this dialectical use of shifting camera roles (for in this film the camera is never a genuine participant in the action; and it is even doubtful whether any real improvisation occurred before it). Nevertheless, the form of the film derives from the possibilities revealed by true *cinéma vérité*, and from this point of view it remains very instructive. For example, during a prolonged long shot, quite ostentatiously *composed* (the camera as a "dictator" of the action), an actor suddenly turns toward the lens and takes the cameraman to task, bringing about an actual shift in the camera's role, for it suddenly becomes a *participant* in the middle of the shot. Later, the camera even becomes a kind of *passive voyeur*, when the cameraman has had a "fix" and the lens wanders idly over the walls. The implications of these shifts extend far beyond the importance of the play and even of the film itself; they have apparently borne fruit even in Europe, particularly in *L'Amour fou* by Jacques Rivette, who is a known admirer of Shirley Clarke's work. He has gone further however and employed true shifts in the camera's role.

Jean Rouch's use of shifts in the relationship between camera and characters in *Moi, un noir* is tremendously complex; any examination of them on the basis of the finished film is quite problematic. The very solid structural framework of the film highlights the apparently completely chance nature of the original material by comparison with the "finished" quality of the spectacle we see. In actual fact, however, the original material, far from being homogeneous, has several levels of "authenticity," combined with an artfulness unprecedented at the time (1959). The visuals, shot silent, consist of scenes alternately more or less staged, more or less improvised, or more or less actually lived; in the first two instances, there is some degree of awareness on the actors' part of the camera's presence, whereas, in the third case, the actors are either unaware of the camera's presence or have simply forgotten it (as in the drunk scene). There are continual transitions from one form of camera-actor relationship to another, often within a single shot, resulting in an enormous variety of shifts in awareness created through visual means. But that is not all. The relationship between the protagonists and their filmed image subsequently becomes the object of similar shifts during the recording of the participants' comments on themselves. Sometimes they forget that a microphone is present, so that it becomes what might be described as an eavesdropper; sometimes they remember, and the microphone then becomes a participant. The whole formal development of *Moi, un noir* hinges on these constantly shifting relationships between actors and the instruments recording their actions, and the result constitutes one of the most remarkable examples of the use of sheer happenstance as a formal dimension.

In the wake of these pioneering efforts in France, several film-makers of the New York underground have attempted to exploit shifts in the camera's role. Aside from the somewhat unusual film by Shirley Clarke that I have already mentioned, the most interesting of these attempts is Andy Warhol's *The Chelsea Girls*. This film, at the time of its making, was undoubtedly one of the most radical versions of the filmed "psychodrama" (Jean Rouch and Edgar Morin being more "academic" proponents of this sort of work in their *Cronique d'un été*). Its great originality lies in shifts in the camera's role (sometimes a voyeur, sometimes a participant, sometimes a "distancing" device through the use of jerky pans and zooms, sometimes merely a director's tool determining what is seen on screen through very conventional setups), these many shifts effectively suggesting the ambivalence of the roles assumed by the characters themselves (is the beautiful girl really a male transvestite, or is she a lesbian playing at being one, or is she perhaps a "straight" who has been asked to play a lesbian playing a transvestite, and so on?).[7] The film is a perpetual interplay of masks, in which the viewer finds it absolutely impossible to determine the part played by improvisation (whether free or within predetermined limits), the part played by the acting out of previously agreed-on gestures, and even the number of lines of dialogue actually decided on beforehand. Despite, or rather because of, this constant ambiguity on every level, *The Chelsea Girls* possesses an unusual tension, often maintained throughout an entire sequence and often considerably heightened by the fact that each of the film's twelve sequences lasts as long as the film-magazine in the camera (thirty minutes). The extraordinarily prolonged continuity that results also makes certain kinds of shifts in camera role possible (as, for example, from a voyeur to an actual instrument of torture when a harassed participant in the psychodrama walks over to the footage counter to determine how long this harassment will continue).

As for the "open" form taken by the film as a whole (two reels simultaneously projected on two adjacent screens with more or less random alternation between their sound tracks), it is so elementary a procedure compared with the richness and complexity of the material generated by the interplay of masks that only a few striking but isolated plastic effects produced by the fortuitous juxtaposition of two images seem worth remembering. In this respect, the film seems to confirm to some extent what was stated at the beginning of this chapter: Although some form of interaction involving sheer chance may prove very worth while in film, the concept of an "open" work is for the moment totally irrelevant to the essential problems of the medium.

The accidental also intervenes in *The Chelsea Girls* in another way that is just as intriguing. The feeling that there is a truly uncontrollable world just off screen (that is to say, just outside the bounds of this on-screen world, which is interesting precisely because the exact degree of control exercised over it at any point can never be determined) plays an intermittent yet powerful role, marvelously weaving in and out of the interplay of masks, until, finally, in one of the very last sequences, when what is apparently a real fight takes place between two of Warhol's protagonists, the "action" moves off screen altogether for some time. In this connection, we might note that the world of sheer chance (which, as I have said, is usually banished by most film-makers to some forgotten corner of off-screen space) seems to be most palpable when it asserts its presence without ever becoming actually visible, when it lurks just outside the visual field without ever actually entering it, its proximity being somehow conveyed by the sound. As soon as this world of sheer chance erupts on screen, a process of integration begins: This contingent reality (in principle beyond control, in any event uncontrolled), when captured on film, slowly becomes a part of a universe that is somewhat more reassuring, not because of the more realistic nature of sound or the more pronounced stylization of the visual image but simply because of the intrinsically threatening nature of anything invisible and uncontrolled off screen (as any horror film will illustrate). This is particularly true when the film-maker leads us to understand that this lack of control is not at all simulated (as in a horror film) but rather absolutely real, that *anything* in fact can emerge from that off-screen space. In short, when we see images (images that we still usually think of as being controlled by *someone*, whether a director or a cameraman), while at the same time we hear their opposite (that is to say, elements of a noncontrolled universe off screen), the result is a genuinely dialectical tension. Yet as soon as a fragment from the uncontrolled world "enters the scene," bidden or unbidden, it remains a "foreign body" for only a few seconds, losing all its strangeness as gradually this new element (this person) becomes part of whatever is occurring on screen. On the other hand, if a person exits from frame and continues to speak or to make sounds of any kind, he still remains an integral part of the relatively more predictable world of screen space, and in fact extends this world into off-screen space. This, indeed, is one of the great lessons to be learned from *The Chelsea Girls*, suggesting yet another extremely complex parameter simultaneously involving the dialectic of materials, the role assumed by the camera, and the relationship between off-screen space and screen space already discussed.

We now come to Jean-Luc Godard, whose entire body of work from *Une Femme mariée* on essentially depends on the successive roles assumed by the camera (and ultimately the viewer) with regard to the actors and vice versa. In *Une Femme mariée*, alternations between the camera as participant, passive spectator, and "ringmaster" or dictator of the action are rather clearly indicated by Godard: At least whenever the camera is a participant, an inserted numbered title announces the fact just as the extreme stylization of the composition indicates when the camera is the "ringmaster." However, as always happens with Godard (and it is in this connection that the interplay of masks becomes important in his work, too), the actual degree to which the actors were allowed to improvise in other scenes is quite difficult to determine, and because of the important part improvisation plays elsewhere in the film this uncertainty takes on an emphasis that it would not have in the work, say, of a Joseph Mankiewicz.

These ambiguities intervene most systematically in *Deux ou trois choses que je sais d'elle* and, in fact, provide the film with one of its essential underpinnings. The relationship between actor and camera may change at any moment, even in the middle of a shot (as in the brilliant sequence in a fashion boutique where both the salesgirls' and customers' asides are admirably combined in a visual pattern that is almost choreographic in its complexity), or in the middle of a line of dialogue (as in Marina Vlady's monologue at the hairdresser's). At times, the transition is obvious; at times, it becomes evident only after the fact; at times, the exact moment it actually occurs cannot be determined, although the viewer is vaguely aware that "there has been one somewhere."

Godard at times seems to lose sight of the structural and formal (that is, aesthetic) possibilities inherent in this interplay of masks, and in *La Chinoise* these shifts have been reduced at best to their simplest expressive form. Godard's contribution, however, is immense. It is quite possible that without him the principal ideas underlying this chapter could not have been formulated.

Yet why conceal from the reader my grave misgivings regarding these selfsame "basic ideas?" Often the views expressed seem mere metaphysical abstractions. This chapter is nevertheless perhaps the most important in the book, for even though it may contain but a single truth—the fact that cinematic material is always refractory—this truth is a primary one. Cinematic material is especially refractory to any preconceived ideas we may have of it.[8] Yet are we therefore to reject any and every preconceptual approach to film form and structure, as certain people would have us do? Is the remainder of the book already outdated then? Must cinematic creation become purely empirical? I believe not. I believe that even if this problem has not been dealt with in a convincing manner, it is nevertheless necessary to discover some way of taking the essentially refractory character of this material into account as part of the conceptualization process *preceding* filming. Surely, if a film is to be absolutely rigorous in every respect, the work must take the function of chance into account as early as the *découpage* stage (rather than only during the editing or during location shooting) and must do so both on the level of filmic "texture" (Eisenstein's approach) and on the formal level (*cinéma vérité*'s contribution). There seems to be a sort of Heisenbergian uncertainty principle at work between the film-maker and what he films. He cannot aim his camera at anything without modifying it, for what he films, life itself, is irretrievably foreign to the artifices of his instruments. Like modern physicists confronted with certain elementary particles, film-makers therefore must take into account the inevitable gap between their instruments and themselves on the one hand, and life on the other (perhaps by some day combining Eisenstein's approach with Godard's), so as to be able to work on life as a raw material and ultimately shape it, despite this gap, through a work that will thereby be all the richer.

Notes

1. Obviously, the reference here is not to the restricted use of chance in music as a means of choosing between different itineraries for a work, as when Henri Pousseur draws lots.
2. And I feel that it is just as much out of place in literature and the plastic arts, although I have less competence as a critic in these fields.
3. This is a hasty treatment, to say the least, of one of the most important film-makers of the 1920's, whose work was relatively unfamiliar to me at the time and whom I hope to deal with more extensively in a forthcoming book.
4. Nine times out of ten, however, this "realism" is partly destroyed through dubbing and sound-mixing.
5. As the unedited rushes of *Que Viva Mexico* show.
6. The Japanese cinema, on the other hand, particularly during the 1930's, was greatly influenced by the Soviet film-makers, as can be seen not only in the films of Ozu, of course, but also in the works of other directors almost unknown in the West.
7. In *Moi, un noir*, this procedure already exists in rudimentary form, as the characters in that film periodically pretend to be Edward G. Robinson, Lemmy Caution, and Dorothy Lamour.
8. Animated films being in principle the one general exception. However, the case of Norman McLaren is of interest in this regard. In his "best period," the famous Canadian deliberately chose a technique (drawing directly on the film) that introduced a contingent, uncontrollable element into the image, something that had previously been considered a technical defect: namely, the instability of the figures so characteristic of the films McLaren made at that time.

8

Structures of Aggression

In preceding chapters, there have been occasional references to the feeling of discomfort created by certain types of "match cuts," ones that until recently had been considered "bad" matches but that could be integrated, it was suggested, into a broader, nonnormative plastic conception of *découpage* wherein the degree and the nature of the resulting discomfort would be taken into account and regarded as parameters. The discomfort created by disorientation in particular (because of "bad" eye-line matches, for instance, or "bad" matches in screen position and direction of movement), the vectors of which can unquestionably be "controlled," can be handled in such a way as to result in a new sense of orientation, thus producing the kind of configuration already described as a "retroactive" or "deferred" match. The important part surprise can play in *découpage* has likewise been referred to. The end result of a "retroactive" match is surprise (we are astonished to realize that we were actually not confronted with the spatial or temporal configuration we thought we were, just before the transition between shots occurred), and a similar effect is produced by any sudden shift in awareness of the relationship between screen space and off-screen space (our surprise, for instance, at realizing that someone was just outside frame when we thought he was quite a distance away).

Surprise and discomfort as defined here might be said to constitute the two most moderate forms of aggression the film image is capable of inflicting on a viewer; they lie at one end of a whole range of aggressions of increasing intensity and of very different sorts that a film-maker is in a position to practice on his captive audience. This undeniable power tacitly attributed to film-makers from the earliest days of cinema (people instinctively ducked their heads when Lumière's train pulled into the station) soon came to be considered a veritable public menace. The various forms of official or unofficial censorship set up to confront this menace always concentrated on the *content* of the images, naturally, and never on their *form*. But the complaints that have been current in France for some time now[1] with regard to the violent style of certain of the most progressive television film-makers (extremely fast cutting, deliriously paced zooms) lead one to believe that censors may eventually concern themselves with more abstract forms of aggression. Film censorship has always been a means of protecting the mass audience from anything it objected to, from anything that threatened its physical and psychic comfort. Despite certain transient forms of political and social censorship, it is a mistake to view censorship as something arbitrarily imposed on the people by this or that regime. Censorship is, rather, a series of limitations imposed on film-makers by the masses, a gesture of self-defense whereby the masses protect themselves against forms of experience that news commentators refer to as "violent sensations" but that can, of course, consist of a good deal more than that.

The problem of censorship is quite beyond the scope of this book, and the analysis of aesthetic aggression to be undertaken here will be conducted as if censorship were nonexistent, or rather as if it were merely the sociological expression, at a given time and for a given society, of the tension that arises when taboos are violated. The degree to which these taboos are violated is, in fact, precisely the measure of the poetic intensity of the various kinds of aggression about to be described. At a certain level, this conceptual approach has a basis in fact. The dialectic of prohibition and transgression explored by Georges Bataille[2] is to some extent exemplified in the relationships of films to their censors.[3]

I have in fact borrowed the general terms of "transgression" and "prohibition" from Bataille, because all really censurable images, whether erotic, repugnant, violent, or truly subversive (as opposed to images that embarrass a party or a regime, though not society as a whole, and therefore inconvenience a government but do not traumatize its constituents: shots of the slums at Nanterre as opposed to shots of a fraudulent election) are, despite other possible differences, forms of aggression.[4] We will now examine how *pain*—for that is what is involved: most often psychic pain, but sometimes physical pain as well—can be considered to be part of an aesthetic experience when the pain results from some form of dialectical transgression and is experienced by "normal" adults, by persons capable both of bearing up under a dentist's drill without any particular psychic trauma and of apprehending, however vaguely, the abstract dimension of a work of art. *Le Sang des bêtes* is certainly not a film for children, but neither is *Last Year at Marienbad*.[5]

As should be obvious, aggression is thus considered due to the actual content of an image to be basically no different from purely optical aggression (certain films by the great American animator Robert Breer, dizzying cascades of images that "hurt your eyes" come principally to mind)[6] or from more insidious forms of aggression such as those resulting from the kind of disorientation already described.

Every one of these forms of aggression, in fact, has its source in that very special, almost hypnotic relationship that is established between screen and viewer as soon as the lights go down in the theater and that Siegfried Kracauer has analyzed quite well. Whatever his level of critical awareness, a viewer sitting in the dark alone and suddenly face to face with the screen is completely at the mercy of the film-maker, who may do violence to him at any moment and through any means. Should the viewer be forced beyond the pain threshold, his defense mechanisms may well be called forth and he may remind himself that "it's only a movie" (that distancing phenomenon to be described in more detail below), but it will always be too late . . . the harm will already have been done; intense discomfort, and perhaps even terror, will already have crept across the threshold.[7]

The first time any "normal" viewer sees *Un Chien andalou*, the famous shot of the sliced eyeball is experienced as an absolute shock, which is all the more overwhelming because everything prior to it is deliberately intended to lull the viewer's sensibilities, to create a perfectly reassuring mood: a man very contentedly sharpening his razor, smoking, looking at the night from a balcony with a woman quietly sitting at his side. The shot is just as shocking after several viewings of the film, and during a second or subsequent viewing the traumatic power inherent in it sends out a shock wave that reaches right back to the beginning of the film, so that the "flat" opening sequence takes on the most bizarre sort of emotional shading in anticipation. *Un Chien andalou* was to my knowledge the first film in the history of cinema to have attempted to use aggression as one of its structural components. The presence of a shock wave simultaneously propagating itself both backward and forward from an image that is the film's undeniable center of gravity, its pre-eminently privileged moment, undoubtedly has as much to do with form as with the creation of a dreamlike atmosphere. After roughly two minutes' running time, this crucial shot appears, the effect of which is to divide the film into two separate parts. At the same time, each of the two parts takes on a poetic meaning radically different from the one it would have possessed had there been no such shot. As proof of this, I need only point out that there exists a bowdlerized version in which this close-up of the eye is missing and that it produces on anyone acquainted with the complete version the same effect as does a black-and-white print of a film previously seen in color.

Despite the capital interest of *Un Chien andalou*, aggression has since been used only rarely in this intense a form as a structural element (see, however, the opening of Buñuel's *Land Without Bread* with its gradual progression from the banal to the horrifying). Were it not for Georges Franju's masterpiece *Le Sang des bêtes* (1949), *Un Chien andalou* would appear to have led to a dead end.

The manner in which Franju's short film opens presents a number of striking analogies with the opening of the film by Dali and Buñuel. The images full of a "populist" poetry, accompanied by sentimental music and a nostalgic narration, lull the viewer, thus performing much the same function as the night sky in *Un Chien andalou*. Once again we have no idea that misfortune awaits us. Were it not for the title of the film, we would be as trusting as the nice horse we see being gently led through the courtyard of the slaughterhouse. Even when a small tube is placed over the horse's muzzle, the whole situation seems too ordinary, too humdrum for there to be any sense of impending doom. A sharp detonation follows and the animal pitches over as if struck by lightning, an image of sudden death more overwhelming, perhaps, than any other previously seen in film[8] because of its stark simplicity. The viewer has undergone his first shock. In contrast to what occurs in *Un Chien andalou*, this shock is repeated with endless variations throughout the film. The entire rhythm of the work is based on a succession of painful shocks felt as directly as the electrical charges once administered to viewers sitting in wired seats by rather naïve exponents of "total cinema" during the showing of certain horror films in the United States. Rhythm seems to be the appropriate term, for these shocks are quite varied in intensity and sometimes are separated by documentary or lyrical sequences of varying length, while at other times they occur in extremely close proximity, as when some ten lambs are slaughtered in the span of a few seconds and their dead bodies then inflated with compressed air and skinned, this being followed by a prolonged shot showing the steaming carcasses, a kind of *fioritura* of an astonishing beauty that nonetheless seems to emit the very smell of death. The somewhat facile black humor coloring certain sequences occasionally mars the purity of the film's structures, particularly in the scene where a butcher "splits his steer as the clock strikes twelve," yet these structures exist, created principally by the editing and the admirable sound effects contributed by Jean Painlevé. Most importantly, from the point of view that concerns us here, they are structures whose very substance is horror, and they are inevitably perceived (except by persons of extremely perverse sensibility) through a cloud of pain. Beyond the humanitarian or vegetarian concerns that may perhaps motivate certain more sensitive souls, each of us is vulnerable to these brutal assaults on bodies that, after all, are terrifyingly similar to our own. What makes the image of the slit eyeball in *Un Chien andalou* so painful if not the realization of our own eyes' vulnerability to the slash of a razor? *Le Sang des bêtes*, in short, undeniably presents us with an almost musical interaction between moments of tension and moments of respite, in the form of more or less closely spaced and more or less pronounced crossings of the pain threshold.

But, in this respect, *Le Sang des bêtes* remains the only film of its kind. In the United States, where the limits set by censorship have receded considerably over these last few years, films have been made that in actual fact are little more than sexual fantasies of human slaughter (*Blood Feast, Two Thousand Maniacs*). It is rather doubtful that the directors of these movies had the sense of form that Franju possessed when he was making his first short films, or that form has any more than an accidental function in their work. These films are nonetheless interesting works, in so far as the traumatic power inherent in their images undoubtedly provides raw material that other film-makers more sensitive to the complexities of form and more conscious of contemporary formal methods could exploit. Aside from the question of censorship, are film-makers in the West willing or able to exploit material of this sort? Generally speaking, the European film-makers most concerned with problems of form— Bresson, Antonioni, Resnais[9]—tend to exclude from their work any painful violations of taboos, or include such violations only reluctantly, inserting any such element in their films in the most gingerly sort of way (the sex in Resnais's *La Guerre est finie*, the violent fights in Bresson's *Au Hasard Balthazar*). On the other hand, when Buñuel rather late in his career becomes conscious of form in the sense in which the word is used here, in works as accomplished as *Diary of a Chambermaid* and *Belle de jour*, he suddenly acquires a sense of modesty; his images are no longer as corrosive as they were in works such as *Los Olvidados* and *El*—less accomplished works, it might be added.

The Japanese, however, are more accustomed to living with their fears: The modern individual probably fears death just as much as his Western counterpart, but Japanese society as a whole seems to have better assimilated the idea of death. Like Franju's great documentary, the Japanese fiction film offers a whole tradition of cruelty in Antonin Artaud's sense of the word, whose specifically structural potential has been sensed by more than a few film-makers.[10] Akira Kurosawa's masterpiece, *Throne of Blood*, is built around a central alternation between scenes of extreme agitation and scenes of an almost unbearably tense quiescence, the most striking of which is an extremely prolonged shot of Asaji ("Lady Macbeth") waiting for her husband, Washizu, to kill their lord. Yet neither this murder nor any of the other violence (war, murders, etc.) in the "story" takes place on screen: A battle scene is *represented* by furious gallopings about far behind the actual front, and Washizu's killing of the assassin is a stylized gesture seen in a very "undramatic" long shot. It is only in the final scene in which thousands of arrows pierce Washizu's body as he dashes along the ramparts of his castle, that the on-screen agitation and hitherto off-screen violence are finally united in images that constitute a kind of "coda" that is both disruptive and recapitulative, releasing as it does the tension built up previously by the evacuation of violence from the screen.

A strikingly similar example of a dialectics of horror may be cited in the work of a less prestigious but very prolific director, Shiro Toyada. His film *Japanese Ghosts* is built around alternations of images that are extremely suggestive in their understatement and others possessed of a very crude sort of horror, these alternations generally involving the same element. A scene in which a bandit kills an old man in the forest is a good example. The fatal blow is barely visible and the body topples over out of camera range. The murderer then leans over the invisible body and performs some vague sort of laborious task; perhaps he is stripping the body of a purse attached to the victim's waist or hanging around his neck. A second bandit appears on the scene and the first bandit tells him of his evil deed, adding that he has peeled the skin off the old man's face so that his victim will be unrecognizable! Fair enough . . . the film-maker's approach seems obvious: horror by suggestion. (This use of off-screen space is a case of "deferred apprehension".) Then two absolutely horrifying shots in rapid succession bluntly show us what has thus far been so carefully concealed, the flayed head on the ground, followed by an image of fierce beauty, the skin of the face hanging in one piece from a small tree. An undeniable formal structure—a kind of reduction of the over-all form of *Throne of Blood*—is involved here; moreover, it is used several times without losing any of its effectiveness. We have difficulty adjusting to the horrifying, and the structure has its *raison d'être* in that mixture of repugnance and fascination experienced by the viewer confronted with these images of horror. He is titillated at first by the suggested horror and thinks he has gotten off easily with a little shiver running up his spine, but then suddenly absolutely everything is revealed to him! This "Chinese-box" technique is rich in formal possibilities. Within a register somewhat below the pain threshold, certain American gangster films take violence as the basic material, dealing with it through a technique that we might call, using a musical analogy, "variations on a theme"; Richard Wilson's *Al Capone* is, in fact, conceived as a series of variations on the theme of murder by surprise, each murder being carried out in a more baroque and unpredictable manner than the one before. The film, however, is a typical Hollywood product—that is to say, one with only a very slight formal awareness; structures of this sort can at best be regarded here as fortunate accidents resulting from commercial practicality.

It would be quite unfair to say the same about the masterpieces of the golden age of American slapstick, a cinematic form based, on the one hand, on obvious forms of aggression, and, on the other, on visible structures. In Mack Sennett's, Buster Keaton's, Harry Langdon's, and especially Laurel and Hardy's best films, structure and aggression almost always go hand in hand. The aggression can occur in a great variety of forms and intensities. Surprise, an essential cause of laughter (as Georges Bataille has put it, "the unknown makes us laugh") is also involved, of course, usually occurring in conjunction with deferred structures of an extremely amusing sort.

One of the most beautiful moments in *Sherlock Junior* is surely the scene in which Keaton, before entering the outlaws' hideout, affixes some kind of hoop covered with paper to the outside of one of the windows of the shack. Once inside, as soon as the bandits become menacing, Keaton does a magnificent dive through the window and the hoop, which turns out to have an old woman's disguise hidden inside it, which Keaton is decked out in even before hitting the ground. As he hobbles off, the bandits burst out the door, quite perplexed at seeing that their quarry has escaped them with such incredible speed, for naturally they pay no attention to the old woman.

We are at once outraged and amazed at this surprising and improbable gimmick, and our laughter is a response to this mild aggression. At the same time, the *beauty* of the sequence derives from its structure. Keaton prepares the window, enters through the door, and dives through the window as the outlaws come out the door; our initial perplexity at Keaton's preparations is the counterpart of the outlaws' confusion when they confront the result of the preparations, and so on. James Agee, among others, has analyzed the gags of this period in this way. But it should be particularly emphasized that the beauty of the structure is experienced through laughter provoked by aggression, in exactly the same way that the beauty of the rhythm underlying *Le Sang des bêtes* is apprehended through the pain created by an aggression of an altogether different kind. However, the laughter caused by the great American slapstick artists is not always as unmixed as it is here, at least not for the sensitive adult. The aggression sometimes comes a good deal closer to crossing the pain threshold. Harold Lloyd dangling over the ledge of a skyscraper is an image out of a nightmare; laughter and terror mingle, giving a very special coloration to some admirably structured acrobatics. And, when Laurel and Hardy in one of those "proliferating" structures that were their own special secret, demolish a whole line of cars, make scores of people double up in pain on the sidewalk by punching them in the solar plexus, or push a whole crowd of people into a mud puddle (scatalogical aggression such as this is extremely common in slapstick films), the viewer feels that he is the direct victim of a *structured aggression*, and his somewhat strained laughter is accompanied by a very pure aesthetic satisfaction. A final altogether admirable example is provided by the sequence in *Long Pants* in which Harry Langdon, after having daydreamed of murdering his fiancée so he can run away with a gangster's vamp, attempts to act out his fantasy. When he asks the ingenuous girl a second time whether she wants to "take a walk in the woods" while attempting at the same time to hide an enormous Army revolver in his pocket, literally repeating a shot previously seen in his daydream, the result is one of the most outrageous surprise gags of the period. And the interminable scene that follows (during which he desperately attempts to distract his fiancée's attention long enough to be able to kill her from a distance exactly as the whole thing has taken place in his fantasy) provides an extraordinary example of variations on a theme occurring within an atmosphere of slapstick nightmare that soon becomes unbearable. Once again acute anxiety mingles with laughter and this ambiguous aggression develops within a formal pattern (the ideal event being established in the daydream, followed by frantic variations on it brought on by all the obstacles that come up in reality) that is almost mathematical in its rigor.

Unfortunately today, the art of slapstick seems dead and buried. It constitutes a genre indissolubly linked with a period of American history[11] that represents the only major collective contribution made by the American movie industry to the art of film, comparable to the contribution made by the French primitives and the German expressionists, and perhaps even comparable to that of the great Soviet experimenters. Until relatively recently, however, the best elements of slapstick survived in a certain tendency of the American animated cartoon, first in Walt Disney's work then, after his decline, in the work of that master of the delirious, Tex Avery. As Georges Sadoul wrote of Avery: "The free play of his imagination, the almost surrealistic gags, the grating humor, the sardonic ferocity evident in the small number of films he made based on a chase and a battle to the death, all to a strange syncopated rhythm, revolutionized the animated cartoon." Avery, who seems to have remained completely inactive after Warner Brothers closed down their animation studios, possessed a sense of excess in everything and of its organization, which distinguish his films from the stereotyped frenzy characteristic of the majority of American cartoons. Two characters hurtle off a cliff uttering horrendous screams; during shot after shot they fall toward the camera and their repeated cries finally become unbearable; the scene lasts for only about ten seconds but appears to go on forever. Then they finally land, as light as feathers, and the chase resumes as if nothing had happened. Elsewhere in the same film (the title of which unfortunately does not come to mind) the Cat hides inside a hollow tree trunk, and the Dog, believing he's finally cornered him, slips his paw into the hole only to grab hold of a tomato held out by the Cat. The Dog squeezes it fiercely and pulls his paw out, smeared with red. Then in one of those crazy reversals, one of those delirious breaks in tone characteristic of Avery's work, the Dog starts to moan, "I crushed him! I crushed him!" and his lamentations go on and on, to the point where we actually feel uncomfortable, and the scene is no longer funny. The moment when the Cat reappears and the chase goes on is almost a relief.

We have now come full circle. Having started with the discomfort created by "bad" matches, we have now arrived at the discomfort resulting from the grating humor underlying Tex Avery's syncopated rhythms. These two forms of malaise are perhaps not as foreign to each other as might initially be imagined. The creation of discomfort as a form of aggression is becoming more and more important in the thematic material of contemporary cinema. One of the most striking recent examples of discomfort created through aggression, a film certain to arouse heated controversy, is Marcel Hanoun's *L'Authentique procès de Carl Emmanuel Jung.* Based on material dealing with the horrible happenings in Nazi extermination camps, the work uses an imaginary trial as a pretext and is filmed in the most stylized manner conceivable (there is no courtroom set; the actors are simply filmed separately against a dark background and confront each other only through the editing). The voices of the actors who are giving testimony about the events in the camps with restrained but obviously intense emotion are never actually heard. The text is spoken for them by the mechanical, neutral, unsynchronized voices of translators, and this distancing already creates a certain uneasiness. What is more, the very subject of the film, represented by the contrast between the gruesome testimony at the trial and the glimpses of the peaceful family life of the fifty-year-old man we are told was a cruel torturer twenty-five years earlier, is naturally one that is highly disturbing to everyone. And finally, both the plastic form and the visual style of the film (in every respect, worthy of the maker of *Une Simple histoire,* even if the style has become more sober) develop quite independently of the horrifying nature of the testimony, sometimes even taking the form of a completely gratuituous visual fantasy, and thus constitute a third source of uneasiness. This discomfort reaches a climax near the end of the film when, after some particularly detailed testimony concerning the conditions inside the gas chambers, a particularly "artistic" succession of shots occurs, showing a nude girl twisting and turning on an unmade bed. The shot has already been seen several times and seems strikingly gratuitous, for nothing in the spare comments of the newspaperman (one of the characters in the film) provides any explanation for it. After several seconds have gone by, the reporter's voice is heard, obviously speaking to the woman he loves (who is clearly the girl on the screen, although she has not previously been referred to), describing a nightmare he has had: He has dreamed that she was one of the Nazi executioners' victims and was dragging herself naked across the floor of the gas chamber. In this particular case the "distance effect" resulting from the viewer's discomfort, on the one hand, and the manner in which the structure has developed in time (through the premonitory shots) and space (organization of matches and frame compositions), on the other, works perfectly. The effect produced, at once disturbing and very moving, could never have been attained without the temporal development, and the almost too meticulously perfect spatial relationships are only beautiful relative to the feeling of discomfort, which controverts our aesthetic pleasure and suddenly makes their beauty horrible.

It is probable that there will be well-meaning viewers who will violently object to Hanoun's film on the grounds that no one has the right to consider the suffering and death of millions of Jews as an aesthetic object, for that in my view is Hanoun's approach in this very beautiful film. There is no intention here of deciding this serious question one way or another. It can only be noted in passing that numerous creative artists, among them many who are far from second-rate, have made evil into an object of beauty, generally through erotic fantasy. (Sade, Genet, Lautréamont, Bataille, and, in cinema, Leni Riefenstahl come to mind.) Those who refuse to accept this attitude (or reject it in cinema, which amounts to the same thing) and therefore reject Hanoun's approach, which is a good deal more restrained and also more ambiguous, are the same people who —for perfectly understandable reasons—are often incapable of regarding Nazi extermination camps and other more recent horrors as part of the "drama of history." But surely every creator has the right to use this "drama" as a source of inspiration and treat it however he pleases. This attitude toward Hanoun is no different from that which led a certain dilettantish leftist critic to accuse Ingmar Bergman of political opportunism for having included a series of shots from a Vietnam newsreel in *Persona*. This critic is so blinded by his own system of values that he does not see that to a mind like Bergman's the sight of a Buddhist monk setting himself on fire is no longer an image with a political meaning, but an image of human violence and injustice, and therefore a poetic element that was necessary at that precise moment in the film. Bergman the man may very well thoroughly disapprove of American policy and its application in Vietnam, but that has to do with politics—that is, with life—and if ever there was a film-maker who clearly let it be understood that for him art and life are two separate entities it is Bergman. Is it that surprising that Bergman is not Godard?[12]

Indeed, one of my aims when writing this chapter was the rehabilitation of taboo materials (often with no other connection between them except the fact that they are taboo), which is both possible and desirable in the light of the particular concept of structure defined throughout this book. As a matter of fact, the other goal in this chapter was to demonstrate, through the example of violence and aggression in all their forms, that even those materials apparently most resistant to the "mathematics of form" and the most highly charged emotionally can be "sublimated" through formal abstraction and still retain their full emotional impact. As Pierre Boulez has put it, "For delirium to become an effective creative factor, it must be taken into account and organized."

Notes

1. In 1967. French television has become considerably more tame since then . . . in every conceivable way.
2. Bataille, however, was not particularly concerned with the abstractions of form, and to my knowledge never derived conclusions of a structural sort from this dialectic.
3. Necessarily in an incoherent form, for in an area as subjective as this it is a good deal more difficult for a group of men to express the desires of society as a whole than in other areas.
4. A hurried reading of the above might give the impression that I am defending censorship. That is definitely not true. Censorship for adults, either for supposedly good reasons or for bad ones, must be fought by every film-maker and film-lover in every possible way. Unfortunately, this is far from always being the case. Film censorship exists in some form or other in every country; the universality of the phenomenon should make us realize that it stems from the very nature of the medium and therefore has aesthetic as well as political consequences that every film-maker should be aware of.
5. American children are permitted to see the most gruesome horror films. Not that horror films of this sort are responsible for American juvenile delinquency; rather, the violence inherent in American life gives children in that country a sophisticated awareness that prepares them for these films. Some psychiatrists believe that such movies, in fact, are excellent cathartic devices permitting children and even certain adults to project their fantasies of aggression without harming themselves or others. In Europe, on the other hand, there is some justification for prohibiting young children from at-

tending certain films (as against banning these entirely), for the European child living in a society where daily violence is rare, is far more sheltered, and therefore more vulnerable than his American counterpart.

6. Today, of course, the "flicker" film is a well-known area of experimentation.

7. It should nevertheless be pointed out that in actual practice this bondage of the viewer has rarely been used for purposes as "noble" as those singled out for attention here. And, considering the part it plays in the alienating function of illusionist, "degree-zero" cinema, it is very important to distinguish between the "good" and "bad" uses of the participative phenomenon (a good use, as implicitly defined here, being dialectical "identification" tempered by "distanciation").

8. A comparable example in the fiction film is Nana's death in *Vivre sa vie*. The role of violence is always quite complex and varies in each of Godard's films, and it deserves a separate study.

9. Ingmar Bergman is the exception proving the rule. His case, however, is a rather complex one that will be touched on below.

10. Recently in Europe we have come to know the film-makers of the post-Kurosawa generation, many of whom are directly concerned with the aesthetic use of violence (see in particular Oshima, Wakamatsu, Yoshida, and above all, perhaps, Matsumoto, whose *Shura* [1972], a neo-Brechtian reworking of a Kabuki drama makes systematic use of extreme violence as both a structural and distancing device). It goes without saying that Western censors, particularly in Europe, keep most of the films containing similar material from the public screen.

11. The contribution made in France by Jean Durand, who at least in his use of aggression has no peer (as in *Zigoto, plombier*, where an entire building is demolished by a clumsily handled ladder, or in *Zigoto, détective*, where a decrepit, old housemaid is brutally knocked unconscious by the Herculean hero) should not be overlooked, however.

12. Written at a time when my views on the ideological implications of artistic practice were confused to say the least, this paragraph is from my present viewpoint very naïve pleading for a badly defined cause. Rather than delete or rewrite it, I have preferred to leave it as specific testimony to the intellectual confusion that explains many of the book's inadequacies.

IV

Reflections on the Film Subject

9

Fictional Subjects

Having started from an area of investigation so circumscribed, so modest, so rudimentary that no one seems to have concerned himself with it in a systematic manner before, we have reached a point as we near the end of this work where I can discuss another realm so vast and "noble" that almost all film criticism has been devoted to it. Even in *Les Cahiers du cinéma*, over three-quarters of the articles published are chiefly concerned with a film's subject, and when problems of film form and film syntax are touched upon it is invariably from this point of view. If, after so much ink has flowed, I nonetheless venture out into such thoroughly explored territory, if I nonetheless reserve a prominent place in this book for a treatment of the film subject, it is because my approach is diametrically opposed to that of all critics and nearly all film theoreticians and historians (though not that of certain film-makers). On the one hand, the film subject will be dealt with in terms of problems of form and discourse, an approach consistent with the over-all attitude toward cinema expressed in this book. On the other hand, and more importantly, I intend to approach the subject as a generic term, whereas ordinarily it is approached as the sum total of specific cases, as a series of subjects.

If one is willing to concede that film has at least partially discovered its inherent structural possibilities and that this fact should be taken into account when the moment comes to choose a film's subject, one necessarily has to ask oneself what a film subject *is*, or rather, what constitutes a "good" film subject, or more accurately still, what a "good" film subject is *today*.

Except for the great so-called primitives (Georges Méliès, Émile Cohl, Louis Feuillade) and some of the great slapstick directors of the early days of the cinema, in whose work the subject fulfilled a certain formal function, traditional film-makers have tended to adopt one or the other of the following two attitudes toward the film subject: Either they have held that only the subject mattered and the manner in which it was handled was important in so far as it enhanced the "content," a position held by most "quality" commercial directors, of whom Claude Autant-Lara provides a good example; or, conversely, they have maintained that the film's subject was not at all important, that only the manner in which it was treated mattered; it is the position not only of a minor artist like Henri-Georges Clouzot, but of a director as important as Sternberg. Paradoxically enough, these two seemingly opposite attitudes reflected a single idea, one that present-day conceptions have begun to refute, namely, that a film-maker is merely a director, someone who takes a script of his own or someone else's creation, which he then renders into images. André S. Labarthe has quite succinctly described this quarrel of vocabulary—which is also a conflict of generations—and shown how this dichotomy conceals a very serious underlying problem:

> Of the twin concepts that allow criticism to "grasp" films (as a lobster claw might), *mise-en-scène* bypasses the subject, so to speak, and refers to its *rendering*. From [Louis] Delluc on, judging a film always involved judging the acting, the quality of the dialogue, the beauty of the photography, the effectiveness of the editing . . . and if, for some thirty or forty years, film criticism has more or less managed to "grasp" its object, it is simply because cinema has barely evolved at all, or rather has evolved only within the limits set by the notion of *mise-en-scène*.[1]

When Sternberg made *The Scarlet Empress*, he was quite aware that his screen play was an insignificant trifle. What was important to him was creating a visual object, and, to fulfill that goal, he had to undertake an operation that in effect involved *putting things into images,* as one might put ships into bottles or pictures on pages. Although Autant-Lara (in films such as *Devil in the Flesh* and *La Traversée de Paris*) was led to create a style as artificial as Sternberg's, it was precisely for the opposite reason: He wanted it to *serve the subject,* which to him was of primary importance. For Sternberg, *mise-en-scène* is an end in itself; for Autant-Lara, it is only a means. The relative importance assigned style and content by the two directors is reversed, but their underlying concept of film is in the last analysis identical: Both believe that there is some hierarchical relationship between a film's subject and its form (or in their words a film's "style"). Other well-intentioned people in the film world frequently refer to a "fusion of form and content," but this merely represents another posture based on aesthetic views that have been outdated for a century now, for these advocates of a "great synthesis" still consider the writing of a scenario and its plastic elaboration as two separate and distinct stages, thereby necessarily implying some form of priority between them. Each view, in fact, sees a film's *découpage* as essentially a process giving visual form to a previously existing content, and, no matter how transcendent this process is to some film-makers and how subservient it is to a film's content to others, it is always performed *after the fact,* is always superimposed upon a pre-existing screen play, which in itself is the *literary* development of a subject of some sort or other.

Obviously there have been exceptions. One of the most significant of these in the period between World War I and World War II is undoubtedly Renoir's *La Règle du jeu*—a masterpiece largely for this very reason. If *La Règle du jeu* is one of the first truly modern films, it is because Renoir chose the subject matter precisely for the interesting formal problems it raised and because the form and even the texture of the film derive *directly* from its subject matter. Therein lies the key to the problem of the film subject in a contemporary context. When film-makers finally become fully conscious of the cinematic means at their disposal, when the possibility of creating organically coherent films in which every element works with every other is within sight, surely the subject matter of a film, the element that is almost always the starting point of the process of making a film, must be conceived in terms of its ultimate form and texture. That at least seems to be a proper contemporary formulation of the problem. Renoir already saw this very clearly when he chose the subject matter of *La Règle du jeu*, as he himself proved by the very relevant comments he made in his conversations with Jacques Rivette in one of the *Cinéastes de notre temps* television series. To state what should be obvious, the mad chases back and forth, the continual comings and goings of all sorts that bring the depth of field and off-screen space into play in a very complex way and constitute the essential formal devices of *La Règle du jeu*, are merely the literal extension (the "augmentation," as musicians would say) of the mistaken identities of lovers and the mutual meddlings of servants and masters in each other's worlds, which provide the film with its content. Even taking the term in its simplest sense, the subject is contained in microcosm not only in each sequence but in almost every shot, on a certain level of analysis at least.

It might perhaps be better to describe how a subject can engender form by briefly comparing two minor films by a director whose formal concerns, although constant, are somewhat more superficial than Renoir's and therefore provide a clearer example: Alfred Hitchcock's *Rope* and *The Birds*, two of the best films from his American period. *Rope* is based on a subject much like that of a classical theatrical melodrama, with the traditional three acts, dramatic entrances and exits, and so on. The actual visual form of the film, however, results from an arbitrary decision, the elimination of the cut. On a poetic level, perhaps, this formal decision is in perfect accord with the subject of the film, but in no sense can the form be said to derive from the subject matter. An altogether different approach is used in *The Birds*. Here the entire structure, even the actual style of the film is implicit in the subject itself, the gradual destruction of the American dream, of the sterile and comfortable fantasies of middle-class life as Hollywood depicts it. Starting with the first peck of a bird's beak on Tippi Hedren's forehead, middle-class reality is progressively contaminated by violence; the film's entire development is based on this spread of violence, which underlies both the individual images and the over-all *découpage*. The film, like the subject on which it is based, has a beginning, but it does not have an end, or, if it does, it is buried under the millions of birds that have invaded the screen (the world). *The Birds* is a film in which everything *at every level* derives directly from the premise laid down by the basic plot.

In this cellular relationship between the subject matter and the way in which it is rendered, we discover another analogy, a particularly rewarding one, between contemporary film forms and the strategies of contemporary music. Serial composers appear to us to have a very similar conception of the relationships between the basic choice of a tone row or tone rows (which provides a musical work with its "subject," what classical musicians called the "theme" of a work, although tone rows function quite differently) and the form of the finished work. Serial composers believe that the entire development of a musical work must be derived from the basic cell or at least be located relative to it, even if the actual cellular unit is never recognizable as such.

To serial composers, the almost biological growth of a musical work from a few generating cells, a conception that originated in the great works of Debussy and Schoenberg, is only part of a broader attempt to endow a musical work with a greater and greater organic coherence.[2] With similar ends in view, certain film-makers have recently begun to concentrate on establishing relationships of the same order between the subjects they choose to film and the final style and structure of the films derived from these subjects.

We have already examined at some length two films, *Cronaca di un amore* and *Une Simple histoire*, which represent, each in its own way, important stages on the way to a definition of the structural function of the subject. Rather than repeat what was already said, the reader is referred to Chapter 6, which can be reread in the light of the remarks that follow.

But first a very necessary parenthesis. Among film-makers, there might seem to be little need to provide a definition of a "film subject," particularly with regard to the fiction film—a film, that is, based on a fictional dramatic narrative. Any film-maker recognizes as film subjects the short summaries he can read any week under the heading "New Films" in the entertainment section of the paper.

However, a contemporary writer might view such items with a certain scorn, as being mere "résumés of the plot." Whereas writers are becoming more and more deeply interested in transcendent phenomena, a film-maker, because of the very material nature of his art, a materiality as great as that of sculpture for instance, must attach himself to the concrete, to *immanent* realities. Thus, for film-makers, the "subject" of Witold Gombrowicz's great modern novel *Cosmos* is not at all "interpretation considered as an approach to the universe" or any other abstract statement, but simply "two men enter into the life of a household in which certain mysterious signs lead them to conclude that some enigma exists, which they then attempt to resolve . . . or to embody." Obviously, it is quite possible that Gombrowicz himself took purely abstract problems as his point of departure, but this abstraction is of no use to the film-maker involved in the task of making the novel into a film; what would interest him would be the concrete visual structures, the theme of the hanging object, the interchanges of roles, and so on. Film is made first of all out of images and sounds; ideas intervene (perhaps) later. At least this is true in the "fiction film." But, as we shall see in the next chapter, for some years now a nonfiction cinema has existed, whose *point of departure* is the interaction of abstract ideas considered as the "subject," and whose final result is that combination of images and sounds known as a film. But let us go back now to the attempt to define the film subject.

One of the most important steps toward a functionalization of the subject is the work of Alain Robbe-Grillet—in his novels as well as his films. His novels constitute an altogether original attempt at "written cinema," although initially this notion of "written cinema" was a bit puerile. Faced with the obvious exhaustion of traditional novel forms, Robbe-Grillet in *The Erasers* rather naïvely employed all sorts of pseudo-cinematic techniques (dissolves, tracking shots, pans, close-ups, and so on). In the novels published after *The Erasers*, long descriptions, so detailed as to border on parody, have contributed to creating what was has been scornfully called "a land-surveyor's aesthetic." He was apparently attempting thereby to create a literary equivalent of the concreteness and "objective" precision *naturally* characteristic of the film image. This aspect of his experimental novels is what has principally attracted the attention of many young writers, although it is really of secondary importance. Be that as it may, as a film-maker Robbe-Grillet obviously has not pursued this line of research. Although his attempt to catalogue objects in his work has no doubt left its mark on the history of literature, it is rather improbable that it will have much effect on the history of cinema.

Robbe-Grillet's contribution to a new definition of the interaction between subject and form is of incalculable importance however. It is probable that his work will have its most far-reaching consequences in film, for, when applied to literature, the techniques he employs run the risk of becoming tedious because of the essential monotony of the printed word as it lies on the page, whereas in film the same techniques can affect a whole range of material on every level. The theme-and-variations principle he introduced into the art of narrative assumes infinitely more substantial possibilities when applied to the composite art of cinema. No doubt, it is for that very reason that this creative artist has devoted himself to film-making with an enthusiasm that is unprecedented among men of letters of his stature.

We might best begin a brief examination of Robbe-Grillet's contribution with a rather simple example, his second novel, *The Voyeur*. The book's plot (what we call the subject) develops in a relatively continuous manner, broken in the middle however by a long time-ellipsis in which the only real action of the novel, a murder, occurs. A continuous development interrupted by some sort of "jump" or abridgement can be found at every level of the narrative, from a single sentence to the entire novel, including every intermediary phase. This is why his novels are so important for film-makers. He creates a proliferating narrative that grows like a crystal from a basic "cell" to form an entity that is completely coherent even in its contradictions, for every one of its facets reflects in a more or less recognizable form the seminal idea in which the whole originated. No novel of the nineteenth-century type could have the formal unity possessed by one of Robbe-Grillet's works, even the least successful of them. If (as it surely can) film, like music, can gain something from progressing toward greater and greater organic unity, the narrative forms that literature so generously furnished film over the last forty years obviously are no longer of any use. The subjects underlying these old narrative forms, however, can still be of some service, provided the film-maker deduces strictly *cinematic* formal and structural consequences from them. If logically deduced, these consequences will result in a cinematic development of the subject radically different from the literary development the same subject might have led to, as can be seen by comparing Musset's *Les Caprices de Marianne* with Renoir's *La Règle du jeu*.

In his first screen play to be made into a film, *Last Year at Marienbad*, Robbe-Grillet took this concern for organic unity even further than in *The Voyeur*. Each shot, each incident, refers the viewer to at least one other moment and usually several other moments in the film through repetition, variation, or contradiction; precisely by appealing to the viewer's memory, by testing the viewer's recollection of the preceding details of the film as it unfolds before him, Robbe-Grillet and Resnais have created a work that reflects its subject in miniature at every moment, a subject that can be summarized, although not adequately described, as "three people's completely different recollections of the same event." This progressive thematic unity is what allows us to follow the extraordinary variety of interwoven threads linking every shot to every other, thus reinforcing the linear movement created by the editing. It is unfortunate, however, that the *découpage* and editing of *Marienbad* do not participate more frequently in the creation of this network of interrelationships, which stem principally from the drama being unfolded, from the actual *content* of the images. The "camera" is perhaps too content merely weaving arabesques around the events, thereby failing to create the sort of genuinely *dialectical* relationship between participation and nonparticipation in the action that underlies *Cronaca di un amore*. In this respect, *Marienbad* also seems perhaps less successful than *Une Simple histoire*. Only certain sequences such as those in the continually transformed bedroom and out on the terrace are really tightly articulated. However, reservations of this sort are of no great moment in the light of the extraordinary step forward *Marienbad* represents in the history of film, particularly with regard to the reintegration of the film subject into the very texture of a work.

The same holds true, moreover, for Robbe-Grillet's first film as a director, *L'Immortelle*, though at the time of its release I (and a good number of my friends) unfortunately underestimated its importance by virtue of a too hasty comparison with the visual opulence of *Marienbad*. On the material, textural level, it is true, Michel Fano's sound track is the only really functional element in what at the time was an attempt at a brand new type of unity; however, we were doubtless wrong to be disappointed in the film, for how could a completely inexperienced film-maker have been expected to create a totally coherent work when so few film-makers with more experience have done so? But looking back on *L'Immortelle* today, the film seems to me to be a complete success from the standpoint of what Louis Delluc meant by *découpage*—the succession of events, scenes, and even individual shots as "containers" or units of meaning. *L'Immortelle*'s "program"—a term that we cannot perhaps substitute for "subject" but one that nonetheless singularly clarifies Robbe-Grillet's approach —consists of a gradual deterioration in verisimilitude, accomplished through a labyrinthine series of coincidences that become more and more fortuitous. This progression exists on every level of the film, in entire scenes as well as in individual shots. As the film unfolds, there are more and more sequences and even individual shots in which there is a progression from an apparently coherent reality to an increasingly pronounced, frozen artificiality as the hero confronts a series of coincidences and contradictions, a formal development perfectly reflecting the narrative progression from an atmosphere of deliberate banality toward an "unacceptable" artifice, a series of supernatural coincidences right out of a H. P. Lovecraft novel. And indeed, this intrusion of "impossible" mysteries into everyday reality has its source in the fantastic novel. But what is important here is that Robbe-Grillet has used it both as a principle of narrative form and of plastic composition—another great step toward the total unity of film.

It is commonly agreed that the subjects of *Marienbad* and *L'Immortelle* are "obscure," but that attitude stems from a grave confusion in terms that merits discussion. The subject of *Marienbad* is obscure only if one persists in believing that the action occurring on screen has a single underlying truth that explains everything, only if one persists in believing, that is to say, that every film possesses a key allowing one to resolve the various contradictions, to opt for what A says rather than what X says, to decide that a given shot has to do with fantasy while another shot has to do with reality. As those responsible for the film have repeatedly said, *Marienbad* has no key. The verbal or visual contradictions are the very essence of the work; they do not conceal the subject, but rather are directly derived from it and furnish yet another example of how this subject is the crucial factor in the film's entire development. In certain respects, both *Marienbad* and *L'Immortelle* are "innocent" films; nothing remains hidden, nothing that is not immediately perceptible in the film exists "somewhere else," above all not in the creators' minds. They are not films that call for interpretation; they demand simply to be seen. In every sense they are films that must be approached naïvely. There is nothing that will do more to spoil the pleasure we should experience by allowing ourselves to become lost in these labyrinths constructed to intrigue our minds and our eyes than the search for a hidden meaning "behind" them.

Hidden meanings, of course, can always be detected; hundreds, thousands of them can be found in these films if the viewer is so inclined. Yet Mack Sennett and Louis Feuillade showed us long ago that great cinema can be a purely immediate experience, and, as paradoxical as it might seem, films such as *Marienbad* and *L'Immortelle* continue that noble tradition. This is simply another way of saying that the subject in its most seminal definition is only a résumé of the action, even if the action in this case is purely mental.

Films that for one reason or another can be described as obscure obviously exist, however—films, that is to say, with a more or less hidden subject. We might ask at this point what the function of such subjects is and how films based on them should be "read."

Without attempting to draw up an exhaustive list of every possible kind of obscure film, one can immediately distinguish several important types. On the one hand, there are films that conceal a simple subject by "going beyond" it, surrounding it with digressions that act as a sort of mask, one that may at times have very elaborate Byzantine contours, or in any case more or less discontinuous ones that enable us now and again to glimpse some fragment of the original subject. This technique is sometimes used by film-makers seeking "honorably" to acquit themselves of tasks they feel unworthy of their talents; some beautiful and relatively "difficult" American films, such as Robert Aldrich's *Kiss Me Deadly,* have resulted. It is Jean-Luc Godard, however, who thus far has derived the most rewarding results from this principle, especially in *Pierrot le fou.* He too starts with a conventional detective story and then proceeds to "cloud the issue" with an extraordinary freedom. A number of events occur in *Pierrot le fou* that are absolutely incomprehensible if the viewer relies only on the deliberately confusing "explanations" offered from time to time. Men of letters will of course maintain that the real subject of *Pierrot le fou* is the love of Marianne and Ferdinand, or perhaps something akin to "the grandeurs and miseries of the modern romantic spirit." But, as was said earlier, a subject is primarily a mainspring of the discourse of a film, a driving force, a seed from which a form germinates; and the detective story that was Godard's starting point, the "plot," provides all these things. Love or a philosophy of life, in and of themselves, are only themes, and a *theme* is not the same thing as a *subject* for a film-maker.

Godard needed the subject of "Pierrot le fou" in order to give *form* to his film. As he structured the work, however, the subject practically disappears from sight in the course of its development. And let it be noted that I use the word "practically" deliberately. The original plot line might, of course, have disappeared entirely, as happened to the de Maupassant story that is supposedly the basis of *Masculin-féminin*. In the case of *Pierrot le fou*, the film might thus have been "stripped down" to the nostalgic wanderings of a man of great inner purity and the woman who will lead him to his death. But stripping the film down in this way would also have deprived it of its underpinnings. Godard has a very different view of the original subject from that of his audience, and he insists on revealing that subject from time to time precisely to remind the audience that he knows it more intimately than they do and has deliberately kept it hidden. On the level of communication, of course, this is tantamount to emphasizing the universal relevance of his story, but more significantly, this narrative method creates a dialectical tension between the subject and the discourse, fragments of the subject appearing and then disappearing in accordance with a rhythm that is quite essential to the discontinuous structure of the film. Godard carried this principle even further in *Made in U.S.A.*, but because of the careless way in which the film was made and perhaps more importantly because of a problem of running time,[3] nothing new is added to the dialectic already contained in *Pierrot le fou*.

As the reader will notice, I use the term "discontinuity" in reference to *Pierrot le fou*. Together with *Vivre sa vie* and *Une Femme mariée*, the film is, in fact, part of the great battle Godard is waging to free himself from the traditional narrative forms of cinema that have their source in the unity and continuity of action of the nineteenth-century novel, and it represents a step toward the creation of new narrative forms based on a "collage" of disparate elements as well as on discontinuity of tone, style, and materials. Although *dis-continuity* of this sort has already been mentioned during my discussion of the dialectics of materials, it must now be viewed from the perspective of the film subject. The choice of a subject for *Pierrot le fou*, or more accurately, the decision made with regard to how the subject was to function, was exercised precisely with an eye to the new narrative form that Godard is intent on creating, whereby the subject of a film will function as a hidden pivot around which *dis-continuity* will become *structure*. The quest for some way in which to give form to the discontinuity that underlies all of Godard's work is diametrically opposed to the approach of Robbe-Grillet, who has attempted in his first three films to create works with marked unity and even continuity (although in the process he completely reformulated the empirical unity previously obtained in the novel through such common devices as sustained characterization, unity of style, and continuity of narrative action) in his search for an all-encompassing type of unity, one bringing every element of a film, both narrative and plastic, into an intimate, symbiotic relationship resembling that of certain "lyrical" operatic works such as *Pelléas et Mélisande* or *Wozzeck*. As completely different as these two approaches might appear to be, they nevertheless constitute the most fertile ones of any in contemporary cinema.

Midway between the "straight" but hidden subject of the sort found in *Pierrot le fou* and the apparently concealed but actually "irrational" subject of *Marienbad* and *L'Immortelle*, another type of concealed subject can be distinguished, different both in nature and in function from those in *Pierrot le fou* and *Made in U.S.A.* This third type of subject involves what we might call "the psychology of intimation." It is not the characters' external behavior or the nature of the external events determining their acts that is kept hidden, but rather their innermost motives, the principles underlying the rather strange world they inhabit, the factors that Maurice Blanchot calls "the secret center of everything."[4] Both Blanchot's essays and novels are full of rewarding lessons for the contemporary film-maker seeking new subjects more in accord with the needs of the new language just beginning to develop in cinema. To adapt one of Blanchot's narratives to the screen would be a patently absurd enterprise; Blanchot's subjects can function only within a specifically *literary* set of coordinates. But other subjects fulfilling analogous functions can doubtless play comparable roles within a specifically *cinematic* set of coordinates.

How can these subjects be properly defined? Working within a literary context, Blanchot has defined these subjects in an infinitely more subtle and suggestive manner than could be done here,[5] but, nonetheless, a definition of how these subjects might function in cinema is not impossible, and, however simplistic my approach may be, such a definition may prove useful. Generally speaking, concealed subjects of this sort, although they remain almost as invisible as those that certain critics think they detect buried in the labyrinthine images of *Marienbad*, can eventually be apprehended through a process of interpretation, through a "close reading." In contrast to a Robbe-Grillet film, a subject that "really exists" underlies such works. It is usually expressed in metaphors so personal in nature, however, that quite probably the person responsible for them would not or could not express himself in any other way than in absolute metaphors, metaphors that have no independent meaning, that simply refer to a completely inner world that is, in a sense, beyond "comprehension." If the resulting films seem to demand interpretation, interpretation nonetheless is no more necessary with them than it is in the case of a Robbe-Grillet film or novel. Endeavoring to determine this "secret center of everything," even though this center may really exist in the author's mind, it is not necessarily a viable approach to a work and will in fact almost surely cause it to elude us.[6]

For obvious reasons few films thus far have used Blanchot's particular type of subject. There is one film however that represents a remarkable step toward a solution of the problem of the subject. It deals with this problem in a way that is personally more appealing to me than any other previously mentioned, for it seems to have inherent possibilities of developing into something extremely fruitful, representing as it does a kind of synthesis of the approaches embodied in *Marienbad* and *Pierrot le fou* and retaining all the advantages of both. The film is Ingmar Bergman's *Persona*, perhaps the most beautiful work thus far from this director whose work has evolved so extraordinarily over the years.

The "plot" of this film is usually interpreted as hinging on an exchange of personalities, but, even if this reading is correct, even if that is what Bergman principally had in mind, it nonetheless is an obstacle to any real understanding of the film. It may admittedly "explain" a large part (though not all) of the mysterious events that take place in this deliberately difficult work. But, at the same time, such an explanation masks a whole network of extremely complex and contradictory interrelationships that connect all of the events together and provide the film's superstructure. The film's "secret center," whatever it might be (and even if it is one involving the much discussed exchange of personalities), is used by Bergman to give an aesthetic, polysemic coherence to images and events that have many potential meanings both because of their ambiguous nature and because Bergman and Bergman alone possesses the key to the film, a key that is hidden from the beginning and that rightfully remains so. In individual sequences, certainly, it would appear that possible interpretations are constantly being suggested. Many critics would find it very easy—and very tempting—to interpret the sexual aggression in the amazing sequence of the broken glass in Freudian terms. But would such an analysis bring us any nearer to the tangible reality of the scene? Surely, it would be better to *experience* this scene as it develops, to feel the growing sense of apprehension in the interminable waiting, which has such a powerful effect: The longer it lasts, the stranger the characters' gestures appear to be, as this scene, which in the beginning was not at all intense because of the very large space the shot takes in, becomes more and more fraught with tension. And surely it would be better to simply *experience* the pain of the cut that ultimately results, a wound in itself minor and completely ignored by the characters yet that becomes as aggressively shocking as a major mutilation because of the place it occupies in the plastic and dramatic progression of the scene. We have already noted how absurd it was to seek a political explanation for the scenes from the Vietnam war that the sick woman sees on her television set. The horror of the images and the woman's anguish as she sees them must be *lived*. Interpreting them is tantamount to no longer seeing them. There are perhaps readers who will object that Bergman obviously wants his work to be interpreted. Admirers of a Raoul Walsh or a John Ford know that these directors make films they insist should merely be seen and heard, not interpreted (and these films are nonetheless endlessly interpreted by these same fans). Why then should Bergman be denied the right to share the ambition of a Walsh or a Ford—namely, the creation of films that must simply be *experienced?*

The principle underlying Bergman's approach seems most evident when he abruptly introduces elements foreign to the "action." In actual fact, this is only a more satisfying extension of Eisenstein's concept of "attraction by affinities," a technique that often assumed a rather naïvely metaphorical character in the work of the Russian master (and that he abandoned entirely in his maturity). One of the most sophisticated examples of this technique occurs in *The General Line,* where a jet of spraying water expresses the peasants' joy at receiving their new cream separators and at the same time commingles with the actual spurting of the cream from the spout to create a visual metaphor. In Bergman's case the notion of the image-metaphor is much more functionally integrated into the work. It is at once more abstract (in that the metaphors have no specific referent in the film) and more concrete (in that these intrusions involve the actual material confronting the viewer: film, screen, and arc-lamp); we are aware of this concreteness, moreover, not only because we are shown the film slipping out of the gate, a burnt-out frame, or a film tear, but also because the ultra-rapid, almost subliminal, style of editing Bergman uses in these passages enables us to experience the material made directly as actual celluloid film than would shots of "normal" duration, where we always have the time (and the space) to lose ourselves a little, to forget that what we are seeing is only light and a strip of film. The fluctuations between our sudden awareness that we are watching a *film* and our total or partial lack of awareness of that fact have as much to do with the dialectics of roles and materials previously described as with the Brechtian "distance effect." In this respect, Bergman seems to have successfully achieved another synthesis, combining two tendencies already dealt with here: one toward a greater organic unity attained through the interaction of overlapping and increasingly complex ambiguities, the other toward a structure based on a discontinuity and disparity of elements. The dialectical interplay between the continuous and the discontinuous is an important component in the underlying rhythm of *Persona.*

It is obvious that an exhaustive outline of the modern film subject and its function in the fiction film has not been presented here. There are, moreover, "nonsubject" films (for example, *The Chelsea Girls*) that present problems of an altogether different order. I feel, however, that I have fulfilled, at least in part, the task I set for myself: that of defining the responsibilities that I and other film-makers must resolutely confront. A film subject must no longer depend merely on our passing literary enthusiasms, on our minor day-to-day concerns, or on our notion of what might be of interest to an audience, even one of our own choosing. We are gradually creating a new cinematic language; let us therefore search out subjects that fit its needs. Moreover, this new language has already resulted in the creation of a totally new type of subject, which I shall call "nonfictional" (primarily in order to avoid its being confused with the old-fashioned documentary), one that functions in an altogether different way from the one I have called the "fictional" subject. The final chapter will deal with this new type of subject.

Notes

1. *Cahiers du Cinéma*, no. 195, p. 66.
2. A unity that is immediately undermined dialectically by the use of a style of musical discourse that is discontinuous and disjunctive. Here, too, the similarities between film form, as it is currently developing, and contemporary music are obvious.
3. *Made in U.S.A.* strikes me (or rather struck me in 1967) as an obvious case of an artificially inflated film, lengthened so as to suit the requirements of distribution. Yet as cinema becomes more and more aware of the organization of durations and the over-all composition of a film, concepts that will make totally new demands on a viewer's memory, it will become increasingly apparent that the traditional ninety minutes' running time that may have been perfectly suitable for the condensed novels characteristic of commercial cinema for so many years will no longer be a satisfactory format. Marcel Hanoun's three best films are each about an hour long and his total intransigence in this and every other respect is one of the reasons his films are not better known (as of 1967; *Le Printemps* (1971), a near masterpiece, runs 80 minutes, but then too *L'Hiver* (1968) is clearly inflated to 80 minutes, which would seem to confirm my hypothesis). This tendency toward shorter films would become more general, I believe, if distribution were organized in a more rational manner. There is, of course, another entirely different type of film that tends to be very long (for example, *The*

Chelsea Girls and other underground films), but only the future will tell whether or not this attempt at making film duration congruent with real duration will be fruitful or not.

4. See his Preface to the French edition of Adolfo Bioy-Casares's novel *El Invención de Morel*. Maurice Blanchot is an important French critic and novelist whose work is thus far known only in France. His fictional writings are among the few significant developments that have grown out of Kafka's "absolute metaphors." An examination of his first novel, quite relevant in this context, will be found in Sartre's essay "Aminadab ou du Fantastique considéré comme un language," in *Situations*, vol. I (New York: French and European Publications, 1969).

5. See in particular *L'Espace littéraire* (Paris: Gallimard, 1955).

6. Susan Sontag writes, in *Against Interpretation* (New York: Farrar Strauss and Giroux, 1966), "In most modern instances, interpretation amounts to the philistine refusal to leave the work of art alone. Real art has the capacity to make us nervous. By reducing the work of art to its content and then interpretating *that*, one tames the work of art. Interpretation makes art manageable, conformable."

10

Nonfictional Subjects

From the earliest beginnings of film, in addition to those pioneers for whom film was essentially a lucrative way of entertaining the public, there were others for whom film principally provided a means with which to inform (and perhaps even propagandize) and educate (and perhaps even indoctrinate) a mass audience. For both Marey during the archaic era of cinema and Lumière during its "primitive" period, it was an article of belief that, in the camera, man had at last found an instrument capable of capturing and recording the "real world" and that its essential function, its sacred mission lay therein. In their view the proper function of film would be the promoting of scientific progress, that great ideal of the beginning of the twentieth century; film would change mankind's perception of the world.

When sound was first introduced, during the heyday of the documentary film whose ideal was this celebration of the "real," John Grierson, the English film producer and theoretician, attempted to base a definitive film ethic on the realistic aspect of the concrete film image, the only one that counted to his way of thinking. In his view, film was necessarily *engagé* (to use a term popular only some twenty years later): "The documentary idea after all demands no more than that the affairs of our time shall be brought to the screen

in any fashion which strikes the imagination and is as rich in observed detail as possible. At one level, this vision may be journalistic;
at another, it may rise to poetry and drama. At yet another level its
aesthetic quality lies in the very lucidity of its exposition."[1] This
belief led him to condemn studio shooting of any kind and to declare
that, when a film director dies, he becomes a cameraman.

This bias, shared for some time by a large number of well-intentioned film-makers, indirectly but profoundly affected the evolution
of cinema in two ways. On the one hand, it imbued a very large
number of talented directors, principally those in England and
America but in Italy and France as well, with a deeply felt sense of
social responsibility (which was presumed to be more imperative
for a film-maker than for other artists, owing both to the popular
nature of his "art" and to its "realistic" nature) that frequently distorted the director's approach to the substance out of which film is
created and that emasculated his work. On the other hand, as the
quotation above demonstrates, this Griersonian ethic presupposes
some form of hierarchy within the very sort of nonfictional film
he advocates, a distinction between a film's message and its poetry, to
adopt Grierson's terminology, the naïve simplicity of which is
fairly characteristic of the whole old-style documentary school—
which for every one of the few works of genuine merit it produced,
such as *Man of Aran* and *Coal Face*, produced hundreds of films
that were as sentimental and insipid as *Louisiana Story*, or as luster-
less and pedantic as the bulk of the films produced by the General
Post Office (GPO) unit that Grierson himself directed.

This takes us to the very heart of our subject. We might ask why
the films produced by the GPO should strike a contemporary viewer
as being so lifeless, so fake, so contrived. It is because the notion of
nonfiction in film has changed radically over the last ten years (a development that has also shed some light on the evolution of the fictional film). Ultimately, Grierson's distinction between the content of
film and its form is no different from the views of an Autant-Lara, just
as Walter Ruttman's approach based on these same hierarchies is
exactly the same as that of a von Sternberg. In each instance, regardless of whether the subject or its treatment is given precedence, the
existence of a hierarchy, of a vertical compartmentalization, is precisely what prevents that fusion of form and content that Grierson

believed he was expounding in his writings and his films but that in actual fact only a few purely fictional films such as *The Blue Angel, M,* and *Vampyr* had attained at the time.

I have already attempted to indicate how this fusion is being brought about in the contemporary fiction films, in a more complex manner than Grierson or even Eisenstein could ever have imagined. This complexity has a specific source: Form and content are two concepts that no longer have any meaning; a vastly more organic synthesis is under way today, based on a notion that is the corner-stone of my own present endeavor; and film-makers are increasingly convinced that everything must function on every level, that form is content, and that content can create form. Contemporary nonfic-tional film subjects often are scarcely different from those of the old-fashioned documentary. What *has* changed, however, is the manner in which these subjects *function* within a cinematic discourse that has become far more Protean through such recent developments as dialectical interaction between different kinds of film material and between the different roles the camera can play, resulting both from technical improvements (lighter cameras and tape recorders) and from a certain expansion in film vocabulary (as, for instance, the recent rehabilitation of the "jump cut," or cut in which no appre-ciable change in angle or shot size occurs, and certain other kinds of "bad" matches).

We have seen what role fiction subjects play. We might now con-sider the function of nonfictional subjects, or at least that of the two types most relevant to contemporary needs: the *film essay* and the *ritual film.* Both types can, of course, assume a great variety of forms and may in fact coexist in the same film, a fact that reveals how arbitrary and oversimplified this distinction is. One hopes it may nonetheless prove useful.

For the contemporary observer, the first significant examples of an essay-type film are Georges Franju's short works. Let us therefore examine how *Le Sang des bêtes* and more importantly *Hôtel des Invalides* differ from the hundreds of films with apparently similar subjects. It should be stressed that Franju's films are only *apparently* similar to previous documentaries. What the old-style documentary-makers took as their "subject"—a passive subject by comparison with the "active" fictional subject—Franju takes as a *theme*, and his subject is, in and of itself, a development or rather, an interpretation, of this theme and it thereby becomes "active."

The aim of the old-school documentary film-makers was an absolutely objective rendering of the world they were filming. They sought to make what they filmed beautiful and clear; for them, this sort of reproduction of reality, as judicious to the mind as it was pleasing to the eye and ear, was its own justification. *Le Sang des bêtes* and particularly *Hôtel des Invalides* are no longer documentaries in this objective sense, their entire purpose being to set forth thesis and antithesis through the very texture of the film. These two films of Franju's are *meditations,* and their subjects a *conflict of ideas.* What is even more important, these conflicts give rise to structures.[1] Therein lies the tremendous originality of these two films, which were to cause nonfiction film production to take an entirely new direction. We might now examine how their subjects function.

A subtle but fundamental ambiguity underlies the sumptuous images of *Hôtel des Invalides;* it can be read either as an attack on war, or (on a level that is perhaps less sophisticated but still perfectly cogent and perfectly "natural" to a good many people) as a flag-waving patriotic film (we must remember that it was commissioned and distributed by the French Ministry of the Army!). The pan showing first a collection of medals on the breast of a veteran and then his hideously disfigured face is obviously an ambiguous, "reversible" figure, as is the device of having the words of a patriotic hymn appear on the screen together with gruesome paintings of military carnage; and what could be more ambivalent than the final shot of the film showing the children of the veterans joyfully walking off into the distance under a magnificent stormy sky.

Historically, *Hôtel des Invalides* represented the first use in the documentary film of a formal approach that previously had been exclusively employed in the fiction film. This, however, does not actually turn the documentary into fictional narrative, as always happened in Flaherty's films, with frequently disastrous results: The young visiting couple in Franju's film cannot be regarded as anything more than a mechanical device providing some sort of continuity, as ambiguous as the rest of the film, whereas the handsome youth in *Louisiana Story* is a fictional character, however fiction may be defined.

Hôtel des Invalides admittedly still possesses certain traits that relate it to the conventional fiction film or documentary: a unity of materials,[2] of tone, and of style, as well as considerable spatial and temporal continuity. *Le Sang des bêtes*, however, already contained the beginnings of a disjunct form because of its breaks in tone and material, and, in the two films that were to follow, Franju carried these explorations in discontinuity even further. These two works (his best ones after *Le Sang des bêtes*) are biographical reflections on the lives of *Le Grand Méliès* and *Monsieur et Madame Curie*. Both films employ what at the time was an almost completely unprecedented alternation between scenes performed by actors (recollections or recreated scenes from their lives), iconographic documents of all sorts, and, in *Le Grand Méliès*, clips from Méliès's films. In this film the authenticity provided by "still-lifes" of actual objects and documents from Méliès's life is carried over into the staged scenes by a surprising yet perfectly logical device: Having Méliès's own son play Méliès. This "historical" presence achieves maximum intensity, with "reality" and artifice becoming one and their dialectical relationship "crystallizing," when Méliès's widow appears during the film's last shots playing herself.[3] Of course, many previous "semifictional" films (such as Dieterle's biographies) as well as later documentaries involving some form of iconographic reminiscence[4] (Resnais's *Van Gogh*, for instance) are based on similar subjects. Because these subjects appear, however, in contexts where dialectics (as I have attempted to define them) are employed only on the most banal "articular" level,[5] they result in structures scarcely more complex than a mere linear depiction of the highlights of a life, organized along the lines of a literary biography or an obituary.

It is not surprising that an artist of Franju's stature could not confine himself for long to the short film without risking losing his creative impetus. Unfortunately, however, the magic that is so much a part of his nonfiction work no longer survives in his fiction features. Though Franju the documentary film-maker has had many imitators, his short films remain unique. In my opinion, he is the only cinematographer to have successfully created, from pre-existing material, films that are truly essays, perfect reflections on nonfictional subjects.

In feature-length film, however, a rather curious attempt of this sort has since been undertaken in Italy, one also involving preconceived (as opposed to purely aleatory) material, Francesco Rosi's film *Salvatore Giuliano*. No doubt the film is less reflective and more journalistic, corresponding more to a "profile," the prose equivalent of Franju's poetic meditations. Using as a basis a subject with such vast implications that it raises fundamental questions regarding the entire social and political situation of Italy today, Rosi, in what would seem to be the one inspired moment of his career, constructs a film whose structure derives precisely from the intricate nature of the subject. Viewed as a whole, the film is very much like a hurricane, if I may be allowed this somewhat far-fetched simile: Fragments of sound and fury fly by, sometimes in nonchronological order, often barely comprehensible,[6] and nearly always contradictory on some level or other. These fragments, moreover, seem to whirl round the calm and empty center or eye of the hurricane, with Giuliano himself never present on screen except as a dead body, thus providing an example of how a metaphor can pass intact from the level of subject to that of form, and be fully functional at both levels. At times the sense of the hero's presence somewhere nearby creates absolutely chilling moments of suspense, with Giuliano in a house not far off or close by behind a door; at other moments this element of suspense is almost completely absent, when events occur that have no direct connection with Giuliano personally. This movement constitutes the principal element of tension and release, as well as being one of the number of ways in which the film differs from previous attempts at historical reconstructions. The essential difference, however, may be this: By choosing a political and contemporary subject, then treating it in a much more scrupulously objective manner than is customary, Rosi endows his subject with the ability to engender form. This approach to a subject of this type is of fundamental interest, and, although the film is often quite academic in texture, the material incorporated quite uniform (new camera roles intervening only secondarily, as when Giuliano's mother plays herself), and the narrative development quite linear, these obstacles are easily avoidable today. We must remember that *Giuliano* was made some time ago, in 1961.

It is Godard, starting with *Vivre sa vie*, who has carried these experiments furthest. In order to transcend the normally constraining function of a film subject, he employs two methods, either alternately or simultaneously: He either uses concealed subjects in the manner I have already described or uses nonfictional subjects, which he deals with as a series of reflections on reality as he sees it. Godard quite frequently is an essayist, or more accurately a polemicist, although of a completely original type—and one perhaps justifiable only within the context of film-making. That the actual ideas expressed in his films are often specious is a fact of less importance than the way in which they are paraded before us; it is this element of intellectual spectacle that is irreplaceable, not the ideas themselves. This might appropriately be called a "cinema of ideas," but his approach is also and principally an aesthetic attitude, in the same sense that Sartre's essay on Baudelaire is a work of art, no matter what one's opinion of the ideas expressed and despite Sartre's own distinction between art and literature.

The first fruits of an endeavor this innovative are often not viable, and, though *Vivre sa vie* is an unqualified success owing to its dialectic of fiction and nonfiction, *Masculin-féminin*, the quite intriguing *Deux or trois choses que je sais d'elle*, and certainly *La Chinoise* are not successful films.[7] Quite probably, they are not successful because they become more and more experimental. Nevertheless they are steps toward a cinema of the kind long ago dreamed of by directors as dissimilar as Jacques Feyder, who hoped to adapt Montaigne's essays to film, and Eisenstein, who wanted to make a film based on Marx's *Capital*: a cinema of pure reflection, where the subject becomes the basis of an intellectual construct, which in turn is capable of engendering the over-all form and even the texture of a film without being denatured or distorted.

As has already been pointed out, Godard has gone a good deal further in this direction than any other cinema *auteur*.[8] Nevertheless, this is the one area in which he has perhaps been surpassed, interestingly enough by directors who are much less well known and who work for television. The two examples that follow were not chosen for any special superiority, but because they are fairly recent and fairly typical. The first of these is Jean-Pierre Lajournade's *Bruno*. By viewing the subject he chose for this strange program alternately from a sociological and political perspective and from a more intimate existential point of view, Lajournade has laid the foundations for a rather cohesive deliberately shifting structure, which tends at times toward a *cinéma-vérité* style (as when the actors, interviewed by real personnel directors, seem no longer to be acting) and at times toward a pronounced and occasionally clumsy stylization (as when the young man wrestles, either alone or in the company of a girl student of his, with the inner torment that has led him to abandon his studies and look for the first job opening available). Sometimes the transition from one style to the other takes the form of abrupt ellipses, and sometimes it is almost imperceptible, as during the hero's encounter with the snobbish girl, where stylization and improvisation mingle in a rather disquieting way (throughout the film, moreover, it is often difficult to determine the exact nature of the relationship between camera and protagonists).

Another possible approach to this sort of subject is illustrated by Danielle Hunebelle[9] and Jacques Krier's television series *Jeux de société*. It is not so much the fact that nonactors are often called upon to play themselves in dramatizations of social problems as the manner in which these programs are structured that is of interest here. Although in certain episodes of the series the narrative is carried forward essentially by staged scenes, ones skillfully intercut with and commented on by interviews involving people directly concerned with the "problem," in the episode entitled "La Mort d'un honnête homme," this procedure is reversed. Here, the dramatic narrative appears only in a very fragmented, allusive form in the acted scenes but is commented on at length by the interviewees, and the shifts in camera-actor relationship characteristic of the series as a whole consequently assume a very perceptible structural role here, the resulting structures deriving very directly from the contradictions inherent in that splendid platitude—the responsibility of the press. Thus even false problems may provide subjects for reflective films and result in aesthetically viable works.

This writer has already mentioned how much he respects André

S. Labarthe's work for the *Cinéastes de notre temps* series. It might simply be noted here that the dialectics of fiction and nonfiction that seem to be characteristic of nearly every one of the great reflective films of the last few years[10] exist in these programs as well, in the form of an alternation between interviews and film clips such as were described in the discussion of the dialectic of materials.

I might now discuss that other important type of nonfictional work, which I have called the ritual film. One should admit from the outset, however, that an analysis of this type is very problematical at this juncture, for this sort of cinema is still in its gestation period.

Although the notion of a cinema of ritual has its source in the experimental film of the 1920's, notably in the films of Man Ray and Hans Richter,[11] the concept did not really take hold until the advent of two successive postwar generations of American experimental film-makers. Almost every film made by the California avant-garde (1940–1955: Curtis Harrington, Maya Deren, James Broughton, Sidney Peterson) has ritual aspects. The formal possibilities implicit in such an approach are exploited with unequal results, a particular feature being the use and abuse of the possibilities of spatial disorientation created through editing. It seems to me that it is Kenneth Anger's two most important films, *Fireworks* and *Inauguration of the Pleasure Dome*, that stand out today as the important contributions. *Inauguration of the Pleasure Dome* involves a ritual in every sense of the word, one freely inspired by the sexual and magical practices of a modern sect and performed before Anger's camera by participants who in some cases were actual members of this sect (thereby peripherally introducing a mixture of the authentic and the fictional). The "inauguration" follows a rigorous symbolic ritual that is completely obscure to the profane spectator (the subject of the film therefore being of the concealed type), and this inexorable progression of symbols provides a framework upon which are grafted luxurious extravagances of color (in make-up, sets, costumes, filtered lights), and at the same time a gradual accumulation of careful superpositions transforms perfectly legible images into pure visual texture. Anger might perhaps be reproached for having let the method employed result in a certain tedium, but, if tedium it is, it is a "heavenly tedium," at least to any sensual eye.

The transformation of a ritual sensuality into visual material is even more successfully achieved in the best film of Ron Rice, whose premature death deprived the new American cinema of one of its most authentic talents. This film, *Chumlum*, superficially resembles certain sections of *Inauguration of the Pleasure Dome*, although here the constant use of multiple superimposed images tends to create a plastic space that at times is quite rigorously articulated (according to the principles outlined in the chapter on editing). The greatest originality of the film lies however in the fact that these spatial articulations become part of a continual flow, in which distinct shots no longer exist; *Chumlum* follows an incredibly complicated rite in the midst of which momentarily emerge extremely complex configurations, color combinations so refined as to be without precedent in cinema.

Stan Brakhage's very interesting film, *Blue Moses*, contains both reflective and ritual elements. Ostensibly a dissertation on the "paradox of the actor," interlarded with considerations that are completely esoteric because they have to do with Brakhage's private life, the film is a kind of ritual essay. Involved in these two inextricably intertwined subjects are constant oppositions between the actor (with make-up) and the actor as man (without make-up), between almost completely abstract images of the surrounding countryside obtained through swish-pans and stable shots "inhabited" by the actor, between the actor and his image on the screen, between the spoken word and silence, and so on, making *Blue Moses* one of the most intriguing attempts at creating a complex dialectic to have come thus far from American cinema.

A final word must be said about the great animator Harry Smith and his feature-length *Heaven and Earth Magic*. Only recently has it been possible to see this film in Paris, and it still is very difficult to write about it. But, if ever a rite, in this case the most compulsive imaginable, has resulted in the direct creation of the form and texture of a film, it is in this enchanting and exasperating work, whose plastic effect is similar to that of Max Ernst's collages and whose obsessive themes resemble the labyrinthine puzzles of Raymond Roussel. Even obsessions here become structures, everything becomes structure, endlessly, systematically, exhaustively, all within a single fixed shot into which objects and people are hurled, simultaneously or separately, as if by the distracted hand of a dreaming god.

Perhaps the most striking conclusion to be drawn from these brief reflections on the subject is that, for the contemporary cinematographer, both fictional and nonfictional subjects assume the same function, the engendering of form. In the fiction film of the past, the subject was chosen either for the literary developments it could lead to or for the visual arabesques that could be woven around it. The documentary film of the past also represented a choice between these two alternatives. There were, admittedly, film-makers who undertook to accomplish *both* ends, but they always approached the tasks *separately*, as the quotation from Grierson indicates. The cinematic revolution now in progress is based on what is essentially a very simple idea: that a subject can engender form and that to choose a subject is to make an aesthetic choice. This idea has a childlike simplicity, yet it is inherently one with incalculable consequences: It is what will enable cinema to become what music has been thus far, the art of arts.

Notes

1. *Grierson on Documentary* (New York: Praeger Publishers, 1972).
2. No doubt because they attempted to prove something, to explain something in *Man with a Movie Camera* and *Triumph of the Will*, Dziga Vertov and Leni Riefenstahl remain the two greatest documentary film-makers of the old school.
3. Although the manner in which Franju uses newsreel shots is quite interesting.
4. We might be told that this is precisely what the GPO unit did with the mail-sorters on the night train and the sailors on the North Sea. Yet what makes this method worth while in Franju's case is that it is used dialectically and is accorded a special place in the structural counterpoint of several methods, whereas in the GPO films the monotonous persistence of a single approach makes them linear and dull, at least to a contemporary viewer.
5. Although Dziga Vertov's *Three Songs for Lenin* anticipates Franju's films to some extent.
6. In the sense that any shot change involves the continuity-discontinuity principle.
7. The film might be less obscure to the Italian viewer, although not necessarily.
8. I would certainly not defend this viewpoint in these terms today.
9. Jean Rouch's ethnographic and sociological films are obviously reflections of

a kind, but I have already discussed his work and do not feel that examining the manner in which the subject functions in his films would contribute substantially to this chapter.

10. Danielle Hunebelle has since produced for American television "Blacks for Neighbors."

11. As indicated in the Preface, this hasty tribute to the new American cinema dates from a period when I was neither familiar with nor very sympathetic toward the bulk of its major achievements. And, though the concept of a ritual cinema may still be a seminal one with regard to the work of Anger, I should not deal with Hans Richter in these terms today, when I am primarily concerned with the problems of perception training and a scientific exploration of the medium.

Index

Actor's Revenge, The, 65
Agee, James, 129–30
Al Capone, 129
Aldrich, Robert, 76, 148
Alexander Nevsky, 34, 95, 115
All That Fall, 66
Alphaville, 60, 74
Amore in città, 79
Amour fou, L', 116
Anger, Kenneth, 164
Antonioni, Michelangelo, 11, 27–28, 30, 44, 54, 75, 76–77, 78, 79, 80, 127
Antwerp, Belgium, 66
Applause, 42
Argent, L', 30
Arroseur arrosé, L', 109
Artaud, Antonin, 127
Astruc, Alexandre, 77
Au Hasard Balthazar, 26, 127
Autant-Lara, Claude, 140, 141, 157
Authentique procès de Carl Emmanuel Jung, L', 132–33
Avery, Tex, 131

Bardem, Juan-Antonio, 46, 75
Barnett, Boris, 54
Barraqué, Jean, 51

Bataille, Georges, 67, 123, 124, 129, 133
Battleship Potemkin, The, 36, 43
Baudelaire, Charles Pierre, 162
Bazin, Janine, 59
Becker, Jacques, 88
Beckett, Samuel, 66
Beethoven, Ludwig van, 98
Belle de jour, 127
Berg, Alban, 67
Bergman, Ingmar, 133–34, 151, 152–53
Bezançon, Micheline, 88
Bezhin Meadow, 38–39
Big Knife, The, 76
Birds, The, 12–13, 142
Blanchot, Maurice, 150–51
Bleu du ciel, 67
Blond Cobra, 57
Blood Feast, 127
Blue Angel, The, 64–65, 158
Blue Moses, 165
Bob le flambeur, 44
Boule de suif, 40–41, 53
Boulez, Pierre, 134
Brakhage, Stan, 57, 165
Braque, Georges, 39
Breathless, 6, 38

168

Brecht, Bertolt, 153
Breer, Robert, 124
Bresson, Robert, 26, 28, 30, 42, 54, 57, 63, 67, 90, 91, 127
Broughton, James, 164
Bruno, 163
Buñuel, Luis, 7, 125, 127

Cacoyannis, Michael, 46
Cage, John, 106
Cahiers du cinéma, Les, 139
California, 164
Capital, 162
Caprices de Marianne, Les, 145
Carné, Marcel, 8, 62
Cavalcanti, Alberto, 110
Chelsea Girls, The, 117, 118, 119, 154
Chien andalou, Un, 124–25
Chikamatsu, 98
Chinoise, La, 120, 162
Chumlum, 165
Cinéastes de notre temps (series), 59, 142, 163–64
Clarke, Shirley, 116, 117
Cleo from Five to Seven, 56
Clouzot, Henri-Georges, 140
Coal Face, 157
Cohl, Émile, 58, 59, 140
Connection, The, 116
Conner, Bruce, 57
Cosmos, 144
Crime and Punishment, 88
Cronaca di un amore, 11, 27, 75, 76–80, 143, 146
Cronaca familiare, 23
Cronique d'un Été, 117
Crucified Lovers, The, 94–99
Cubism, 37

Dali, Salvador, 125
Debussy, Claude, 15, 99, 143
Delluc, Louis, 140, 147
Deren, Maya, 164
Deux ou trois choses que je sais d'elle, 56, 100, 120, 162
Devil in the Flesh, 141
Diary of a Chambermaid, 63, 127
Diary of a Country Priest, 42, 63, 67
Dieterle, William, 160
Disney, Walt, 58, 131

Divorce Italian Style, 54
Dovzhenko, Alexander, 11, 29, 54, 57
Duchamp, Marcel, 107
Duckweed Story, 23, 25
Dulac, Germaine, 41, 53
Dupont, Ewald André, 24

Earth, 11, 29
Éclisse, L', 80
Eisenstein, Sergei, 7, 34, 36, 37, 38–40, 42, 43, 53, 54, 71, 95, 111–12, 114–15, 121, 153, 158, 162
El, 127
El Dorado, 53
Éloy, Jean-Claude, 98
England, 157
Enthusiasm, 111
Entrée d'un train en gare de la Ciotat, L', 110
Epstein, Jean, 41, 53, 57–58
Erasers, The, 144
Ernst, Max, 165
Example Étretat, 55
Exterminating Angel, The, 7

Fabulous World of Jules Verne, The, see Invention diabolique, L'
Fano, Michel, 96, 97, 98, 146
Femme est une femme, Une, 61
Femme mariée, Une, 60, 98, 119, 149
Feuillade, Louis, 140, 148
Feyder, Jacques, 162
Filipone, Piero di, 77
Fireworks, 164
Flaherty, Robert, 159
Float Like a Butterfly, Sting Like a Bee, 61
Force of Evil, 96
Ford, John, 152, 153
France, 4, 59, 96, 106, 117, 123, 157
Franju, Georges, 125, 127, 158–61
Freud, Sigmund, 152
Fuller, Sam, 38
Futurism, 37

Gance, Abel, 41, 53, 55, 59
General Line, The, 36, 38, 153
General Post Office Film Unit, 113, 159
Genet, Edmond, 133
Geography of the Body, 91

Germany, 62
Glasgow, 113
Godard, Jean-Luc, 6, 38, 42, 56, 59,
  60–61, 74, 110, 115, 119, 120, 121,
  134, 148–50, 162
Goldman, Peter Emmanuel, 61
Gombrowicz, Witold, 144
Grand Méliès, Le, 160
Grierson, John, 156, 157, 158, 166
Gris, Juan, 37
Guerre est finie, La, 127

Hanoun, Marcel, 8, 14, 42, 56, 80–85,
  88, 132, 133
Harrington, Curtis, 164
Heaven and Earth Magic, 165
Hedren, Tippi, 12–13, 142
Hegel, Georg W. F., 51
Heisenberg, Werner, 121
Hidden Fortress, The, 96
High and Low, 40, 43, 56
Hiroshima mon amour, 54
Hitchcock, Alfred, 11, 12, 74, 142
Hollywood, 75, 113, 129, 142
Horla, Le, 73–74
Hôtel des Invalides, 158, 159–60
Huitième jour, Le, 56
Hunebelle, Danielle, 163

I Am Curious (Yellow), 51
Ichikawa, Kon, 65
Immortelle, L', 97, 146–47, 148, 150
Inauguration of the Pleasure Dome,
  164, 165
Invention diabolique, L', 59
Italy, 157, 161
Ivan the Terrible, 39, 44, 95, 115
Ivens, Joris, 110

Jacobs, Ken, 57
Jannings, Emil, 24, 65
Japan, 54
Japanese Ghosts, 128
Jetée, La, 58
Jeux de société, 163
Jour se lève, Le, 8, 62
Joyce, James, 15
Jules and Jim, 58

Keaton, Buster, 129
King Kong, 59

Kiss Me Deadly, 148
Klein, William, 61
Kracauer, Siegfried, 124
Krier, Jacques, 163
Kurosawa, Akira, 40, 42, 43, 56, 58,
  96, 127

La Ciotat (France), 109
Labarthe, André S., 59, 60, 140, 163
Lajournade, Jean-Pierre, 163
Land Without Bread, 125
Lang, Fritz, 14, 63
Langdon, Harry, 129, 130
Last Year at Marienbad, 8, 14, 52–53,
  54, 62, 65, 100, 124, 146, 147, 148,
  150, 151
Laurel and Hardy, 129, 130
Lautréamont, 133
Leenhardt, Roger, 59
Lepeuve, Monique, 55
L'Herbier, Marcel, 30, 41, 53
Life of O'Haru, The, 98
Lille (France), 82
Lloyd, Harold, 130
Long Pants, 130
Louisiana Story, 157, 160
Lovecraft, H. P., 147
Lower Depths, The, 96
Lumière, Auguste, 109, 110, 123, 156

M, 14, 63, 158
Maas, Willard, 91
Macbeth, 88
Made in U.S.A., 149, 150
Malle, Louis, 6
Mamoulian, Rouben, 42
Man Escaped, A, 26, 42
Man of Aran, 157
Mankiewicz, Joseph, 120
Marey, 156
Marker, Chris, 58
Markopoulos, Gregory, 53, 91
Marx, Karl, 162
Marx brothers, 114
Masculin-féminin, 149, 162
Mastroianni, Marcello, 28
Maupassant, Guy de, 73, 74, 149
Méditerranée, 71–74
Meerson, Lazare, 30
Méliès, Georges, 55, 90, 140, 160
Melville, Jean-Pierre, 44, 57

Mr. Hulot's Holiday, 64
Mitrani, Michel, 66
Mizoguchi, Kenji, 94–97
Moi, un noir, 116, 117
Monsieur et Madame Curie, 160
Montaigne, Michel de, 162
Moreau, Jeanne, 28
Morin, Edgar, 117
"Mort d'un honnête homme, La," 163
Mouchette, 26
Movie, A, 57
"Music of Changes," 106
Musset, 145

Nana, 18–19, 20–22, 23, 24, 26, 29, 30
Nanterre (France), 124
Napoleon, 55
New York, 117
Nicht Versöhnt, 14, 62, 100
Night and Fog, 55
Night-Mail, 113
Notte, La, 28, 44–45, 80
Nun, The, 98

October (Ten Days That Shook the World), 7, 11, 38, 112
October in Paris, 61
Odessa (Russia), 36, 43
Olvidados, Los, 127
Only Son, The, 25, 54
Opéra-Mouffe, 61, 63
Ophuls, Max, 77
Othello, 29, 45–46, 94
Ozu, Yasujiro, 19, 23, 24, 25, 54

Painlevé, Jean, 126
Paris, 66, 80, 81, 84, 90, 165
Peau douce, La, 7
Pelléas et Mélissande, 150
Persona, 100, 133, 151–53
Peterson, Sidney, 164
Pickpocket, 26, 42
Pierrot le fou, 60, 148–50, 151
Place Pigalle (Paris), 44
Pointe courte, La, 94
Pollet, Jean-Daniel, 71, 73
Polonsky, Abraham, 96
Prokofiev, Sergei, 95

Ray, Man, 164

Ray, Nicholas, 24
Reflections on Black, 57
Règle du jeu, La, 64, 141, 142, 145
Reisz, Karel, 32
Renoir, Jean, 18–22, 23, 24–25, 28, 63–64, 141, 142, 145
Resnais, Alain, 8, 14, 42, 52–53, 54, 55, 127, 146, 160
Rice, Ron, 164–65
Richter, Hans, 164
Riefenstahl, Leni, 133
Rivette, Jacques, 98, 116, 142
Robbe-Grillet, Alain, 8, 66, 97, 144–47, 150, 151
Romm, Mikhail, 40–41, 42, 53, 54
Rope, 11, 74, 142
Rosi, Francesco, 161
Rouch, Jean, 110, 116, 117
Roussel, Raymond, 165
Ruttman, Walther, 110

Sade, Marquis de, 133
Sadoul, Georges, 131
Saga of Anatahan, The, 96
Saludos Amigos, 58
Salvation Hunters, The, 54
Salvatore Giuliano, 161
Sang des bêtes, Le, 124, 125, 126, 130, 158, 159, 160
Sansho the Bailiff, 98
Santos, Pereira dos, 98
Sartre, Jean-Paul, 162
Scarlet Empress, The, 140
Schoenberg, Arnold, 96, 143
Schwitters, Kurt, 107
Sennett, Mack, 129, 148
Sherlock Junior, 129
Simple histoire, Une, 8, 13, 14–15, 80–88, 100, 132, 143, 146
Sjöman, Vilgot, 61
Skolimowski, Jerzy, 74
Smith, Harry, 165
Smith, Jack, 57
Sontag, Susan, 61
Soviet Union, 111
Stalinism, 10
Sternberg, Joseph von, 54, 64, 96, 140, 141, 157
Straub, Jean-Marie, 14, 62
Strike, 43, 111
Surrealism, 72

Technique of Film Editing, 32
"Tentato suicidio," 79
Terra trema, La, 11
They Live by Night, 24
Throne of Blood, 127–28
Toyada, Shiro, 128
Trans-Europ-Express, 66, 97, 98
Traversée de Paris, La, 141
Traviata, La, 98
Trial of Joan of Arc, The, 63
Trou, Le, 88
True Confessions, 82
Truffaut, François, 7, 58
Twice a Man, 91
Two Thousand Maniacs, 127

United States, 110, 126, 157

Van Gogh, 160
Varda, Agnès, 56, 61, 94
Variety, 24
Venanzo, 77
Vertov, Dziga, 58, 110, 111, 157

Vidas secas, 98
Vietnam, 133, 152
Violin and Guitar, 37
Visconti, Luchino, 11
Vivre sa vie, 60, 149, 162
Vlady, Marina, 120
Voyeur, The, 145, 146

Walsh, Raoul, 152, 153
Warhol, Andy, 117, 118
Warner Brothers, 131
Webern, Anton, 51, 56, 99
Welles, Orson, 29, 30, 45, 94
Wilson, Richard, 129
Wozzeck, 67, 150

Xenakis, Iannis, 106, 107

Zavattini, Cesare, 80
Zazie dans le Métro, 6
Zeman, Karl, 59
Zéro de conduite, 58, 64, 158
Zurlini, Valerie, 23

CRADLE TO GRAVE

Cradle to Grave

Comparative Perspectives on the State of
Welfare

RALPH SEGALMAN
Emeritus Professor of Sociology
California State University, Northridge

DAVID MARSLAND
Professor of Sociology
Brunel University

St. Martin's Press   New York
in association with THE SOCIAL AFFAIRS UNIT

First published in the United States of America in 1989

Printed in Hong Kong

ISBN 0–312–025343

Library of Congress Cataloging-in-Publication Data
Segalman, Ralph.
Cradle to grave: comparative perspectives on the state of welfare
Ralph Segalman and David Marsland.
p. cm.
Bibliography: p.
Includes index.
ISBN 0–312–02534–3
1. Public welfare—Cross-cultural studies. 2. Social policy—
Cross-cultural studies. 3. Welfare state—Cross-cultural studies
I. Marsland, David. II. Title.
HV31.S37 1989   361.6—dc19   88–15861

Contents

Preface   vii
Foreword   xi
Acknowledgements   xiii

PART I   THE WELFARE STATE IN THE
         WESTERN WORLD: AMERICAN, BRITISH
         AND SCANDINAVIAN EXPERIENCE

1 Introduction: The Price of Solutions   3
2 Welfare Dependency   9
3 Education in the Welfare State   14
4 Health in the Welfare State   20
5 Housing in the Welfare State   26
6 Employment in the Welfare State   33
7 The Welfare State and the Family   38
8 The Tenets of the Welfare State   56

PART II   THE UNUSUAL CASE OF
          SWITZERLAND

1 Introduction: The Swiss Approach to Poverty   65
2 The Swiss Welfare System   69
3 The Family and Other Limitations on
    Welfare Dependency   78
4 The Extent of Welfare Dependency in Switzerland   86
5 Negative Factors   91

PART III   WHAT ARE THE LESSONS?

1 Is Switzerland a Special Case?   99
2 What Really Makes Switzerland Different?   101
3 The Autonomous Local Community   107
4 What the Swiss Have Taught Us   109

PART IV   TOWARDS REFORM OF BRITISH AND
          AMERICAN SOCIAL POLICY

1 Welfare State Societies in Decay   115
2 Reform of Taxation, Incentives and the Work Environment   118

v

Contents

3 Support for the Family   121
4 Reinvigorating the Local Community   125
5 Reform in Housing and Education   129
6 Towards a Culture of Freedom   133

Bibliography   135
Index   139

Preface
Digby Anderson

When the Social Affairs Unit was formed in 1980, it chose as its first publication *Breaking the Spell of the Welfare State*. Until then, few social scientists outside economics had been prepared to present the arguments against state welfare and even fewer had had the opportunity to put those arguments to a wide audience. It was not surprising: most sociologists and social policy academics owe their salaries to the welfare state or that branch of it which is state or state subsidised higher education. (Incidentally, it called for and still calls for a degree of courage for a sociologist such as Professor Marsland to criticise state welfare while continuing to teach in the state system.) The fashionable wisdom, reinforced by the enormous vested interest state welfare creates, was that all was well with the welfare state, or would be if yet more taxpayers' money were injected. It is true that Marxists produced 'critiques' of state welfare but only in the name of a utopian state which would run the whole economy on welfare principles.

Today there is general agreement that there is a welfare state problem, even a crisis, though there is much disagreement about its nature and solution. That is some progress. And especially from economists have come studies showing at least the inefficiencies of state welfare, at most its failure to help the poor and the very high cost of that failure. Sociologists, Professors Segalman and Marsland go one further: the welfare state is not just a failure, it causes damage, damage to society and damage to the poor. In combination with 'progressive' policies on divorce and wider 'rights', it subverts the family and local institutions which are potential sources of a welfare far greater than it can deliver. It thus threatens the successful socialisation of future generations, transmitting to them a culture of crime, despair and dependency.

This scholarly but very readable study is highly original in its combination of economic and sociological analysis. It is also unusual in its scope, covering the United States and countries in Western Europe as diverse as Sweden, the welfare utopia, and Switzerland's minimal welfare system. Nor is it just a critique. Using the Swiss

example, the authors propose ways to reform education, health and
social security, to re-invigorate decaying communities, strengthen
the family and, through the encouragement of self-discipline and
independence, produce true welfare – after the welfare state.

The Unit's task is to generate, enliven and inform public debate
on social affairs, and it is with those objectives in mind that I warmly
commend *Cradle to Grave* to the widest possible readership.

Digby Anderson
The Social Affairs Unit
London 1988

Foreword

In the past few years several critical accounts of the welfare state have been published. They have successfully challenged the welfarist assumptions on which social policy in America, Britain, Scandinavia, and many other Western societies has been based for decades (Anderson, 1981; Gilder, 1981, 1986; Seldon, 1981). Building on this critique, this book attempts to take the argument an important stage further.

We have examined the literature of welfare in America, Britain, Scandinavia and the other welfare states systematically. We have conducted interviews with welfare administrators and other key personnel in most of these countries. What we have discovered is that the solutions commonly adopted throughout almost the whole of the Western world to deal with the problems associated with poverty have a high price. They cause more damage and much worse damage than the original problems. Bureaucratic state welfare creates dependency, hurts the poor, inhibits real solutions, and threatens to undermine the foundations of civilised, democratic societies.

One of our major themes is the process by which this damage is done. State welfare, in combination with liberal welfare state policies on divorce and on 'rights' more generally, undermines the family by making fathers redundant. With the family destroyed, its essential role in the socialisation of children goes by the board. In consequence the attitudes and skills required of independent adults in a free society are progressively attenuated. Commitment to self-sufficiency and capacity to achieve and maintain it are sabotaged.

A swelling population of welfare dependents is created. Economically supported outside the labour market, they have little interest in work, and are deprived of the support and discipline which work provides. Inhibited by central state welfare from any real stake in the neighbourhoods in which they live, they watch their local communities decay around them. Educational, health and housing programmes in the inner cities are close to collapse. Employers are frightened off by environmental conditions, by the costs required to maintain what they see as excessive welfare provision, and by the lack of skills and commitment in the demoralised population, and so establish themselves elsewhere. Crime escalates. The life of welfare

ix

dependency is institutionalised and normalised, and the fractured family re-creates new generations of children incapable of disciplined and independent lives.

This destructive process is apparent in America, in Britain, in Scandinavia and wherever welfare state policies have been adopted. Unless some radical alternative is found which gets big government off the backs of the people, an increasing proportion of the population will be sucked into welfare dependency. Democratic societies cannot afford the financial costs of state welfare, which drive up taxes, rates and inflation, and squander resources which are needed for productive investment. Still less can the socially destructive effects of excessive state welfare be afforded. Unless these policies are reversed, we are embarked on nothing short of cultural suicide.

THE STRUCTURE OF THE BOOK

The book is in four parts. Part I describes the destructive effects of welfare state policies in the USA, Britain and other countries in Western Europe. We examine education, health, housing, employment and the family. In each case we draw on official statistics, research studies and interviews. In each case the evidence is incontrovertible: welfarist solutions have made social problems in all these areas worse.

We expose the principles underlying such policies as muddled, contradictory and implausible. We reveal how their effect has been to create an ever-expanding sub-class of welfare dependents incapable of supporting democratic freedom or of benefiting from it. We examine the damaging effects of these developments on the economy and culture of free societies.

As a contrast to the deep-seated malaise caused by state welfarism, we turn in Part II to an examination of the exceptional case of Switzerland. On the basis of careful field research we show how the Swiss have managed to avoid overblown state welfare, and in consequence escaped the destructive penalties other Western countries have paid for it.

The Swiss approach insists on individual, family and local responsibility for welfare. It avoids confusing poverty with inequality. It acknowledges the need for effective control of socially damaging deviant behaviour. It presumes that the State's responsibility is to

help people towards independence from State support as quickly and as effectively as possible. The result is a free and prosperous society with high levels of social mobility, negligible unemployment and little poverty. The canker of welfare dependency, which elsewhere threatens general prosperity and democratic freedom, is absent.

Part III examines the lessons which comparison of the Swiss case with the welfare states of America, Britain and the rest suggests for countries infected with the welfare virus. We show that Switzerland is not, as is often argued, a special case. Principles, approaches and strategies adopted by the Swiss are entirely compatible with economic, political and cultural conditions in other countries.

All that is required is a decision to reduce welfare provision drastically, and commitment to new policies which solve problems without causing worse ones. Small-scale local communities should have their autonomy, including their financial independence and responsibility, restored. State sabotage of the family should be ended. Redistributive egalitarianism should be abandoned. Help for individuals and families in need should be in the form of loans, temporary, and locally administered. It should be presumed that individuals and families are capable of making arrangements for their own and their dependents' welfare. The power and scale of the central state apparatus should be drastically reduced.

In Part IV the specific implications of our analysis for social policy in Britain and the USA are delineated. Established policy approaches to income maintenance, health, housing, employment and the family are examined. The extent to which these approaches generate welfare dependency, increase poverty, and inhibit any consistent advance towards general prosperity is exposed and criticised.

To answer these weaknesses, radical changes in taxation policy are recommended, together with restoration of more positive attitudes towards the family, education and individual initiative. The dangers of municipal socialism in the conurbations of Britain are also examined, and suggestions made for restoring the power of genuine localism.

The damaging consequences of the welfare policies adopted all over the Western world after the Second World War are now apparent. Governments of left and right alike are reaching around for solutions to the decay and chaos which increasingly characterises all our major cities. Our argument is that nothing less than a reversal of these policies is necessary if we are to avoid a deepening crisis.

The welfare state has proved a damaging distraction and shown itself dangerously counterproductive wherever it has been tried. Instead, we should follow the clue provided by the Swiss, by common sense, and by principles long established in free societies, to reach beyond the welfare state towards real welfare.

Acknowledgements

The authors are indebted to Praeger-Greenwood Press for their permission to use material from the work of Segalman, Ralph, The Swiss Way of Welfare: Lesson for the Western World (New York, 1986) and to the editors of The Public Interest for permission to use material from the article 'Welfare and Dependency in Switzerland', (Winter, 1986) pp. 106–21.

Professor Segalman also wishes to express his deep appreciation to his wife Anita for her help in reading and revising the manuscript.

Acknowledgements

The authors are indebted to Praeger/Greenwood Press for their permission to use material from the work of Aaron Wildavsky, *Searching for Safety*, used by the Praeger Books (New York, 1981) and to the authors of *The Public Interest* for permission to use material from the article "Welfare and Democracies in Switzerland" (Winter, 1990), pp. 106–27.

The authors/research team would like to express its thanks and gratitude to Ms. Ann Liu for her help in reading and reviewing the manuscript.

Part I
The Welfare State in the Western World: American, British and Scandinavian Experience

Part I

The Welfare State in the
Western World:
American, British and
Scandinavian Experience

1 Introduction: The Price of Solutions

In the United States there is a metaphoric aphorism, namely, 'Edsel's Law', which states that if a commercial enterprise produces a bad product line (the 'Edsel' of the Ford Motor Company), it soon learns that it has made a mistake. The corollary of the law indicates that if a government establishes a policy which fails, it will probably add to the policy, or build more of such policies, but, in any case, the policy will never be cancelled.

'Edsel's' corollary probably explains why there are so many problems in the welfare states without much discussion of the need to go back to the drawing-board. For what do we find?

High unemployability
High unemployment
High government deficits
A huge body of centralised bureaucracy resistant to cutting
An extensive social pathology in the form of low educational achievement
Increased illegitimacy
Criminality and drug addiction
Extensive alienation
Intermittent riotous behaviour
Emigration of skilled employees

Yet with inflation waiting offstage ready to appear as soon as the temporary recovery is over, most welfare states have lost sight of their goals, and seem to be frantically redoubling their misdirected efforts.

PROBLEMS IN THE WELFARE STATE

Most of the welfare states are beset with large populations of youth and young adults who are generally idle and less than minimally prepared for employment. They seem reluctant even to consider beginning employment which their parents' or grandparents' generation would have taken as a 'first rung' on a lifetime employment ladder. The employment offices, by and large, do not consider these

3

young people as part of the workforce because they are not actively seeking work. For the most part, these young people depend either on the dole and government allowances or on someone else with whom they live, who is also usually a dependent of some government programme. For the most part, these young people live in geographical areas with a high rate of welfare dependency, in subsidised housing which is damaged by years of tenant misuse and mismanagement. The area in which they live often has a high rate of crime, delinquency, drug addiction, alcoholism, violent behaviour, broken families and illegal immigrants. These areas have schools which have a high rate of absenteeism, children who are difficult to control, and a demoralised set of teachers with a high rate of staff turnover. Intact families, especially those with employed heads, either move away from these areas as quickly as they can or they avoid moving into them in the first place.

The dependent population, especially those who live in these areas, have a falling marriage rate, an increasing divorce and desertion rate, and a declining rate of family formation. Children in such areas make up a sizable population. They are a matter for serious concern because they are increasingly being reared in disorganised homes with only one parent. The mother is joined from time to time by intermittent men who are introduced as 'the boyfriend' or 'Uncle John'. Their stay in the home is short in time and they cannot, in any sense, be considered as a father substitute for the children or as a financial or familial support for the mother. The birth rate in such families far outpaces the birth rate of intact, complete families in the population.

THE EFFECTS OF ECONOMIC CHANGES

In addition to these ills, most of the welfare states are suffering a loss of heavy industries to Third-World countries, where unskilled manual labour is cheaper and without the extra employment benefits required by the welfare states. As a result, there is a substantial shift in the employment pattern in the welfare states of those not in government employment. This shift causes a shrinkage of unskilled and 'blue-collar' positions, and the new jobs which do open up have increased requirements of education, job-conditioning, and technical training, often at less pay. Such jobs as do appear are usually located not in the geographical areas of the dependent unemployed, but, in

new locations near suburbs and new developments. Moreover, they are concentrated primarily in the service industries. This has already begun in the United States (Eisenstadt, 1985, p. 3), and signs of it have appeared in other welfare states too. This change in future employment patterns causes increased strains on the welfare state. For it represents a cutback of a major population base upon which the welfare states have become increasingly dependent for tax income. The new employment population base will be less well equipped to provide adequate tax income. This new employment pattern is also a matter of serious concern for the future because the replacement birth rate derives from a population which provides inadequate and unsuitable familial socialisation for employment in the new industries.

POLITICAL SUPPORT FOR THE WELFARE STATE

Most of the welfare states have developed extensive programmes of income redistribution which provide substantial grants – euphemistically renamed 'benefits' – despite the fact that they do not require prepayments during prior employment. Many of these grants have been provided because of pressures by groups of proposed beneficiaries. They tend to support the welfare state only to the extent that they continue to benefit. In time, these groups withdraw their political support when proposals are posited to benefit other population groups, or when efforts are made to offset current benefits with increased taxes for such established beneficiaries. Thus, as the welfare state ages, it begins to take on the shape of a gigantic pyramid selling scheme or pyramid swindle – with the older investors benefiting from the support of the newer entries, until, eventually, new support disappears as new entries to the society inherit only guaranteed obligations without benefits. Observers report continued acrimony as each group seeks to maximise its share of command over goods and services.

THE COMPLEX UNCONTROLLABLE WELFARE STATE

Many of the welfare states have also developed an intricate mosaic of social services and welfare income administration. These are both highly centralised and rigidly controlled by a complex of regulations originally installed to protect various political, regional, and/or

economic interests involved in the legislative compromises which made possible the policy. Many of these regulations are no longer applicable, or else they have been offset by counter-regulations in later legislation. This has resulted in a maze of requirements satisfied only by a large bureaucracy and private and public lawyers and social workers, whose services are required to keep the constipated system functioning. In France, for example, it is impossible to find one's way through the system without the use of specialised service workers (Fondation pour la Recherche Sociale, 1980).

The colossal bureaucratic centralised funding, adjudication and distribution mechanisms are apparently impervious to electoral and political choices (Eisenstadt, 1985, p. 2). As a result, these pro-grammes have become impersonal, massive in operation, and unable to individualise the services because of the complex of national and regional regulations, and also because of the difficulty of processing decisions through the multiple control complex. For example, in the United States, there are numerous instances where people have been incorrectly reported as deceased, with an unintended stoppage of benefits of over six months. There have also been instances when reports of death of beneficiaries were not processed, with multiple posthumous cheques received by the family of the deceased. With complexity has come a continued burgeoning of staff.

WELFARE AS A RIGHT EQUALS PERMANENT WELFARE FOR MANY

Yet another continuing problem in the welfare states derives from the assumption that welfare is a right, rather than a privilege. A corollary of this assumption is that the beneficiary need do nothing to receive this grant, except to apply and to express (or prove) his neediness. If a claimant gambled away his assets, or even gave them away, it would not make him ineligible. If he refused employment or refused to educate himself for employment or refused to accept training, it would make no difference. He could continue to receive the aid. Any attempts to change the regulations to require him to do otherwise would be doomed, either because of the difficulty of changing the law and regulations, or because of the resistance of the bureaucracy to persuasion.

This conflict between the intent of welfare as a temporary aid (as so understood by most of the public) and welfare as a permanent

right (as understood by the welfare bureaucracy and welfare state planners) has serious implications. The welfare state nations, by and large, have given up on the concept of client rehabilitation for self-sufficiency, an intent originally supported by most welfare state proponents. What was to have been a temporary condition has become a permanent cost on the welfare state. As a result, welfare discourages productivity and self-sufficiency and establishes a new mode of approved behaviour in the society – one of acceptance of dependency as the norm.

PRODUCTIVITY AND THE WELFARE STATE

Yet another associated problem of the welfare state is related to productivity. Evidence has accumulated that the welfare state is less productive than the free-enterprise economy. The American experiment in providing a guaranteed minimum income in controlled tests in Seattle and Denver indicated that the guarantee of even a limited income results in sizable reduction in work hours for men and women. Even more damaging consequences of the minimum guaranteed income were indicated in the social realm, with a large percentage of families, particularly among the working poor, being dissolved during their period of subsidy. Thus, helping families with supplementary funds and income guarantees weakens the position of the father in the family to the point where he is actually encouraged to leave. This, in turn, means that the children will not have the socialisation provided by an intact family. These studies also showed that there are psychological and emotional disruptions among those supported under the income guarantee experiment, which were not evident in the control group.

This destructive effect is not limited to the United States. In Sweden, where a guaranteed income has been in force for many decades, and where the pursuit of gender equality has led to abolition of the joint income-tax return, the two-income family is almost mandatory if the couple wishes to stay above the poverty line. Couples seeking to care for their own preschool children are taxed for, but ineligible to receive, benefits such as subsidised meals, which accompany daycare. As a result, marriage among young Swedes is falling, but cohabitation is rising. The Swedish total fertility rate has fallen to 1.5 children per family, despite increases in child allowances (Carlson, 1983).

Thus, among the dependent poor, the working poor and even the middle class, the welfare state has the effect of discouraging the socialisation of children by parents. In its absence, social control becomes difficult and expensive, and the need for a heavily policed state becomes gradually inevitable.

2 Welfare Dependency

Another product of the welfare state experience is the growth of welfare dependency which is transferred from one generation to another. For over 25 years, evidence of this phenomenon was quietly, but firmly, repressed in the United States behind a façade presented by the welfare establishment, the sociological, psychological and economic scholars of poverty, and the social policy formulators. This myth was, for the most part, supported by the media (William Julius Wilson, 1985).

The picture of the welfare-dependent population presented by these people was that the poor were basically all alike. They were supposed to be similar in behaviour to the rest of the population, imbued with the same Protestant ethic and valuing education, work training, employment, self-improvement and self-sufficiency as much as the rest of the population. The behaviour of the poor was supposed to reflect these values.

Indeed, it was claimed by these proponents of the poor that welfare dependency was only temporary in almost all cases, and that the poor would move into self-sufficiency as soon as opportunities became available. In the meantime, all they need is more money to improve their situation.

Their purposes in repressing discussion of the true picture of welfare dependency was no doubt compassionate. Welfare experts, public, academic and journalistic, feared that a contrary view of welfare poverty might lead to more robust management and constraint of welfare, and, perhaps even a revised administration of the policy.

EVIDENCE OF POVERTY

In the meantime, data began to accumulate in the form of Sheehan's *Welfare Mother*, Auletta's *Underclass*, Sharff's *Ghetto Family*, Segalman and Basu's *Poverty in America*, and Murray's *Losing Ground*. In addition, persistent poverty and dependency was reported in England by Townsend, in the Low Countries by Schaber and associates, and others.

In the latter studies, however, the description of the poor tended to define the condition as entirely the results of social factors beyond their own control. It was claimed that it did not in any way derive

9

from individual behaviour, lifestyle or choices. In these European studies, as in the picture of dependent poverty presented in the United States, the poor were depicted as victims of conditions beyond their control, rather than as independent agents who deal with – or choose not to deal with – the problems they encounter.

Two studies made in West Germany by Strang (1970, 1984) found that the poor are not monolithic at all. Some people faced with poverty are able to surmount the problem and can mobilise themselves to do so, while others tend to fall into a life of dependency which persists into subsequent generations. Studies in the United States on residual poverty were numerous, but they persistently claimed that welfare dependency was a myth rather than a fact. In the 1960s, chronic dependency was estimated by scholars and researchers as 'less than 10 per cent'. By the 1970s, they were still reported as insignificant, although the figures indicated about 20 per cent, and this population category represented over 60 per cent of the costs. By the 1980s, they were reported as not a major problem even though some reports indicated a figure of as high as 43 per cent.

In summary, we can conclude that welfare dependency is a major cost to the welfare state, and that the problem can be expected to grow.

DESTRUCTIVE EFFECT OF WELFARE DEPENDENCY

It is important to examine how welfare dependency affects children and society. The Sheehan study, we believe, is typical of the reports of chronic welfare dependency. The Sheehan welfare family had the following characteristics. They are very similar to those reported from other ghetto sources:

(1) a matriarchal pattern of family structure;
(2) many children of different fathers;
(3) childbirth by mother at an early age;
(4) only a tenuous relationship between the family and community, religious organisations, community resources, schools and centres of community services, including employment programmes, and a general fear and suspicion of agencies of community responsibility;
(5) only a tenuous relationship between the immediate family and relatives (particularly male relatives) in the extended family. The only extended family strengths derive from

grandmothers, who were, themselves, reared in a welfare-dependent setting;

(6) a view by the mother which expressed no hope of, or aspirations for, eventually getting her children out of poverty, either by seriously supporting efforts at their education or by encouraging their acquisition or vocational skills;

(7) a child-raising orientation by the mother which lacks authority and purpose, and which is generally disorganised and confused. The mother's control of the children is usually ineffective and episodic, and relies entirely on physical punishments – an option no longer open when the children became physically larger than the mother;

(8) a point of view towards all matters which was fatalistic;

(9) a present-time oriented life pattern which promoted impulsive behaviour, and short attention-span activity, except in the matter of watching hours of television soap opera programmes;

(10) a life history containing a series of poor marriages and/or male liaisons;

(11) behaviour patterns of older children which indicate a continuation of residual welfare dependency. In the case of one daughter, she was already a welfare recipient with her own child, and, in the case of a son, he already had an expensive heroin habit and a history of repeated violations of the law;

(12) a history of missing or unemployed husbands or fathers of the children, each of whom had had only a fluctuating, unclear and temporary place in the family constellation;

(13) a disorganised and impulsively-operated home, with little meal planning and very little organisation of familial duties or clear division of family responsibilities;

(14) a pattern of financial management and credit use which is chaotic and not operated on a basis of purposeful or economic survival priorities;

(15) a relationship with the welfare authorities which is based less on the true facts of the family's situation and more on an attempt to gain maximum financial aid with as little follow-up investigation as possible.

GHETTO DEPENDENCY

Sharff's anthropological study of East Harlem provides a similar

family picture. Here, a female-headed matriarchal welfare-dependent family, seemingly without planning to do so, directs its children towards coping models which adjust to welfare dependency and life in the ghetto, rather than towards models related to moving into self-sufficiency and employment. In addition to the 'mother-matriarch', the Sharff family constellation consisted of:

(1) an elder son who is encouraged to free himself from school requirements as early as he can so that he may become the 'street representative' of the family, helping to protect the family from harm by his gang alliances, and helping to supplement the family's disposable income by contributing his street earnings and his share of gang booty. The gang also serves the family in keeping the matriarchal 'boyfriend of the moment' under the matriarch's control. The gang derives its income from various rackets, including 'protection of local merchants', which means that the family is, in part, supported by illegal activity and is tied into a crime syndicate;

(2) a home and childcare manager, a daughter who takes over the care of the younger children and who, in turn and in time, becomes pregnant and brings in her share of welfare support. As in the case of the older son, this child is also encouraged to free herself from school as soon as possible so that she may relieve her mother of home duties;

(3) a family advocate, usually a son, but sometimes a daughter, who alone among all the children is encouraged to stay in school. This is the child who accompanies the mother in all contacts with authorities, whether welfare, school, or police. This child learns to present the family's needs to authorities, to ask for services and benefits, and to protect the family in case of trouble with authorities;

(4) understudies are developed for each of these roles as younger children become available. This is particularly important in the case of the 'street representative', who cannot be expected to be available indefinitely in view of the hazards of gang conflict, delinquency and periodic incarceration. Similarly, as younger girls become available, they learn the roles of welfare mother-hood.

It should be noted that these learned roles become instilled in the children and, in time, in *their* children. Their life pattern contains not only a modus vivendi for living in the ghetto, but also a modus vivendi of continued dependency on society. It perpetuates an

apartheid condition between the welfare poor and the productive elements of society.

COLLUSION WITH DEPENDENCY

It should be noted that the representatives of mainstream society in contact with welfare families also participate in the perpetuation of the dependency pattern. Examples found in Sheehan's 1976 report include:

(1) provision of money by the welfare agency for moving expenses, which was not used by the family for moving and was never returned by the family, or even requested by the agency;

(2) provision of extra food stamps without checking when the family reported that the first supply was lost. In the process, the client had a double allotment for the period.

(3) acceptance of the client's feeble excuses for not becoming involved in the work-training programme;

(4) the purposeless relationship between the welfare representative and the client, and even a reluctance by the worker to discuss the client's questions on how she might handle her problems;

(5) the systematic separation of social services from eligibility determination provided no opportunity to discuss with the client her continued dependency and the likelihood that her children would follow in her pattern;

(6) the agency's frequent ignoring of obvious lies and manipulations by the client. In several instances this kind of client relationship was rewarded by additional agency grants. The plethora of welfare workers known to the client, all of whom had short and only occasional contacts with her, ensured that the client would not be affected by any relationship with the welfare agency.

The design and structure of the welfare agency is so ineffective in helping the client escape from the welfare trap that it might appear to have been designed by a permanent civil servant in the British television programme 'Yes – Minister'.

3   Education in the Welfare State

A clear connection between the female-headed family to be found in chronic welfare dependency and inadequate educational and school socialisation, inadequate school progress and inadequate preparation of children for necessary purposes of social control has been reported by Dornbusch, *et al.* (1986). Various researchers have tied welfare dependency to hard-core delinquency and have indicated a connection between such families and psychosocial dependency. There are various reports from police agencies that drug addiction is frequently found in broken families and families without suitable fathers. Reports abound from ghetto schools which indicate that only a small proportion of children of broken families are able to complete their education in a satisfactory manner.

THE IMPORTANCE OF EDUCATION

Education is a critical dimension of intergenerational welfare dependency in that it is basic to an individual in preparing for and accepting an occupational role. Without a job he cannot expect to achieve autonomy and a self-sufficient status. Education provides the individual with the necessary verbal and written skills of communication without which work is not possible. Education trains the person for thinking rationally and independently. It provides the learning of social skills and norms necessary for productive interaction with others, and for the acquisition of self-discipline and self-restraint without which learning is impossible.

Education prevents dependency by providing knowledge and skill upon which employment and involvement in the market-place can be built. When it is successfully mastered, education provides substantive human economic capital. It also provides psychological human capital, by strengthening the individual's self-concept and sense of self-worth, and by providing problem-solving skills. The appropriately educated individual knows which doors to knock on, and what to say when they are opened. Because of self-confidence derived from past learning achievements he is ready to risk himself in an encounter with an opportunity. Many less-educated people, because of the low

14

expectations they hold for themselves in mainstream surroundings, tend to avoid such experiences or are lost in making their way in new surroundings.

Education is important in other critical realms of life as well. In health research, for example, it has been found that health conditions of individuals are directly related to the level of education achieved. This correlation can be explained by the role which the individual plays in choices related to his health. The informed patient is all the more likely to be a health-preserving patient. In the absence of knowledge, emotion and myth all too often take control.

RESPONSIBILITY FOR EDUCATION

Most people believe that the main responsibility for education rests on the schools. However, careful examination of the theory and research of learning suggests that it is the early learning years of the child, rather than the school years, which are most critical for successful preparation for later life. Erikson, indicates that every child must successfully surmount a series of struggles, such as trust (versus mistrust), autonomy (versus doubt and shame), initiative (versus guilt), and industry (versus inferiority), during his early years. These mainly precede the usual school experience.

Brown and Madge (1982, p. 97) indicate that family background and experience has an increasing impact over the whole life cycle. The Coleman (1966) and Jencks (1973) studies found a strong basis for concern over family background and experience in relation to successful learning achievement. Bourdieu (1980) and Hinde (1980) demonstrate that the 'cultural capital' provided by parents determines the degree to which educational success, and then occupational success, becomes possible.

FAILURES OF EDUCATION

Careful analysis of the Sheehan (1976) welfare family or the Forman (1982) families in the United States and Britain, and other residual welfare studies in the western nations, indicates that probably the most serious weakness in the welfare-dependent family is its failure to prepare its children for life in the mainstream and for making the most of what schools have to offer for upward mobility.

In the United States, inadequate socialisation of children for schooling has converted ghetto schools from learning centres to behaviour control centres. Desegregation by bussing and other mechanisms has lowered the educational productivity of many American schools, with the result that many middle-class parents (minority and majority) have fled to private, tuition-charging schools, where learning productivity and educational standards are high. Thus, the 'mediocritisation' of American public education has been achieved, a sort of educational redistribution by the welfare state to match its income redistribution goals. This has contributed to the apartheid effect of American income redistribution – a separation of the residual welfare-dependent poor from the self-sufficient society.

In Britain, the early Labour governments supported grammar schools, modern schools and technical schools to match the different talents of students, and to satisfy the variety of preparatory demands of commerce, industry, and universities. Most of these schools have, in recent decades, been replaced by comprehensive schools, which, in the name of democratisation, bundle students with mixed abilities and talents together. These schools usually fail to satisfy the requirements of employers or universities. The homogenisation of schools parallels a similar pattern in the United States.

Both in the United States and Britain, there are private schools with high standards. Private schools are, in both countries, now becoming almost the only entry to better-quality university education and continued upward mobility. With falling standards and educational productivity in the state schools, it is becoming less possible for a student to graduate from a state school and then to enter a prestigious university. Under the new 'egalitarian' system in the state schools, the bright poverty child, who is held back by a class of dullards and misbehaviour-prone children, is outstripped by the dim middle-class or rich boy in the private school. So much for the educational social justice of the welfare state. Middle-class parents soon learn the trick of moving to a neighbourhood where a good state school still functions, despite the high costs of relocating and buying a house in such neighbourhoods. Either that, or they take on extra employment to cover the tuition costs of private schools.

EDUCATIONAL IMPASSE

The educational impasse in public education in the United States and

Britain is not easily resolved. Once the mass of parents in a school district fall behind in appropriate socialisation of their children for learning in the school setting; once they lose (or abdicate) the function of 'policing' their children's learning attitudes and school progress; then the school adopts a defensive position of limited accountability for its progress with the children's learning goals.

Concurrently, as the schools relax their pressure on students and parents for learning achievement, parents and students begin to blame lack of learning progress on the schools and their personnel. When a school or school district begins to fail in its reported and reportable achievements, such as interdistrict exam results, then the funding authorities at all levels make less stringent efforts for teacher salaries, school operational budgets, and so on. In time, teacher and staff morale losses are matched by increased dropout and truancy rates. With the loss of teacher morale comes the disappearance of teacher enthusiasm for teaching and promoting learning.

There is a 'tipping point' in school clienteles and in teacher quality, just as there is in public housing, public hospitals, and other public institutions. As quality of clienteles and staff diminish, and as additional 'difficult students', and/or substitute teachers enter the school, the better students and their parents and the better teachers turn elsewhere. The contemporary problem school district presents similar dynamics to the failing family, in that each partner blames the other for failures which have been created by all of the participants. The solution lies not so much in failure analysis, but in resocialisation of and reimposition of responsibility on parents, children, teachers, and staff. The educational situation provided by the suburban neighbourhood and local school ensures interactive cooperation between parents and teachers, with responsibility, taxing authority, and community accountability resting in local hands. This kind of neighbourhood regulation and structure is sadly anathema to the highly centralised, regulation-ridden bureaucratic welfare state formula for social order.

EDUCATIONAL FAILURE IN SWEDEN

In Sweden the schools have also been affected by welfare-state activity. Because of the high tax rate occasioned by welfare-state services and benefits, both parents are employed in most Swedish families. Thus, Swedish children have less attention from their

parents, and school progress has been affected. Reports by Rydenfelt (1981, pp. 41–4) indicate that because of welfare-state legislation, which now restricts the freedom of teachers to control student behaviour, 11 per cent of the teachers in the system left it in 1980, and an additional 22 per cent took early retirement. Twenty per cent of the current teachers are really substitutes, primarily college students. Every tenth teacher in Stockholm was reported to have been beaten, attacked or threatened.

Rydenfelt's report of Swedish schools parallels the frequent reports of violence and vandalism in American schools, where a major part of the cost of the educational system is tied to policing and control procedures unrelated to teaching goals. The ineffectiveness of Swedish schooling is now reflected in increased youth unemployment and unemployability, and a growing population of sex-offenders, alcoholics, drug addicts, and other social outcasts isolated from the mainstream labour market.

ELSEWHERE IN EUROPE

In Holland, the schools have long been 'pillarised', that is, taken over by voluntary or religious sponsorship, but subsidised by government funds. At first, the subsidies were limited to 20 per cent, but by the 1980s these had reached 100 per cent. With full federal payments, school operation has become a matter of negotiation between the centralised voluntary agencies and the government, with parents generally omitted from the equation. Thus, the education of children in the Netherlands Welfare State has become less, rather than more, democratic, and less related to preparation for competence in the market-place (Van Doorn, 1978).

In Denmark (Gress, 1982) the state pays up to 85 per cent of teachers' salaries in the private and independent schools (as compared to 100 per cent in the state schools). Although the schools function reasonably well, Gress notes that there is a loss of commitment and professionalism in the educational establishment, along with an increasing involvement of the schools with political campaigns and group rights. Gress describes the school ethos as one of 'amateurism', a refusal of teachers to teach with authority, an inculcation of anti-business values and a rejection of history. This ethos, Gress reports, has weakened all the public schools in the Scandinavian countries. Even the evening schools or 'second-chance' schools for workers

have been politicised to the point where many are now merely centres for the new 'peace movement', and are no longer offering serious substantive learning.

EDUCATIONAL COLLAPSE IN THE USA

A similar malaise has affected many of the public schools in the United States. The Berkeley, California, school system was formerly a bulwark of high educational standards. It coordinated the work of teachers with police and social agency efforts for maximised socialisation of children, even to the point of intervention, in order to improve parental performance and enforcement of community norms, yet, in recent years, it has become involved in an ethos of student freedom and pluralism to the point where truancy is no longer considered a problem by teachers, truant officers or others. Instead of punishment for unauthorised school absences, children are asked to 'rap' with school personnel. The police are no longer involved in the matter and social agencies are no longer associated with the problem of school truancy. An atmosphere of permissiveness and a 'do-your-own-thing' ethos prevails to the point where a serious drug culture pervades the schools (Zellman and Schlossman, 1986).

A similar drug scene is apparent in most American public high schools. Part of the control problem in American schools is the stringent efforts of civil rights advocates (tied to the welfare state) who seek to protect the rights of children for privacy. These rights, however, run counter to the need to search children for drugs and weapons, which is essential if drug and violence problems are to be kept out of the public schools. Until these problems are controlled, little education and child socialisation will be achieved.

4 Health in the Welfare State

In the United States, the Federal government has so far limited itself to Medicare and Medicaid in terms of health service provision. Before the establishment of Medicare in the mid-1960s, medical delivery in the United States still retained a considerable degree of charity work by most physicians, with a heavy involvement of voluntary and philanthropic agencies in the operation of clinics and hospitals. With the introduction of Medicare, which supported a large proportion of medical and hospital costs for the elderly, and which was based on a fee-for-service system to doctors, medical purveyors and hospitals, there was a rapid rise in medical expenditures and medical delivery. Seemingly overnight, with rises in costs and volume, there was a diminution of charity and voluntary medical services.

This increase in prices affected not only Medicare fees (which were social insurance benefits offset by a payroll and member contribution), but also affected the prices of other third-payment services, such as Blue Cross, Blue Shield, and commercial medical insurances. To meet these medical costs, labour unions negotiated for increased medical employee coverage, and this was encouraged by the exemption of such employee benefits from income tax – better to accept a raise in tax-exempt medical care benefits than a wage increase, which would be less than 55c in the dollar after taxes.

On Medicare, there was a partially deductible, limits of service co-payment partially to constrain overutilization, but, on Medicaid, the new programme for welfare beneficiaries and other needy, there was no deductible or limits of service co-payment at all. Under Medicaid, the states would contract to provide payment to physicians, hospitals and other medical purveyors for all services rendered to persons certified as poor or on welfare, and the federal government undertook to underwrite a major portion of these costs. States made individual contracts with the federal government with various service provisions and services based on state programme plans.

CONTROLLING COSTS

The addition of Medicaid spurred an increased impetus to the medical

cost inflation rate, which far outran the general inflation rate. The introduction of new technologies and federal funding of additional hospital beds in areas believed to be already amply supplied led to even further medical cost inflation. Finally, medical and hospital costs grew to the point that the federal government began to design methods to restrain costs.

Programmes, such as the establishment of Professional Service Review Organisations, to restrict excessive services, and the Regional Health Service Agencies, to limit authority for unnecessary expansion of health service facilities, were not effective. Nevertheless, they continue to operate and in the process, by their own procedural additions and administrative costs, add to the overhead.

Finally, the federal government established a Diagnostic Group Rate Plan, under which hospitals (and soon doctors) are paid a set amount for each diagnostic category, regardless of time involved in service to the patient. This, in turn, encourages hospitals to discharge patients as soon as possible, and there are complaints from patients who are sent home with no one to provide care for them. The Medicare DGR rates are now being applied to Medicaid rates as well, and other third-party payers (insurance companies, etc.) are adopting the plan in many areas of the United States. With increased limits on amounts and types of care, along with the DGR, welfare clients, who were once overserved in some locations, are now receiving reduced medical services, and what is delivered is unrelated to their specific needs.

There are other mechanisms which are offered to restrain medical inflation without neglect of patients. Health maintenance organisations, such as Kaiser Permanente, have apparently operated effectively in this regard. The HMO provides full care for each patient enrolled, regardless of his condition or medical needs.

HEALTH CARE FOR WELFARE DEPENDENTS

The welfare-dependent, because of his lifestyle, often finds himself lost in the complex of HMO medical services, and has difficulty in following the instructions of medical personnel in the treatment of his problems, in the prevention of medical difficulties and in the building of a healthful lifestyle for himself and his children. The middle class and the working poor, however, usually find themselves well served in HMOs.

Another mechanism to control medical inflation has been encouraged by the Blue Cross and Blue Shield organisations. These are Preferred Provider Organisations, made up of individual general practitioners, specialists and hospitals which agree to provide full medical care for each patient enrolled in the organisation for a set fee. It is too early to determine how effectively these programmes provide high-quality medical care at restricted costs.

In the United States, more than 80 per cent of the population are covered by medical and hospital insurance. It is not too clear how many of those who are not covered are really unemployed and unemployable, and how many are employed in the underground economy (small marginal shops, cocktail waitresses, black-market untaxed services, and illegal enterprises), whose attitude regarding medical and hospital insurance is that they can always be certified for Medicaid if they need it.

It should be noted that the provision of medical care at no cost under Medicaid prevents the development of medical self-sufficiency behaviour among a substantial portion of the American population. Similarly, it is difficult to know how many people during their employable years are impelled to accept employment for fear that they will not be covered by Medicare in their old age. After all, if they haven't worked enough for coverage, they can always be provided with Medicaid as well as Supplementary Security Assistance for the Aged.

THE DRUG PROBLEM

In the United States, yet another problem has occurred in the realm of drug addiction control. A major unit of the Federal government has taken it upon itself to make a study of drug addiction. It undertakes door-to-door sampling, questioning householders on whether or not they use drugs regularly. With increased governmental undercover arrests of drug users, it might seem doubtful that a drug user would admit to the use of drugs. It is not surprising, then, that this federal study reached the conclusion that the drug addiction problem is declining and under control!

Many state and local agencies laugh at the federal study, which is obviously planned to be used as a proof of the administration's effectiveness before the next national election, and a few have likened the study's conclusions to the 'Emperor's Clothes'. Should national

policy on something as important as drug addiction be based on an invalid study? Yet none of the local and state authorities and their research, clinical or police personnel are ready to make their questions public for fear that they may make enemies at the central government level and thus miss out on the renewal of their federal grants or their applications for new federal grants. In this way, centralised federal government radically weakens the rational planning and control of health policy and resource distribution.

PROBLEMS WITH THE NHS

In Britain the national health service is almost 40 years old. Health care, at great expense to the economy, is available to all residents without cost, except for minimal fees for particular items. Despite this, observers indicate that there is no evidence that the gap in health standards between socio-economic groups has been narrowing.

One example is that the daughters of blue-collar workers are four times more likely to die before the age of one year than the daughters of managerial and professional classes. For sons, the ratio is five to one. The reason for this disparity is that the deciding factor on mortality rates in industrialised nations (Wilensky, 1975, pp. 95–6) is *not* the availability and quality of health care, but, rather, the cultural life patterns and the health behaviour activity of the affected population. Thus, the manifest function of the welfare-state health service, which is purportedly provided in order to equalise the life chances of all people in the population, is, in reality, not directly related to health care delivery for all.

Just as a 'good' education as an egalitarian goal is not achievable through an intensively funded school system, and education can be improved only by motivation and involvement of the parents, so the most modern and complete health system cannot achieve the egalitarian goal of good health for all without motivation and involvement of the patients.

According to Daniels (1986), nearly ten per cent of the British population is privately insured, and half of these pay for their insurance out of their disposable income. The health care delivery system is ridden with ill-maintained, dirty facilities, with long waits for service, delayed service, inefficient and uncoordinated pro-grammes, low morale among professional and staff workers, and

all this despite increasing budgets taking increasing portions from the gross national product.

By and large, there is in Britain a virtual monopoly in the health care system. For those who cannot afford to pay for their own health care, there is only one source – the National Health Service. If its quality is low, there is nowhere else to go for this population. If one has to wait, what alternative is there? Either the patient waits or, worse yet, delays or omits the care, even when it may be vital. In this sense the National Health Service actually prevents people from obtaining the best care available.

NHS AS A MONOPOLISTIC MONSTER

Public criticism from welfare state supporters complains that the very existence of private care (a growing element) draws valuable resources from the public programme. Yet careful analysis of the problems of the public programme forces one to conclude that more money will not solve the problems of the system.

Daniels, in fact, fears that the NHS will become an 'insatiable monster, capable without difficulty of devouring the entire national product', without, of course, delivering good-quality services to all. Daniels is concerned about the attitude of 'democratic masochism', a public attitude towards the health service which requires the patient to *accept* the indignities, delays, impersonality, inefficiency, dilapidation, employee dissatisfaction and staff malaise – a condition similar to the loss of commitment and professionalism identified by Gress in Scandinavian health and school services.

Waugh's (1985) application of the 'Gammon Law of Bureaucratic Displacement' to the National Health Service is appropriate in that increase of expenditures in a bureaucracy will be matched by a fall in production. It is quite possible that with a 24 per cent annual increase of expenditure, the system may fall further in quality and effectiveness, will increasingly be challenged by private medical systems and, finally, will lose the support of the middle and upper income levels of population and become a poor people's health service, but without a means test.

Thus, the charity health programmes for the poor, which were probably quite good in comparison with the current system, and which were eliminated by the National Health Service, will again be available to the poor under the NHS, but without the individualised

compassion and professionalism of the earlier time (Green, 1986).

SCANDINAVIAN HEALTH CARE

Health Service in Sweden is also in difficulty. In 1978 the universal health service used 12 per cent of the GNP, and the system is experiencing recurrent emergencies deriving from low productivity, long waiting lists, impersonal treatment of patients, low staff morale, and staff malaise (Rydenfeldt, 1981).

Similar problems have been experienced in other European countries, and, generally, these derive from a basic structural incentive defect, namely, a low level of efficiency and staff interest which extends from the balance sheets to the bed sheets. Having a governmental intermediary somehow removes the invisible controls without which the programme meets no one's standards.

5 Housing in the Welfare State

One of the myths of social work which has been widely adopted by proponents of the welfare state is that the provision of attractive and safe housing will positively affect the behaviour of the poor, and encourage them to adopt a productive, clean, healthful lifestyle, bringing peace and good citizenship to the community.

It was assumed in terms of this myth that residents of subsidised housing would respect such a housing environment, maintain it in pristine condition, and defend it against vandals. For a time, this assumption proved valid, as long as care was taken, in publicly supported housing programmes, to select the tenants from among the working poor, including only families without a record of crime, delinquency, prostitution, unmarried motherhood, child abuse and neglect and drug addiction. This policy of selectivity was installed in housing projects in the early years of their establishment, when philanthropy led the American nation in such enterprises. Planning and managerial staffs were primarily drawn from the private housing field, where tenant selectivity was critical in preventing the bankruptcy of the projects.

The idea of these programmes was to make livable housing possible for limited-income families, who were struggling to improve their lives, exhibiting hard work on the part of the parents, consistent educational effort by the children, and careful housekeeping, home management and budgeting by the mother. Such families were often imbued with the dream of some day owning their own home or, at least, being able to afford rental housing in the private sector. Many of these families did succeed in achieving these goals and were able to improve their economic status as their grown children moved into the society as professional people, educators, civil servants or in other upwardly mobile employment.

CENTRAL STATE INTERVENTION

In the United States, with the onset of the economic depression in the early 1930s, the federal government entered the housing field for the first time, primarily for the purpose – unconnected with housing –

26

of providing jobs and revitalising the economy. It sought to do this in a number of ways. The first method, which can be considered similar to the social insurance approach, consisted of a special mortgage arrangement to make it possible for the working poor and middle-class workers with limited assets, but a regular income from earnings, to buy a house of their own with a small downpayment, an extended mortgage period, and a limited rate of interest.

The mechanism for this was the reinsurance of loans made by banks to approved applicants, so that the banks could offer such loans on more generous terms than if the bank were to be responsible for the risk. The applicant was required to pay a $\frac{1}{2}$ per cent mortgage insurance fee in addition to the interest. This mortgage insurance fee went into a fund which reimbursed banks for any losses they might experience with FHA loans. This system worked effectively for over fifty years, and the mortgage insurance programme actually made a profit.

In addition to this system, parallel loans were set up through the Farm & Home Administration of the Department of Agriculture, the Veteran's Bureau, and special loan programmes were established for home repairs, remodelling and improvements, and for purchase of cooperative apartments and multiple resident ownership of cooperative homes, and so on.

The reasons the home loan system worked so well were twofold: (1) There was a system for discretionary selection of borrowers; and (2) each of the applicants was required to make a downpayment on his loan, which may have been limited in the eyes of the bankers, but was sizable from the point of view of a family with a limited income. This downpayment represented the family's stake in their home, and that, plus the monthly payments they made, which represented, at least in part, their own payment on principal, encouraged the family to care for their property. Over the years, observations of home owners and tenant use of property, when controlled for comparable income, indicate that the home owners not only maintained their property, but saw to it that their children did not vandalise their own or neighbour's homes. Tenants by comparison did far less for their homes. Similarly, home owners were shown to be more concerned about protection of the neighbourhood and were generally more responsible citizens.

A MORE DIRECT METHOD OF INTERVENTION

The second method of providing housing for families with limited income was the mechanism of the federal housing project. In each community, the local authorities passed legislation or ordinances creating a local housing programme board and providing for its election or appointment. This housing board planned a low-cost housing project or a collection of such projects in order to provide housing for families unable to afford to purchase their own homes or to rent adequate housing at commercial rates. The local community or city usually contributed land for the project and the board secured a loan at low interest for the purpose of building the project. These loans were provided by banks or from bonds subsidised and reinsured by the federal government. Because of exemption from city land taxes, because of the government's low interest rates, and because of the provision of only basic facilities within the housing structure (such as the omission of closet doors and so forth), lower rental rates were charged than would have been required in privately owned units.

The fundamental policy for this type of subsidised housing was based on the marginal income of families in most American cities, who were employed, highly employable for the jobs opening up after the depression, and who were rearing children who were attending school regularly – people, that is to say, who were securely on the path towards eventual self-sufficiency. During those years, there were few multi-problem, chronically dependent families. To be admitted into a low-rent housing project, most families had to have at least one employed wage earner and not have any member who had been involved in crime, drugs, alcoholism or other behaviour which might be a problem.

The rentals were set at approximately one-fourth of the family's monthly earnings, and thus the rentals differed for each family. Families were assigned to apartments on the basis of their size, with large families assigned to the larger apartments. Each family was given to understand that the low-rent apartment was theirs only temporarily, and, as soon as their economic situation improved, they would then be expected to move on to the purchase of their own home or to commercial rental housing. Each family was given to understand the rules by which the project would be operated, and families which broke the rules or whose children damaged project property or interfered with other families would be required to leave

the project. Management was usually held in the hands of salaried personnel with rental or other business experience.

During the 1930s and 1940s, most of these thousands of projects operated well and without difficulty. Some of the national policymakers and interested academics did object to the lack of tenant advisory councils in many projects, under the assumption that public housing should be operated more on a social relationship rather than a business basis. Where housing advisory councils did exist, some critics of the housing boards complained that the councils lacked leadership because the potential leaders were usually the tenants who had to move from the projects as their economic situations improved. In time, housing board policies permitted over-income families to remain, but at a somewhat increased rental.

TRANSFORMATION OF THE SYSTEM

The nature of the public housing programmes, which provided a needed temporary shelter for the working poor as they moved upwards on the socioeconomic ladder, changed radically with the entry of a number of external forces. The first of these invasions of community autonomy on the housing front was drastically felt in the 1960s and 1970s. The growth of AFDC welfare programmes for millions of children without stable fathers or father surrogates in families led to many families being without suitable housing. These welfare families were homeless not only because of limited income but also because of past damage to rental housing, rental non-payment, and other problems which made them less than attractive to commercial landlords.

Many of these families were being housed in expensive hotel rooms by the local welfare departments. Pressure from the legislators at state and local levels resulted in revision of the public housing selection guidelines which previously limited the percentage of welfare-dependent tenants in the projects. Concurrently, under instigation by neighbourhood legal programmes (funded by the War on Poverty), a number of class action court cases were pressed to ensure the right of prostitutes, ex-criminal offenders, drug addicts, couples without marriage, and unemployables to be granted housing facilities in the project. As the less-desirable and welfare-dependent families moved into the projects, a tipping point was reached, and the upwardly-mobile working-poor families left the projects.

In time, these housing projects became dilapidated and physically dangerous to live in, especially in the high-rise projects, where elevators, doors and stairways were vandalised. Some projects, such as Pruitt-Igoe houses in St Louis, were deserted even by the residual welfare tenants because the project hallways were infested by rats and insects and terrorised by dangerous gangs of children and youth from the families. In time, all tenants moved out, the fixtures were stolen by the gangs, and, eventually, the buildings were demolished and the federal losses were written off.

In other projects, the Pruitt-Igoe fate was averted by training and employing special housing project police forces in large numbers, at great expense. Despite this, most American public housing projects have not been safe places in which to live. In a South Los Angeles project, for example, there is a murderous gang made up of youth and adults who were reared in the project who terrorise the families who live there. It is almost as if the women who entered into a life of welfare dependency and housing project residence have, by their own acts, created their own rapists and muggers. No apartheid area in South Africa can be considered more separate from the normative mainstream population than such a project.

The only successful public housing projects are those in the few cities where federal funds were not accepted and where tenant selection and housing management remained entirely as a prerogative of the local community. In these instances, the projects continued to be a method of serving the transitory poor. Another sector of public housing has succeeded in the specialised programmes serving selected aged and handicapped adults, especially where these were managed by local civic and church groups and provided with federal loan guarantees.

DESTRUCTIVE RENT CONTROL

Still another area of government involvement in housing has had disastrous results. This is particularly evident in New York City, where the colossal megapolis operates a welfare state which is even larger than many nations. Under a 'temporary' measure originally imposed by the federal government in the 1940s, during the Second World War, and extended ever since then by the City of New York, residential housing operates under rent control.

Rents in New York are regulated in two ways. In buildings built

before 1947 no increases were allowed until 1969, and many tenants are still paying 1940s prices. In 1969 'rent stabilisation' was applied to all buildings, both those built before 1969, as well as those built later. Only limited increases were permitted for pre-1969 buildings, based on increased operational costs proven by the landlords. Those built after 1969 had rents based on proven landlord costs at the time of opening. Thus, most rents reflect early 1970s costs, despite the multiple inflations which have occurred since then. When a tenant of a rent-controlled apartment moves or dies, the family is often successful in moving in a relative or friend, often collecting a generous amount of 'key money' under the table. If this transfer does not succeed, then the apartment falls out of rent control (1940s prices) and into 'rent stabilisation' (1970s prices). There are also 'vacancy allowances', and other complex regulations which protect sitting tenants and push up rent for newcomers.

Tucker (1986), after careful study, concludes that people who move to New York now pay higher prices than they would have to pay without rent regulations. He reveals that rent control and rent stabilisation primarily protect upper-middle-class people who 'know the ropes' about rental housing and who could easily pay commercial rentals or purchase their own homes or condominiums if rent controls were not in operation. A large proportion of these tenants are participants in the underground economy (artisans who work overtime for cash, couples who are in retail businesses which report only marginal taxes, and so on), and who are reluctant to undergo the credit or tax analysis involved in a housing purchase.

Another factor which perpetuates unnecessary housing bureaucracy is the size of the force of employees of the Department of Housing Preservation and Development, originally established as an enforcement agency, but now operating primarily as tenant advocates before the New York City Housing Courts. Tucker found instances of housing judges and city officials and HPD civil servants (city and state) who also live in bargain rent-controlled apartments and who have a vested interest in perpetuating the system, both in order to preserve their cheap housing deal and to perpetuate their status as high-level civil servants.

The rent-control system in New York has effectively achieved the following conditions:

(1) it has made the building of new housing for the middle class and the working poor so unprofitable that new residential housing has become a rarity;

(2) it has economically discouraged and prevented the maintenance of good housing so that much of it has fallen into an unsafe condition;

(3) it has caused many responsible landlords to sell out to less responsible, 'fly-by-night', 'corporate-ghost-entrepreneurs', who collect all the rent they can and then abandon the properties. These houses then become unsafe and unlivable and are soon abandoned by the tenants and become victim to squatters, vandals and gangs.

(4) it has prevented new capital from entering the housing rehabilitation field because of the concern that such investments will be lost by present and future housing regulations of the city. As a result, New York City has been exempt from the wave of 'gentrification' of inner city housing which has occurred in other cities. As a result, vast areas of the city remain devastated for decades, resembling bombed-out sectors after a major war. These areas become an expense to the city, provide no taxes, and cost large sums in terms of crime control, public health danger and potential for fire hazards;

(5) it has effectively prevented the availability of housing for the poor and near-poor, causing overcrowding and extremely hazardous conditions.

Wherever, throughout Europe, welfare-oriented rent control has been imposed, the same destructive effects have been observed.

6 Employment in the Welfare State

Just as important as family, schooling, and housing in social control is employment. To the extent that welfare, charity, wealth or social insurance make employment unnecessary to the individual in the long or short run, these grants or benefits are desocialising in their effect on individual behaviour.

The achievement of completed training for a job, and the continued acceptance of a person in his job provide a sense of self-worth which equips people for other life endeavours and for retaining a sense of pride in self-sufficiency and in the maintenance of his dependents. The sense of being a productive participant in society promotes the individual's investment in community life, promotion of social order and fulfillment of the norm of reciprocity. It keeps the person in touch with both material and social reality.

Levenstein (1964), in his explanation of *Why People Work*, maintains that 'individuality simply cannot exist without a structured community' in which work and jobs have an important role. Without work, one has no tie to the community except perhaps as a low-valued dependent. Our freedom to be ourselves depends on our work. Work is the process by which one refuses to allow one's life to become a mere vanity.

Pavalko (1971) argues that through work a person gains standing and a place for himself in society. In the modern world, occupational roles are achieved through one's own efforts, rather than inherited, and having an occupational role is proof of one's having made something of oneself. Work thus provides the person with an identity, a set of expectations of how people will interact with him, and with a validated approach to others in society. Without employment, the person is a 'nobody'.

Social indicators reveal that the recently and involuntarily retired have a high mortality rate; the unemployed and the under-employed have a high incidence of mental illness and emotional distress; and the unemployed have a high rate of suicide, divorce, desertion, and separation from mates. Among unemployed and unemployable youth, we find a high incidence of anomy, delinquency, violence, drug addiction, vandalism, and general anti-social behaviour.

UNEMPLOYMENT MEANS LACK OF WORK

In every developed nation except one (Switzerland), there has been chronic unemployment, under-employment, inadequate occupational youth training and high unemployment compensation and related costs.

In the United States, an average of 8 per cent unemployment of the labour force has been consistently reported, without taking into account the millions of discouraged workers and unregistered, outdated workers. Some minorities are reported to have an estimated 16 per cent unemployed, and minority youth have been reported to have a rate which doubles even that.

Those who are employed are themselves in a less than enviable situation, in that in American manufacturing industries, the American family real income has increased only 1 per cent per year over the last 18 years. Conditions in West European nations, Canada, Australia, New Zealand and other developed nations have not been much better. In many of these countries, the minimum wage and restrictive constraints on employers have been maintained and even strengthened, despite studies (such as those reported by Segalman and Basu, pp. 335–42) which indicate that these depress employment, raise production costs, and prevent the availability of employment entry for many young people who end up permanently unemployed, dependent, and frequently part of counter-productive, anti-social activity.

In West Germany, Strang (1970) reports that the productivity problem is tied to the phenomenon of having so many unemployed protected from having to accept a lower status position, if it is offered, that the unemployed remain on unemployment compensation or on the dole longer than is economically appropriate. According to Ferdinand Mount (1986) and others, 'trade union monopoly power' operates to damage employment and economic performance. As a result of these developments, despite the productivity gains of the economy by rationalisation and mechanisation of industry, there has been a great slump in 'smokestack industries' in the older developed countries and a mass exodus of manufacturing to the newer 'miracle-developed' countries where labour is cheap and unregulated and government restraints are generally absent.

DESTROYING EMPLOYMENT

An example of how industry has been beleaguered by government

constraint in the developed countries is offered by Roger Starr's *The Rise and Fall of New York City* (1986). In 1946 New York was without doubt the most favoured city in the world. It had profited from the Second World War and was unscarred by it. The city was rich in assets. Its geography served it well. Its harbour was among the best and busiest. It had the finest transportation of any large city. It concentrated millions of workers in the central business district and got them home at night. The city had a high quality of population with almost every talent or skill and a state school system rated among the best. There was a large housing supply and a generally lawful and voluntarily compliant population. The city had a health system foremost in the world, built of public hospitals and clinics buttressed by a network of voluntary and proprietary hospitals and clinics. And best of all, the city had great manufacturing importance, ranking alongside Chicago and Detroit, insuring the city against the risk of depending on a service economy.

What happened to New York? First of all, the manufacturing rampart began to crumble almost immediately, losing 600 000 jobs in ten years. Neighbourhood associations, environmental groups, lawyers, ambitious politicians, and many others joined in the work of moving industry out of their neighbourhoods or the neighbourhoods of their constituents. With the loss of jobs came a loss of work-related transportation. Efforts to economise and rationalise the subways and suburban trains meant cutting out stations and trains, and this was fought against in the name of minority rights. Smaller ridership meant more opportunity for crime, especially violent crime. With this came greater fear among the public and further decreased ridership. Less availability of safe, usable transportation and increased transportation rates have caused factories to move to other locations. Ridership shrank further.

Manufacturing was also affected by housing shortages for employees who could not find or retain housing in a city with Byzantine rent-control regulations. The very rich were not affected – they could pay the price. The very poor were also provided for in public housing. But the middle class, the historic foundation of social order, responsible citizenship and productivity, was so beleagured as to leave the city in droves. This exodus of the middle class was speeded by the desegregation of schools and by enforced bussing, which lowered the educational standards of schools used by the middle class.

AN INFLUX OF WELFARE DEPENDENTS

The subsidy of the welfare-dependent population encouraged an influx of dependent minority families. This, in time, increased the numbers of unemployed and unemployable youth on the streets, and the violent crime and drug addiction rates rose to a point where whole neighbourhoods and public transportation became deserted by the very population elements which ensured social order.

Robert Nisbet (1986) indicates that 'there are no real villains' in this scenario. 'None are needed. The harm that good men do has been ample . . . the eager, pious, nobly-intentioned politicians, administrators, foundation executives and all-purpose intellectuals ready on a moment's notice to spare no effort in coming up with solutions on the grand scale, underwritten by the taxpayers.'

This coalition of 'good men' is, of course, the same destructive element found everywhere in the welfare state acting as futile surrogates for the normative processes of community decision-making.

THE UNEMPLOYMENT BUREAUCRACY

In most of the developed nations, the employment market is serviced by both public and commercial employment placement agencies. Most of the public agencies are funded or subsidised by the central government and are operated by massive civil service rules and regulations, which have had the usual bureaucratising effects. Registration for employment placement or checking for new openings depends primarily on the applicants waiting on long lines, only to be served in a less than effective information exchange. There is no follow-up to check on whether the employment referral was successful, and, if not, on an analysis of why the placement had not occurred. Seldom is the system able to secure 'feedback' so that applicants can be more effectively prepared and referred to employment.

As in all mass programmes, considerable anomy exists, both in the placement bureaucracy and among the applicants. The least socially competent and the least oriented to the employment system and those whose skills are marginal and not in great demand soon fall in to the category of 'discouraged workers'. They who drop out of the labour market and are then subsidised indefinitely by unemployment compensation, disability manipulation (as in Holland), and public

welfare. In time, these people and their families become a continuing financial and social cost to the society, often on an intergenerational basis.

The existence of numbers of private commercial employment agencies and their expansive growth in most developed nations is, we believe, an indication of the failure of the welfare state's employment placement system. The success of the commercial agencies can be credited to their greater structural and functional elasticity, the built-in motivation of their staffs to perform competitively, and the necessity to operate productively, without which the agency would die.

YOUTH UNEMPLOYMENT WORSE

The scene among unemployed and unemployable youth is even more serious than among the adult unemployed because it is damaging to society, not only in the here and now, but in the future. Male and female youth unemployment and unemployability has been linked with the growing problem of unmarried motherhood in the United States and Britain. Unemployment and unemployability among youth in all of the developed nations has been tied to growing problems of drug addiction, alcoholism and crime. The growth of female-headed dependent families with children has been tied to problems of non-formation of legitimated families among young people who are unable to support themselves and, nevertheless, produce children whom they cannot adequately socialise. Many of them have been described as a 'no-hope' generation, who, according to Van der Vat (1980), 'lack the incentive to seek work because they came from families' which have accustomed them to the acceptability of unemployment. They leave school too soon, unprepared for the disciplines of work, 'depriving the society of their talents and unwittingly helping to create and enlarge a "bottom of the heap" element.'

Waugh (1985) has concluded that Beveridge was wrong in offering people the welfare option. It may have temporarily arrested the momentary hunger and physical deterioration caused by disease, but it has, by its removal of motivational dynamics, given rise to idleness, ignorance and squalor, the three other giants which Beveridge sought to remove and prevent. Waugh believes that the welfare state has brought about an entirely new dimension of moral deterioration which may make the nation inoperable and indefensible.

7　The Welfare State and the Family

Almost everywhere in the developed nations (again with the possible exception of Switzerland), final eulogies are being written on the passing of the family as an institution. If this were true, it would be a serious matter in the light of the civilising effects of the family in the history of mankind.

What are these civilising effects? There are a number of basic values which are ingrained, both by role example and by didactic indication, in the children of effective families. These include the following.

PLANNING AND WORKING FOR THE FUTURE, RATHER THAN SEEKING IMMEDIATE GRATIFICATION

This includes going to school regularly, doing one's homework, cooperating with the teacher, and using school learning for the purpose of building one's later career. It also includes carefully considering occupational and career choices realistically, undertaking an appropriate training programme at the appropriate time, and completing it; careful examination of employment prospects, and choosing some job, no matter how menial, as long as it offers a beginning step on the employment ladder; and establishing oneself as an honest and sincere employee so that an employer will be ready to provide recommendations for more advanced and remunerative employment.

This may sound like the 'Horatio Alger' legend or a sermon from Samuel Smiles, but it must be noted that those who operate as if the legend were true seem to make more progress than cynical entries in the labour market. This kind of behaviour facilitates the building up on one's personal human capital, even at the expense of immediate comforts and pleasures.

DEVELOPMENT OF A MORAL, SOCIALLY RESPONSIBLE SET OF PERSONAL RULES OF BEHAVIOUR

This means behaving in ways that make trust possible when trust is

defined as the reciprocal ability to predict the behaviour of others and oneself and to make choices accordingly. It also involves constantly taking into consideration the perceived wishes and concerns of others, even at some expense to one's own energies and gratifications. This kind of behaviour includes familial and community cooperation and a rejection of attitudes of dependency on others as long as one can care for oneself.

Because trust is a two-way process, this relationship taught to the child by its parents involves expectation of specific behaviours of his parents by the child, as well as expectation of increasingly mature behaviours of the child by his parents. As the circle of the child's world grows, his trust of others and their trust of him grow in parallel. This process defines the child's loyalty and membership in a family, an extended circle of friends and relatives, a neighbourhood, a community, a region, a nation and, ultimately in the human race.

Just as the tie of trusting others and being trusted by others is in a continually dynamic balance, so are the forces of loyalty to and membership in circles of human relationship. Without this reciprocal tie to others and dependence by others on oneself, the consequence is anomie. It is not enough for the person to claim loyalty and love for an undefined and amorphous humanity, as is the case with many disturbed revolutionary or anarchic individuals. The truly civilised person must necessarily retain two-way ties with humanity through direct interaction with others, beginning with a concern for those about him and reaching to all others who are tied to him or her by the human condition.

THE DEVELOPMENT OF BEHAVIOUR WHICH EMPHASISES THINKING OUT THE SOLUTION OF ONE'S PROBLEMS

Rather than resolving problems by evading them or by aggressive confrontation – the primitive 'fight or flight' behaviour exhibited in less civilised populations – civilised behaviour involves self-constraint, rather than self-indulgence, saving more than spending, productivity rather than maximisation of one's pleasures.

It was this complex of behaviour which made the family and the community possible as enduring institutions, and it was these institutions which reinforced appropriate behaviours and thus made

the democratic-capitalist market-place and society possible. It is this kind of behaviour which kept masses of the temporary poor during the American depression from becoming permanently dependent, and it is the attenuation of this kind of behaviour which perpetuates welfare dependency which threatens the social order.

THE FAMILY'S INCULCATION OF VALUES

How does a family instil such autonomous, socially-responsible values in a child? It does this by providing the child with two distinct and countervailing dynamic nuclei for his developmental life.

Each of them is equipped by biological, psychological, anatomical and hormonal qualities to perform the necessary services for the child.

The first is a parent whose primary mode of relationship with the child is an ever-ready acceptance of the child and an overriding concern for his or her welfare. This may even reach the point (the child may well believe this) of rejecting all others in her attention to the child. Upon her, at least in the early months, the child can completely depend, and she will support, comfort, provide for, and defend the child with all her energy.

The other countervailing dynamic nucleus of the child's life space is a very different type of parent. This parent's primary mode of relationship with the child is not an ever-ready acceptance of all behaviour. On the contrary this parent seems constantly to test the child. 'What have you learned? 'What have you accomplished?' 'Might you have had better results if you had done thus and so?'

As the child matures, he or she raises the expected level of acceptable behaviour and achievement. In a sense, the first parental model is one upon whom the child depends for protection, nurturing and comfort, and the second parent is one upon whom the child depends for the coaching he requires to enter into autonomy and social responsibility. It is the second parental model who is constantly testing the child and being tested by him who aids the child in learning how he is expected to behave in the world of social reality.

These two models are not always found separately in one or another parent, but, in an effective parenting situation, enough of the qualities of each model exist in a balanced relationship of stability to provide the kind of support and guidance required by the child.

NECESSARY FAMILY RELATIONSHIPS

It should be noted that the child must perceive that despite the differences between the parental models in his life, the path before him is clearly defined by agreement between the two foci of his governance and direction. Here, we need to make a distinction between having a set of interacting and purposive adults in his life versus a collection of non-interacting, unrelated adults. There are many two-parent families where the requisite harmony is missing.

The adults in a child's life must also be perceived as being in firm control of the major parameters of his or her life. If not, the child may see the adult as an 'other' in his life, but not as a *significant* other. Similarly, the parents must be perceived as 'competent' by the child, based on the child's observations of the adult as he or she performs in and out of family, peer and societal situations. If not, the child may 'feel sorry' for the parent, but view him or her as weak and unreliable. The child must also perceive the parent as consistent in his or her demands in terms of constraints, supports and rewards. If this is not the case, the parent is likely to be viewed by the child as manipulable, and therefore of lesser importance in his life space.

Parents of this sort have been described as 'doormats', who can be programmed to provide gratifications on demand, and such adults can hardly be considered 'significant'. The parent, if he/she is to be of significance to the child, must be perceived as primarily rational, a good planner and goal-oriented, especially in his or her concerns for the child. A disorganised parent, unable to control his or her own life space, or unable to postpone his or her own gratifications, will be perceived by the child as less than significant in his life, and an alternative role model will be sought.

The parent must also be perceived by the child as seeking 'success' for the child in the pro-social mainstream. To accomplish this, the parent must be knowledgeable about, familiar with and involved with the societal mainstream, and particularly with the employment and civic market-place. Without this, the child will probably have no avenue of entry into self-sufficient, autonomous, social responsibility.

Again, the parent must be perceived by the child as sufficiently active in and concerned with the child's life and activities. If the greater portion of the child's life and time is spent with servants who have little stake in the child's long-range development, or in day-care, boarding facilities or public institutions, or frequently changed foster homes in which the child has no discernible, consistent and

continuing adult figures, then to that extent the parents or surrogate parents become mere portions of an untouchable and unreachable firmament. One cannot shape one's personality around the model of a distant star, or a shifting star, or an intermittent star.

THE NECESSITY FOR TWO PARENTS

Now obviously, no one person can demonstrate all of these qualities full-time. Even if all of these roles could be played by one person, there is neither time nor energy for one person to provide effectively all the necessary models for his or her child. Just as it requires two different humans in collaboration to conceive the child, so it requires at least two different humans to collaborate in shaping him for effective performance in society.

An absent father who is the host on the intermittent excursions permitted under many divorce custody arrangements is insufficient. A stepfather is equally fallible as a parent if his authority is circumscribed and his responsibility is limited. Least of all is the 'mama's boyfriend' of the moment likely to be an effective father. If mama and her 'boyfriend', sharing a household and children, have so little commitment to each other as to avoid marriage, how can the child depend on their even more tenuous commitment to him?

PARENTS COMMITTED TO SOCIETY

Still other requirements have been specified for parents in research reported by Hirschi (1983). He shows that

> if a child is to be reared in a manner which will deter him from force or fraud, the parents must themselves be allied to the values of the social mainstream and of the established marketplace of employment and citizenship. In addition to this, the parents must be in a position to continuously (1) monitor the child's behavior in his interactions with others, (2) recognize deviant behavior when it occurs, and (3) punish such behavior.

The competent parent 'who cares for his child will watch his behaviour, see him doing things he should not do, and correct him'. But, if the parents do not care for the child or do not have the time or energy to monitor the child's behaviour, or if they do not see

anything wrong with the child's behaviour, or if they do not have the inclination or means to punish the child, the child is then given the wrong signals and concludes that wrong acts, or unnecessarily dependent acts, or anti-social acts are acts which are either approved of by parents and other social authorities or are at least condoned by society.

According to Hirschi, 'parents of stealers [and other deviant behaviour children] do not track [their children's behaviour], [they] do not interpret stealing [and other anti-social behaviour] as deviant, they do not punish and they do not care'. The surprising finding of these researchers is that child delinquency and crime are caused by both affluence and poverty, in that these two conditions weaken the family's hold on and attention to the child's behaviour, particularly during adolescence.

In a sense, affluence and poverty provide a family with conditions for inadequate, lax or poor child supervision. Among the poor, punishment tends to be 'cheap' on the part of the parent, yelling, screaming, slapping, and hitting, with little or no follow-up, rather than invested with extended parent energy, time, and concern.

CRIME AND THE FAMILY

The single-parent family, these researchers found, is among the most powerful predictors of crime rates. Also children of reconstituted families with step-parents had more crime than children from biological, unbroken families. Involuntarily broken homes, such as by death of a parent had consistently less delinquency than where the home is broken by a parental decision to divorce or separate. The school was also found to be less a factor in delinquency because 'the school can punish only those students who see education as important to them, and many of the delinquent children have never embraced education as a goal, or have given up on it'.

Somewhere, somehow, effective parenting requires not only the ability to teach the child the differences between right and wrong, but also to perceive the multitudinous instances in life where choices must be made. Without these perceptions, the child cannot affect what occurs in his life. Without these, he is equipped with only a kind of learned helplessness by which he will blame everything that has happened to him on 'fate' or 'the system'. The 'poor little me' self-concept will then control his destinies the rest of his life. Only

the competent, alert and motivated parent can help him learn to sense the critical crossings in his life when he has to stop, analyse the alternatives, and use caution. This is how the child learns to control what happens to him, to his career, to his marriage, to his health, to his status as a person and citizen, and to his freedom to make decisions in the future. Without this skill in making choices, most children will not be able to enter the mainstream, nor will their children.

The importance of these findings is made clear when one considers that it is inadequately-socialised children – whether from affluent, middle-class, or impoverished families – who enter into delinquent and anti-social behaviour, eventually becoming part of the inner city jungle culture.

When the family as an institution is considered in relation to problems of welfare dependence and social disorganisation it is difficult to determine which comes first – the lack of effective socialisation of children within a complete family, or the prevalence of social pathologies which prevent the adequate formation of effective families.

THE DYNAMICS OF SOCIAL PATHOLOGY

The dynamics of social pathology are generally not well understood. What is clear, however, is that the child without active, effective parenting is more at risk. Unmarried motherhood, alcoholism and drug addiction have been posited, in many instances, as an attempt by a child to fill a void in his or her life. A missing father, a working or otherwise involved mother, may leave the child without the kind of supervised companionship he needs for emotional growth and learning, and thus a 'side track' is chosen by the child for the remainder of his life.

Similarly, the child who chooses gang membership instead of school and job training (or who is pressured into gang membership through the seeming partial or full abdication of his parents) ends up with a choice which may well represent a lasting life pattern. Parental non-involvement, inactivity and abdication is frequently found in families with absent or non-existent fathers, with working mothers, in reconstituted families, and in other units of weakened structure.

The argument that at the least a two-parent family is required for the adequate installation of a super-ego in the child is persuasively

made by the Bergers (1984, p. 162). Without it, the child has few behavioural controls, and without these it is impossible for a democracy to persist (p. 172). The Bergers indicate that it is only in the family and community that a competent, responsible personal identity is developed. Without such family socialisation, the product is more animal than human.

The findings of the Bergers on life without the father are supported by Mitscherlich (1970). Without the values provided for the child by the complete family, the very survival of society is threatened. As Durkheim has argued, society's continuance is dependent on a widely-shared moral consensus. Without such common values, the only way a society can be continued is by coercion at all levels.

CHILDREN OF THE WELFARE STATE

It is necessary, at this point, to shift our attention from what children need in the way of values to what the children of the contemporary welfare-state society are provided with. The first family model we need to examine is the welfare-dependent family.

The shattered, welfare-dependent family in the urban ghetto, which we have described in earlier pages, is unable to produce children adequately equipped to re-enter society and the labour market without considerable difficulty and social disturbance. This condition is further aggravated by cultural developments of the past three decades, in consequence of which sizable proportions of the population are likely to lose their capacity for self-sufficient, productive and socially responsible behaviour. This effect is at least in part caused by features of the welfare state.

For example, the availability of welfare has itself contributed to welfare dependency and ghetto social pathology. Either it eliminates the economic function of the father or it provides an economic substitute; with the substitution of the state for the father in the economic process, the father has also been eliminated as a functioning, responsible parent.

This has been reported in so many studies in the Western nations as to make their listing almost superfluous. The welfare state has also served in other ways to weaken the family as an institution. One of them relates to the explosion of civil rights and individual protections which has been promoted in recent years as a function of the welfare state.

THE DANGERS OF 'CIVIL RIGHTS'

The major obstructive effect on the family of the civil liberation movement derives from the relaxation of divorce laws. The 'no-fault' divorce laws are destructive because they provide a right for partners in a marriage to break up without provision for past or future responsibility for the children or for their best interests. This arrangement provides for automatic dissolution of the marriage without in any way ensuring the social and psychological care of the children. Neither does the procedure ensure that the participants in the divorce will learn why their marriage broke up, where the mistakes were made, and what part each partner played in the failure. As a result, neither partner learns from his or her mistakes. Neither do the children gain any lessons from the experiences of their parents, except perhaps how to avoid marriage or how to get out of a marriage so that you can be free to 'do your thing'.

Having made divorce easier by law, we have also made it more acceptable to individuals and the community by the removal of any associated guilt or shame. Couples now make less effort to make their marriages work than they would have otherwise done. After divorce they tend either to avoid marriage or to repeat the same mistakes.

'No-fault' divorce was supposedly enacted to eliminate the rancour of contested divorces, but this has proved false. Instead of contested divorces, we now have prolonged contested resolution of property settlements, child support payments and custody. This sometimes reaches the point where many children from divorces are not responsibly dealt with by their parents, instead becoming pawns or spoiled love objects in a seemingly permanent domestic war.

Some recent data suggest that more than one out of every three children has not seen his or her father in over three years, and the proportion of step-orphans is growing.

IRRESPONSIBLE SEX

The right to divorce at will has been matched by the right of an individual adult to have intercourse with another consenting adult without being answerable to anyone else including the grandparents of children from either the father's or mother's side. These liaisons often are limited to sexual exchanges without too much investigation

by either partner of the other's suitability as a potential marriage partner and potential step-parent for the children. Much of the epidemic of child abuse and child neglect stems from the limitations which the children are perceived as setting on the custodial parent's desire for social life.

The removal of legal, social and cultural restraints on sexual intercourse among consenting adults has also contributed to the spread of venereal diseases including the growing epidemic of AIDS. Along with these problems, there has been a growth of drug addiction and related abnormalities in babies caused by the addiction and inadequate self-care among pregnant women. In the past, this was also a concern of the husband, grandparents and other members of the extended family, who have been eliminated from the family by divorce or nonmarriage.

Meanwhile the divorced or absent father, having avoided child support by legal or other means, is free to become someone else's boyfriend, without responsibility, or new husband. Commonly he establishes a new family, which will also be left in time to live on the meagre earnings of a working mother or on public welfare subsistence.

SEXUAL MODELS

The loosening of constraints on sexual intercourse among adults has had further deleterious effects on children. If a child observes that behaviour of this sort is acceptable among divorced parents, it becomes difficult for the divorced parent to teach the children that it is not also acceptable among adolescents. Thus, the familial dissolution explosion has led to an epidemic of sexual intercourse among children. It should be noted that, although sexual intercourse among consenting adults is legally and to some extent, morally acceptable, sexual intercourse by adults with minors is legally described as 'statutory rape'. This is so because intercourse is legally possible only with informed consent, and minors are, by definition, not able to give informed consent. Thus, the legal expansion of sexual rights for adults has led to an explosion of serious criminal behaviour among children, who cannot give informed consent for intercourse and who are not controllable by their parents or society.

GILDER'S VIEWS

George Gilder (1986) has recently written influentially about 'The

Sexual Revolution at Home', in which he describes the effect of the beliefs of Marx, Engels, Women's Liberation and the welfare state on the modern family. He describes the specific roles of mothers and fathers, without which the family cannot function and civilisation begins to falter.

According to Gilder, the mother's role imposes continual challenges, exacting constant alertness and attention, which 'none of the sexual liberators (or welfare-state planners) remotely understand'. With fewer children who remain longer in the household, the focus on each child has increased. He has examined the complaints of women writers about the mother's alleged isolation, her unstimulating environment, her sexual deprivation, her 'entrapment by babies', her boredom, drudgery, and exploitative enslavement by her husband and the capitalist culture. The situation of the American housewife has been proved, according to Gilder's reading of sociological studies, to be different.

These studies suggest that the role of the housewife actually provides the mother with a base for a many-faceted life, which is not tied down to a single organisational structure and a single set of goals, as would be the case if she were employed. Fewer than one-tenth of suburban housewives surveyed report frequent loneliness or boredom. The family and community roles carried on by women could not be assumed by outside agencies. In fact, Gilder believes that 'the woman's role is nothing less than the hub of the human community. Most of the characteristics which we define as humane and individual originate in the mother's love for her children.' Men simply do not have the same deep ties to their children as mothers.

Moreover, according to Gilder, 'the mother assumes charge of the domestic values of the community, its moral, aesthetic, religious, social and sexual concerns', and the success of civilised society depends on how well the women can transmit these values to the men. Thus, the woman and children in the home are the last bastion against the amorality of the technocratic market-place.

Gilder concludes that there is no way to shunt off child care to society, or substantially to reduce its burdens. When children lack the close attention of mothers and the discipline and guidance of fathers, they tend to become barbarians or wastrels who burden or threaten society, rather than do its work. Furthermore, the reports of a number of women researchers are summarised by Gilder to show that motherhood does entail difficult sacrifices of freedom and autonomy, that women are not content with mere influence, power

and wealth, and that they are happiest when the female roles of wife and mother are exalted.

THE FATHER'S CRUCIAL ROLE

Gilder also examines the position of the man in relation to the family and society. He argues that it is the man who makes the major sexual sacrifice by renouncing his dream of short-term sexual freedom and self-fulfilment in order to serve a woman and family for a lifetime. The man's propensity for 'the exciting hunt and predatory chase' must be surrendered, just as the woman's destiny as mother requires reining in of her individualistic aspirations. Neither the male nor female role can be shared or relinquished, except at the cost of familial breakdown.

Men who accept the family as destiny cannot support a family on a 40-hour week, so they train at night and on weekends for better-paying jobs or work at two jobs, while saving to enter a small sideline business and performing house repair chores in time they snatch from posited 'leisure time'. They must turn away from alcohol, drugs, extra-curricular sexual opportunities, and other avocations all in support of the provider role. In addition, the family man must pay close attention to the needs and concerns of his wife and children. Other pressures rest on the female as wife and mother.

While a woman at home can remain uncircumscribed and individual in her relationships, the male at work must keep himself replaceable in his earlier years. He must sacrifice his individuality as an obstacle to earnings and settle down to become a functionary defined by a single job, 'a father whose children are earned by his work', and the value of his work is defined by the market-place. The male is likely to succeed in the market-place to the degree that he represses his individual idiosyncrasies, subordinates himself to the narrow limits of his speciality, and avoids the distractions and impulses of his full personality. He has to accept the postion of a 'barbarian of specialisation', an object of his occupational role and career. Men must give over their lives to unrelenting work, day after day, and look ahead to goals in the distant future, struggling with continued fervour against scarcity, chaos and disaster.

By contrast, the man's role which feminists seek is not, according to Gilder, the real role of men at all – it is a fantasy role in a Marxist dream in which 'society' supposedly does all the work.

FEMINIST DELUSIONS

Gilder is concerned by the dangers to the family posed by sexual liberals, who seek to reshape the norms which have ensured that women will perform the indispensable work of the family and induced men to support their families. The welfare state has apparently embraced the feminist vision of the two sexes no longer needing to make the necessary sacrifices to sustain society. Thus, many men are rejecting available jobs and, instead are doing sporadic work, interspersed with vacations on unemployment compensation. Others work episodically in the underground economy, or enjoy the benefits of free (or almost free) board and room 'boyfriend' status with someone else's ex-wife or a welfare client. Many men and women are passing up the marriage rite, remaining on the uncommitted sidelines of childhood and not accepting responsibility for the actions of their adult bodies.

According to Gilder, the pursuit of promiscuous sexual pleasures offered as an alternative to the duties of the family can only lead to misery and despair for the individuals concerned, and social, political and economic anarchy for society. Without a tie to the family, masculine activity can only degenerate into a game. Gilder concludes that the self-sacrifice of women, rooted in the familial 'web of relationships' in the home and community, finds a perfect complement in the self-sacrifice of men within the institution of the family, – self-sacrifice which is essential for effective childrearing.

INDIVIDUAL 'RIGHTS' AND THE NEEDS OF SOCIETY

The welfare state's contemporary emphasis on individual rights has had its most damaging impact on the family. In enforcing the rights of individuals to escape marriage, it has caused the break-up of millions of families. Many of these dissolutions have created single-parent families in which the mother is putatively in charge – but the children no longer listen to their mother, and their father is, to all intents and purposes, completely absent from the scene.

Few fathers contribute to their children's support, and contact with their children tends to be infrequent. The mother now has to support the family, at a lower standard of living and with even less time to devote to the children. Because of her weakened power, lacking reinforcement by the father and paternal relatives, her control of the children's activity is weakened.

School influence on children is effective only as long as the children remain committed to learning and occupational aspirations. But these are tied to school attendance, and this soon disappears in broken families, where children quickly sense an opportunity to 'do their own thing', with parental wishes no longer enforceable.

CHILDREN WITHOUT FAMILIES

The children of such families are in effect parented by their peers, and the moral level of peer-parenting is usually that of the lowest common denominator. The question that needs to be asked is not so much how children are reared for anti-social behaviour as how so many avoid a life on the street. For even the reconstituted family, where divorced parents with children remarry, offers little hope for resolution of the problem. Maggie Gallagher (1986) for example indicates that pre-schoolers in a home with a step-parent are *40 times more likely to be abused* and far more likely to run away than children from homes with two natural parents.

With the father gone and the mother now involved in increased familial responsibilities, in the emotional diversions and handicaps deriving from her renewed single status and with re-entry into the dating and pairing world, the children are likely to have even less contact with their mother. The limited-quality day-care ordinarily available at typical income levels, the problems of finding and balancing a job with family responsibilities and the breakdown of the full family support group, commonly overwhelms the mother altogether.

THE DOMINANCE OF YOUTH CULTURE

The action of the welfare state in making divorce easier, in easing the status of sexual activity without constraints and in permitting and condoning the production of children out of wedlock has had the effect of denigrating the values of sexual fidelity and devotion to familial life. By freeing the family of its father, the welfare state has created an atmosphere which encourages a footloose youth culture and celebrates the pursuit of trivial childish goals throughout life. The right to be 'different', to be oneself, to do what 'feels good', regardless of the consequences to others and without responsibility

or consequences for oneself, has had a deleterious effect on the family, on public health and on social order.

RIGHTS WITHOUT RESPONSIBILITIES

In some American states, the right of teenage children to receive an abortion, treatment for venereal disease, or birth control equipment has been upheld even though the child's parents have not been informed, let alone given their consent. In those states – as indeed in Britain and in many European countries – it is illegal for physicians to notify the parents. Thus, ironically the welfare-state ethos still requires parental consent for a child to have her ears pierced or an appendix removed, but not to have an abortion.

This trend toward individual 'rights' is strengthened by the mother's right to leave home (with or without the children), and a child's right to run away without being apprehended or detained. Yet by contrast there are few familial rights for children in a family where one or both parents want to be relieved of their responsibilities. The trend towards the exercise of rights without responsibility is also apparent among young males, who have increasingly adopted aggressive roles beyond parental control. Girls differ only in their stance, which is more frequently passive-aggressive, rather than overtly aggressive.

In American juvenile courts, public defenders are supported by an ethos which insists that neither the parents nor the child is at fault; rather, it is 'the system' which causes juvenile delinquency and crime. Parents are not pressed by the courts for responsible control of children, and they are returned to the streets, where they operate in 'packs'.

PSEUDO-FAMILY CARE

With the breakdown of family and community relations has come a growth in the therapeutic professions and government-supported social services. When people are troubled, it becomes the job of the welfare state to look after them. Originally, the social services were founded on the need to help people solve their problems and to learn better how to function in their families and communities. In time, as the therapeutic professions and social services became more strongly tied to the welfare state and its 'third-party' medical insurance,

providers of counselling turned their attention to helping the client 'feel better'. As these professions became more distant from the economic and employment market-place, they lost sight of the goal of guiding their clients back towards life in society.

Until recently, the therapeutic goal was to help the client do better, as a result of which he would then feel better because doing better usually resulted in greater appreciation by others as well as pride in one's achievements. Newer perspectives have shifted the focus to helping the client feel better, regardless apparently of whether or not he did anything to improve his situation. This approach is well suited to the twisted therapeutic philosophy which supposes that all ills derive from society. If anyone has problems, then all that is required is for the 'system' to pay more, or do more for the problem individual.

Along with this viewpoint, the welfare state-cum-civil-rights ethos requires that nothing should be done against the client's wishes. Thus, to press the client to find a job, or train for a job, or to go to school regularly, or to support his family, or to care for her children, or to live by the consequences of his or her choices is somehow supposed to be undemocratic, and an unfair imposition of one's own values on someone else. Of course, this therapeutic stance of helping the client feel better, while not doing better, fits in well with the psychiatric payment method, where the professional is paid by a third-party employer's insurance company, Worker's Compensation programme, or government agency on a fee-for-service basis. To press the client might dissuade him from returning for more help and this is obviously a financially irresponsible act for the practitioner.

THE IMPACT OF SOCIAL WORK

In public and private welfare, social workers, especially in the United States, have tended to follow the lead of the psychiatrists and psychologists, whose status many envied. In their service to public welfare clients these workers had little or no success in rehabilitation of the chronically dependent. Other clients who were not chronically dependent needed little or no help in working out ways to leave the welfare rolls. The Public welfare workers tended to find little purpose in their roles except as agents in the processing of government paper. As the purpose of welfare work became less involved with rehabilitation, although heavily weighted by administrative processes, and as pressure from public sources grew for cutting back on

administrative costs, the usual bureaucratic reaction occurred.

Bureaucracies seldom cut back on staff, but the more vacuous or purposeless a bureaucratic job becomes, the more the central office will load workers with informational inquiries to answer public complaints. The additional paperwork is really a futile attempt to tie the chaotic levels of bureaucracy together, to cover the gaps in unanswered and unanswerable questions. This extra paperwork merely adds to the meaningless weight of the job, still further diluting its purpose.

In time the tie between eligibility and social services was broken, removing the unexercised requirement on the client to become rehabilitated or to bring up his or her children in a rehabilitative manner. It also removed the requirement of the eligibility worker to see that the client moved toward self-sufficiency. Helping people become self-sufficient was simply dropped as a goal of the welfare state. Thus, the welfare state has largely succeeded in convincing the public that the role of welfare client is to continue being dependent and that the role of welfare workers and psychotherapy and social service workers is to help the recipients feel better about staying on welfare.

WELFARE APARTHEID

The promotion of a dependent category of population set apart from the taxpayer-independent population has had enormously destructive effects on the community. When apartheid is created by the welfare state machine, the next institution to suffer is the local community. With increased demand for services to keep the economic machine functioning in a situation of dependent populations and populations without adequately internalised social controls, comes increased taxation of the self-supporting population and/or inflation.

With increased demands come increased centralised taxation and increased centralised regulatory mechanisms. With this flow of power to the central government, the local community and local region loses its power. And as the community wanes, it loses it capacity to serve as protector of the local family and neighbourhood. The centrality is unreachable, incompetent, and yields only to narrow, single-issue campaigns, which tend to be expensive and ineffective. Anything the family and community can do, the mass government can do *less* effectively and *more* expensively.

Homeless children roam strange streets under the control of 'loving' pimps, who succeed in directing them where parents have failed. Doorkey children abound in the city. Children wait late at day-care centres for mama's new boyfriend to pick them up – he's a replacement for last year's stepfather. The once healing, cohesive and constraining community and neighbourhood are now without substance and power. We have seen the brave new world, where everyone is provided for and controlled, and we are appalled by it.

8 The Tenets of the Welfare State

We have examined how the welfare state has led the western nations towards the destruction of the institutions and values upon which civilisation and democracy depend. It is important to examine why the planners seek the establishment of a welfare state despite its destructive effects.

Bethell (1985) suggests that 'Western societies are not so much penetrated as infested by people who dream of human nature as-it-might-be. [These people] wield considerable power.' These proponents of the welfare state make a number of unproven assumptions, which they blithely claim to be self-evident. Anyone who dares to question these assumptions is accused either of ignorance or of being an enemy of the poor and the helpless. In fact those who question the value of the welfare state are entirely sincere in their concern for the less affluent. The difference is their belief that the welfare state is ineffective in helping the poor, and damaging to society, as a whole.

These are the assumptions of the welfare state:

Anything that the free enterprise system can do in productivity and skill can also be effectively done by a well-planned welfare state and its civil servants and at no greater costs;

Benefits granted by the welfare state to the population need do no harm to the citizenry, their institutions and their quality of life;

Actions of a welfare state will not cause productive and creative citizens to leave or to want to leave a closed-border society;

Any welfare state can be as efficient and functional as a non-welfare state. This assumption presumes that the bureaucracy of the welfare state will be constrained in its actions and responsive to the needs and interests of the citizenry;

A welfare state can be operated in a manner which is just and fair to all of its citizens;

It is possible for a welfare state to carry out the necessary domestic and international functions of government, and in addition provide economic security for all without inflation, unemployment, or onerous taxation.

56

MARKETS AND STATES

The facts are that all of these assumptions have been proven invalid. No bureaucratic mechanism, no matter how well equipped with staff and skills, can possibly match the productivity and cost savings of what Adam Smith described as the 'hidden hand' of economics. The competitive market will always, somehow, find a better way to produce saleable goods and services yielding sufficient affluence for many more people than any planner.

The extension of benefits to 'the relatively deprived' cannot be effected, except at the cost of a weakened, costly labour market. Roger Freeman (1981) for example has made it clear that there are severe limits on how far the state can go in transferring huge resources and in redistributing enormous amounts of income without inflicting serious damage on the economy; it produces lowered incentives and efforts, less economic growth, high rates of inflation, tight regulation of people's lives, and intensification of social problems and internal conflicts.

THE ROAD TO SERFDOM AND BACK

The propensity of the welfare state to interfere with the lives of the mass of population in its attempt to manage the market is much greater than the impersonal mechanisms of the market-place. The former is more resented by the population; the latter is either accepted as normative economic process, or else it gives rise to counter-economic action, which usually restores the balance by automatic process. Where the former is bound to be unfair to many, the latter, in the long run, operates in a pattern of fairness for all. Newhouse (1986) has described conditions in Britain and West Germany and suggests that many people take one half of democracy and neglect the other half – they opt for freedom without responsibility. The facts are that responsibility can be learned only in the family; the family can teach it effectively only in a community to which it is responsible; and the community can function effectively only if it is not overwhelmed by the dominance and power of the central government.

Nathan Glazer (1983) has reported that there are increasing pressures both in the United States and in France for decentralisation of social services. This is not only because of the need for adminis-

trative efficiency, but because of a growing concern on almost everyone's part about big government and because of disenchantment with distant professionals in the public service.

TOWARDS DE-CENTRALISATION

This reaction has come with the expansion of the self-help movement and local involvement in voluntarism. As education has spread, and as the average citizen has come to see himself as at least the equal of the average social worker, policeman, teacher or civil servant, it was inevitable that he or she would demand a greater role in government. For social services, this meant a taste for less central government and more local government. In Britain too, this shift in attitude from professionalism to self-help has occurred in the housing field, where the view of the public now is that private housing and home ownership are to be preferred on all counts to council tenancy.

In the United States, the shift has been apparent in the left's slogan 'Power to the people', and in the right's pressure for community control of local schools in the suburbs and for decentralisation of large urban school systems. Superintendants of schools no longer stand aloof. They have had to learn to satisfy their citizenry or leave the smaller communities. Physicians are no longer dominant in matters of community health or health-care policy. Social workers are no longer, on the national or local scene, predominant in social policy; their credibility has been almost destroyed by their promotion of a service-dominated solution for welfare reform. There is everywhere at the local level a clamour for professional accountability.

THE NEED FOR FREEDOM

But this is impossible as long as power and real control rests in a distant centrality. The complexity of central government, with its laws, rules and regulations governing every realm of human activity, creates an attitude of confusion and dependency. As the government confuses social insurance and welfare, earnings and taxation, the individual citizen loses track of right and wrong. It would take a savant, rather than a moral hero, to find his way in the legal maze. As a result, the citizen becomes dependent upon a mechanistic,

routinised and often, senseless, civil service to understand his duties and rights.

The dependency of the citizen on the bureaucracy has increasingly destructive effects on the economy and confuses parents in their attempts at teaching their children. Right and wrong, under the welfare state, have given way to technical 'black-letter', 'small-print' law to the point where complex, centralised definitions of right and wrong are not well understood, even by the civil service which is supposed to interpret it.

Stan Gebler Davies shows how the more the state cares, the more damage it does. He relates this in particular to public housing, which is not only worse than private housing, but destroys private housing as well. The same goes for public education, public industry, public welfare, public health, public transport and public wealth. The caring, centralised state becomes irresponsible, uncontrollable, bungling, dangerous and unwieldy.

A typical example of the way in which the welfare state operates counter to its manifest purpose occurs in California. Here the welfare state has as one of its purposes the employment of the handicapped. The central government has a large staff of state civil servants involved in vocational rehabilitation offices, vocational education offices, social services and employment placement agencies, scattered all over the state and all centrally responsible to state centralised direction.

Once a year, usually before elections, the Governor's committee for employment of the handicapped holds a huge meeting at a hotel in an urban setting, amid affluent accommodations. State employees all come to the three-day meetings at state expense, including representatives of state agencies with only limited involvement in employment of the handicapped. To this meeting, representatives of key corporations are invited to present their ideas and to hear a replay of all the reasons why the handicapped should be employed, why the handicapped make better employees (they usually want to work), and what the cost benefits of handicapped employment are. After hearing these accounts and pleas (which they have heard many times before), all the participants, having had a good time and a few days off from routine responsibilities, go back to their offices, in which they will again be isolated from other colleagues in similar agencies with the same purpose, and scarcely any additional handicapped will be employed.

Suppose the power, money and control of these agencies were at

the local level, and local taxpayers and their representatives were directly concerned with the costs and concerns of the handicapped. Then it would at least be *possible* that vocational educators would really have to work with vocational rehabilitators and employment placement officers for increased employment of the handicapped. But, with power, money and control at the centralised level, the only result of an 'employ-the-handicapped' conference is to make the politicos of the welfare state 'look good'.

PROSTITUTING VOLUNTARISM

Still another way in which the centralised government-cum-welfare state gains control over local communities is by major subventions of local voluntary agencies. Thus, a programme which begins with local volunteer efforts and local policy control and demonstrates local human relationships with its clients is seduced into acceptance of a federal grant. Soon the shape of the local agency is redesigned, its volunteers are now employees following federal rules, and they behave like the impersonal employees of any civil service bureau. The policies of the agency are reshaped to fit federal guidelines (Glazer, 1983) and in time there is no genuine private sector left in the field of welfare policy. Indeed, Rein and Rainwater (1981) maintain that public and voluntary programmes in combination constitute the welfare state society. However, it is the powerful central state apparatus which tends to have the whip hand.

Centralised, over-powerful government makes of the local community a client state with matching bureaucracies to 'interface' with the national administrative forces. With this proliferation of the welfare state, local enterprise and genuine social care are snuffed out.

TOWARDS AN ALTERNATIVE

Patently we cannot continue with an approach which is so thoroughly destructive in its effects. The only feasible alternative is an open, free-enterprise system. But the issue then is whether and how a civilised society so organised can take care of the 'deserving needy' without encouraging them to become 'undeserving'.

How can a society do good without engendering vice? We shall

approach this question by considering the unusual case of Switzerland. For there a people seems to have found a way of avoiding the inevitable problems of the welfare states while at the same time providing real care for those in need and genuine welfare for all.

Part II
The Unusual Case of Switzerland

1 Introduction: the Swiss Approach to Poverty

Switzerland is definitely not a welfare state as generally understood. There is, for example, no national health service, and most of the populations are covered by voluntary health insurance. There is no central programme to provide a minimum guaranteed income for all. There is no concept of a right to state support. Nevertheless, it has achieved what nations traditionally defined as welfare states have not: it has successfully avoided welfare dependency and intergenerational poverty, and it has succeeded in this by methods which are strikingly different from those adopted elsewhere. Just *how* Switzerland deals with its poor and shapes its policies to encourage self-sufficiency offers lessons for others which we should not ignore.

The Swiss begin with a view of poverty which is radically different from that in the other developed societies, Their approach to any problem, whatever it is, starts with these questions: 'What needs to be done to change the situation so that the problems will be alleviated, rather than suppressed? What can be done to resolve the problem under consideration, in a way that does not itself bring about unsought results contrary to our purposes?'

Accordingly, the Swiss, in the manner of the highly inventive minds of the industrial revolution, have arrived at a remarkably rational arrangement for the care of the poor, which is strongly utilitarian in approach and intent. This policy is designed to meet two requirements. First to aid the poor in such a way that they would be helped temporarily, without being encouraged to become dependent by the help offered them. Secondly, aid was to be tied to a policy of encouraging the poor to help themselves as much as possible, and moving them as rapidly as possible out of poverty, if not in the current generation, then, at least, in the next.

SWISS SOCIAL INSURANCE AS A PREVENTION OF POVERTY

Still another requirement was to encourage people to provide for their time of need. Most people, unfortunately, are afflicted with

65

what Karen Horney called 'the neurotic exemption', in that, in good times, they never expect to fall into bad circumstances.

Because of this, the Swiss installed a far-ranging and expanding programme of compulsory social insurance. This imposes on each worker and his employer a compulsory shared-risk programme to provide for both expected and unexpected financial needs. Thus, a primarily self-earned insurance programme provides workers with old-age retirement, disability and sickness insurance, survivors' insurance, accident insurance and unemployment compensation.

Unlike the social insurance policies of most other industrialised nations, these programmes are so designed that the beneficiary cannot control the outcome. Unemployment compensation is given only if the person is validly out of work and readily available for employment as it opens up. Disability is strictly defined in such a way that it has not, as in many other nations, become an alternative to work. If a person were to claim a disability, and if he were to work 'on the side', this would soon be revealed in various ways.

In the first place, income tax reports are open to all and the extra income would soon be reported to the social insurance authority. In the second place, neighbours and fellow members of the community would notice this kind of 'double-dipping', and it would soon be reported to the social insurance agency. Finally, there is no underground economy in Switzerland, so it would be impossible to earn an unlisted employment income. If a person were to stay on disability income while training for an athletic event (which did occur in an American city), this would become common knowledge in the Swiss community and would soon be questioned.

GENUINE INSURANCE PRINCIPLES

Social insurance in Switzerland is operated as a true insurance programme, and the only difference between the Swiss programme and the commercial form of insurance is that the Swiss programme covers amost everyone. No commercial insurance company would remain solvent if the clients were allowed to insure themselves against a house fire if they had a hobby of collecting inflammables. Similarly, no social insurance programme can remain viable and generally unsubsidised if the definitions and responsibilities of clients are allowed to be amended after the fact. The lesson which the Swiss have learned from the insurance business generally is that *client*

behaviour usually changes in relation to administrative actions, unless such changes are subject to control.

Thus, administrative policy for social insurance has to operate in such a manner as to keep people working and contributing to the fund until a real (not client-fabricated) crisis occurs. Even here, Swiss social insurance requires client rehabilitative activity for the infirm (during the benefit period) so that a return to self-sufficiency will occur if it is possible and feasible. Otherwise, the client care can suffer a lessened benefit.

PREPARING FOR WORK

The emphasis on prevention via social insurance is matched by a heavy emphasis on prevention of dependency via employment preparation. No one in Switzerland, apparently, can avoid efficacious schooling and occupational training. If a child should begin to falter in such preparation for adult self-sufficiency, the whole community becomes concerned – not just the school's personnel, but the whole gamut of formal and informal social control mechanisms become actively involved.

Truancy and dropping out of school before completion is little known in Switzerland, and childen not in school during a school day become the concern of the local youth programmes, the local police, the neighbours, the clergy and anyone else who might be around. Educational-occupational offerings are varied and broad. There are options at every level and far into the adult years, and these are effective.

In Zurich, for example, Swiss males have an educational or apprenticeship completion rate of 97 per cent. Swiss females have a 91 per cent rate, which means that only a small proportion (much smaller than in most developed countries) break off their training in preference for early marriage. Even the resident Italian children of former *Gastarbeiter* have rates of 87 per cent for males and 78 per cent for females, even though many of them experience parental resistance to higher education

The old concept that Switzrland has few resources other than its people is matched by a national policy which ensures that its people are educationally and technologically prepared to take their place in the productive economy.

PREVENTION OF POVERTY BY CONTROL OF IMMIGRATION

Prevention of native poverty is also ensured by strict control of immigration. The Swiss have long realised the limits of their national resources. They hold to the view that they cannot provide for everyone in the world, or even for everyone who would seek to come to Switzerland. They have therefore carefully selected a limited scope of responsibility. These limits, whatever the rest of the world may think of them, begin with a strong concern for 'their own', and with charity to others only after all of their own citizens have been cared for.

While this may seem harsh, it probably produces no worse results than more open-door policies which tend to encourage intergenerational dependency on government aid. In any case, Swiss policy on immigration is stringent, operating almost as if it were controlled by a calibrated spigot, which is opened only when negative unemployment exists, and is quickly shut when Swiss natives begin to draw excessively on unemployment compensation.

2 The Swiss Welfare System

Despite all of this preventative effort, some Swiss do find themselves at times in poverty. Such people are served, not by the federal social insurance programme, but by the local communities and the cantons. The differences between Swiss social insurance and public assistance are carefully maintained because *these differences serve a necessary function*. The social insurances are administered by the central (Federal) government, but public assistance is operated by the local communities and cantons. Social insurance benefits are distributed on the basis of prior coverage during employment, with matched contributions by employee and employer.

SOCIAL INSURANCE

Unlike social insurance policies in other countries, there is no ceiling on social insurance payroll deductions and employer contributions, so that a bank president earning 200 000 Swiss francs per year, and a bank clerk earning 48 000 per year, each pay $4\frac{1}{2}$ per cent into the social insurance fund, namely 9000 and 2160 Swiss francs respectively per annum. This is matched by equal amounts from the employer. But, on retirement, both bank president and bank clerk each receive the same amount in benefits, about 24 000 Swiss francs per annum, or 36 000 per annum if married. This is the benefit from the so-called 'First Pillar', (see below) which is supplemented by much higher benefits from employer retirement funds, which now cover all of the population.

Social insurance benefits are generally much larger than public aid, but seldom at a level equal to full time employment. Thus, social insurance coverage has an attraction to potential workers and yet is not so attractive as to discourage full-time work. Social insurance benefits (unlike public aid) are based on a right on the part of the worker and his family (whether it is for retirement, survivors' support, accident or invalidity support, or unemployment compensation). There is no social stigma attached to acceptance of social insurance

benefits, since the employee is merely collecting insurance for which he and his employer have paid.

The benefits are such as to provide for a relatively comfortable survival. Thus, the policy and administration of social insurance in Switzerland is, in many ways, similar to the policies and administration of social insurance in other countries, to the degree that the latter have not been integrated with their public assistance programmes. This is an important proviso.

There is just one exception to the strict separation of social insurance from public assistance. This applies in the case of aged or invalids with an income of less than 12 000 Swiss francs (after deductions of medical costs, excessive rental costs and other special needs). This programme (the *Ergänzungsleistungen*), similar to the Supplementary Security Income programme in the United States, is federally administered, and requires no prior pre-payments.

A limited, but flexible, means test is required, as in all public assistance programmes. The federal government thus provides, in essence, a guaranteed income, on application, for all aged and invalids who are without resources. However the Swiss have wisely avoided setting up such a minimum guaranteed income for employable adults and for families with children. This is because of their concern about the deleterious effect on employment incentives for those who should be self-supporting, and the negative effect on children in families where their role model is an unemployed parent. Thus the income package of social insurance for the aged and infirm consists of a First Pillar (basic earned benefits for old age, disability and survivors), a Second Pillar (a country-wide retirement programme with transferability), additional cantonal social insurances, plus minimum supplementary security income assistance for the aged, sick and handicapped, and individualized welfare programmes for others at the community and cantonal levels.

SWISS PUBLIC ASSISTANCE PROGRAMMES: LOCAL RESPONSIBILITY

Public assistance, unlike social insurance, is not a concern or responsibility of the federal government. By contrast with welfare states, central government is kept out of it entirely. There is not even a federal data-collecting service about public assistance. Control of public assistance by the local community and the cantons has been

jealously guarded ever since the creation of the state. Although all individuals have freedom of movement within the country, the individual's home community or canton carries the responsibility of providing for his care, either directly, if the individual is residing there, or on a reimbursement basis for the first five years, if he resides in another community. A person's established place of residence is that community or canton where he has been economically self-sufficient for a specified time, or where he has been aided on a reimbursement basis by another canton for the specified time.

There is an inter-cantonal concordat which prohibits the 'passing on' of any individual or family to another community. This concordat also requires reimbursement by the community of residence to any communities where its residents may move until they become self-sufficient in the new community or until five years have expired.

Because public assistance is funded from local and cantonal sources, it becomes a matter of concern for each local community to prevent public dependency, if possible, and to work with those who are dependent so that they can become self-sufficient as soon as possible. If a family is so beset with problems as to be unable to become self-sufficient in a short space of time, then the community authorities make special efforts to see to it that the children in that family are reared in a manner which will make them self-sufficient as they reach adulthood.

SWISS PUBLIC WELFARE POLICIES

The public welfare programmes of the local communities have a number of policies which they hold in common. Administration of these policies does vary from community to community, but the general effect, in terms of how the welfare workers view their assignments and how they carry them out, is similar.

These policies include the view that all public welfare aid is temporary, and will continue only as long as the cause of impoverishment lasts. Only in the case of the elderly and some of the physically or mentally handicapped, for whom eventual self-help may be ruled out entirely, supplementary public aid may last a lifetime (over and above the national supplementary security aid income described above).

Although the social welfare system is viewed by proponents of the welfare state, as an income-redistribution mechanism, this is not the

case with Swiss public welfare. Thus, for the Swiss (other than the handicapped and the aged) any aid plan, once developed individually with the client, is immediately followed by a discussion of how long the aid is to be given, and how soon the client will be able to become self-supporting again.

This kind of a discussion involves questions of education and training completed, past employment and work skills achieved, further education and training required and plans for finding employment again. If full-time employment is not immediately possible, because of child-care arrangements, then school and day-care resources are provided in order to make part-time work possible. Even part-time employment is usually viewed as temporary, in that the client is expected eventually to become fully self-sufficient. There is essentially a 'contract' between the client and the agency which covers the client's and the agency's responsibilities with regard to the amount and manner of service to be given by the agency, and the client's movement toward independence.

The nature of the public aid given in Swiss programmes also differs from that of many other western countries. In Switzerland, it is incumbent on the client to work toward his rehabilitation and toward self-sufficiency. If he does not, his grant can be cut or eliminated. His children also must be reared to become self-sufficient. No such responsibility is placed on the welfare clients of other western nations.

Swiss aid is described in most local community welfare ordinances as 'advice, counselling, information, and other social services, including, if necessary, financial and material aid.' There is usually no uniform schedule of grants, merely a set of guidelines which are considered along with the client's goal and plan. Considerations in calculating the amount of temporary aid include not only the general and special needs of the client, but also the amount of money he can eventually earn, and whether a welfare grant larger than the beginning salary might discourage efforts toward training and employment.

SWISS PATTERNS OF WELFARE ADMINISTRATION

Patterns of welfare administration in Switzerland are radically different from those of other welfare systems. In welfare state societies public welfare is generally given on the basis of equality for each category of clients. The delivery of the welfare grant tends to be seen as the primary purpose of the agency, rather than as merely one of

the tools of rehabilitation. Again rehabilitation and social services in other countries are elective, if available at all, and grants are made to clients without any account being taken of the responsibilities of others to help them. Finally welfare grants in other countries remain the same for as long as there are no reports of a change in the client's situation. It can go on indefinitely – and it frequently does. This is not the case in Switzerland, where the amount of the grant is related precisely to the client's progress.

RESPONSIBILITY OF RELATIVES

Another major policy difference between the Swiss and other welfare systems relates to the responsibility of relatives and family. This can extend even to affluent brothers and sisters who are called on to provide aid for needy siblings. Parents and grandparents are always required to provide for their children and grandchildren, if they are able to do so. In the case of grown children in need, parents are called upon to provide aid if they have the resources. Adult children are also required to aid their parents and grandparents if they are in need. Ex-husbands, in cases of divorce (and husbands and fathers in cases of separation), are required to supply adequate spousal and child support.

Where child payments are not forthcoming on a regular basis in such cases, the public welfare agency is required by law to deliver the court-specified sums to the mother and then press for repayment. This system is unlike the American and British experience in that these payments are usually effectively recovered, for a number of reasons which will be discussed later.

THE MEANS TEST

The enforcement of the 'means test' for public welfare in Switzerland is carried out without difficulty. This is facilitated by the tax collection system, which is located in the individual communities. Each year, every person files an income and wealth tax report. Local assessments are first levied on this basis, then cantonal assessments are made, and finally the federal assessments. *For the sum of five francs (exempted in the case of welfare authorities) in most communities, a copy of any individual's tax reports can be secured by anyone and*

without having to state a reason. If a report contains inaccuracies, these can be challenged by any other taxpayer. Thus, the tax record is an unusually authentic source for information on a person's resources and economic ability to support himself or his family.

PUBLIC ASSISTANCE AS A LOAN

Public aid, in Swizerland, by contrast with other western countries, can be recovered by the authorities from an adult client or his direct relatives if he later becomes affluent. As a result clients tend to ask for less aid than they would otherwise, because they know that it may have to be reimbursed. Similarly, because public aid funds which are secured under false pretences or by the use of false information can be recovered with interest by the local community, fraud is kept down to a minimum.

CONFIDENTIALITY AND DISCRETION IN RELATIONS BETWEEN WELFARE WORKERS AND CLIENTS

Public welfare is conducted on a confidential basis in Switzerland, as it is in most other western nations. It is illegal under most community ordinances for a public welfare worker to release information without client permission, even if such information is requested by the local public welfare board members. Neither may a public welfare worker interfere with the constitutional or personal rights of a client. This is similar to the public welfare policies of other western nations.

The difference in the Swiss case, however, is that the client is required to co-operate with the welfare worker not only in regard to determination of needs and resources, but also in relation to improving his own situation and that of his family. Thus, a client who does not co-operate in working toward self-sufficiency may find that the nature and extent of his welfare grant has been changed, or that his welfare grant is to be dispersed in small increments by an appointed guardian, or that it is now to be the form of materials and vouchers only. His only recourse is to appeal beyond the worker or supervisor to the public welfare commission or town council. Under these circumstances, the matter of confidentiality becomes moot.

Similarly, the welfare worker is authorised, when necessary, to release information to youth and community authorities *without*

permission of the client, where the client has not been acting responsibly and where guardianship is to be considered. Here too, the issue of confidentiality becomes moot.

Swiss public welfare workers and administrators thus exercise considerable discretion in their relationship with clients. This is quite unlike the client-worker relationship in most other western nations, where the interaction is routinised and focused primarily on regulations of eligibility for aid, and the authorised levels of grants. In the Swiss public agency, almost no aspect of the client's life, or that of his family, is prohibited for discussion by the worker.

Unlike the restrictions on public welfare workers in other countries, in Switzerland the worker has generally unlimited controls in requiring interviews with the client, in the terms of collateral visits with the relatives, employers, teachers of the client's children, and others who may, in any way, affect the client's progress toward again becoming independent. Thus the welfare worker can shape, both formally and indirectly as well, the way in which public aid and public social services are used by the client and his family. If a client seeks to go beyond the welfare worker's constraints, or even beyond the agency's constraints, he then comes face to face with community authorities who are almost always in agreement with the goals of client self-reliance. In our interviews with public officials, we learned that they are even more imbued with the need to reduce client dependency than are the welfare workers themselves.

STIGMA

The matter of confidentiality is particularly important in Switzerland because of the issue of 'Stigma'. Welfare in most western countries is somewhat stigmatised by the general public, and this serves to hold down the extent of claims for welfare made by most ordinary people in need. This stigma has the opposite effect, however, on the chronically welfare-dependent, in that it ensures their cultural separation from the world of work and upward mobility.

In Switzerland, where most of the population is 'middle class' in its values and where public welfare dependency has a general air of stigma, there is considerable danger that becoming known as a welfare client may negatively label a person among his friends, neighbours, community and potential employers. Thus, in Switzerland, stigma serves to promote self-sufficiency and client co-operation towards that end.

THE VIEW OF SWISS PUBLIC WELFARE ADMINISTRATORS

The view of Swiss public welfare administrators towards their clients seems quite different from that of most public welfare officials in other western countries. On the causes of poverty, most western public welfare writings emphasise the circumstances and conditions of poverty. It is a view which focuses on the structure of society, unemployment, the lack of attractive low-level employment, the failings of public education, inadequate vocational training opportunities, and lack of adequate housing opportunities for welfare clientele.

Swiss public welfare writings and discussions by contrast reflect the view expressed by Heinz Strang (1970) that poverty is often caused by a variety of factors; these include structural unemployment, individual problems, and conditions which prevent adequately remunerative employment, as well as dependency. It tends to be presumed that at least some of these factors may be interactive with the availability of public aid.

Swiss welfare personnel, unlike their counterparts in other developed countries, tend *to individualise interpretations of why a particular client is in need*. The major difference between the two views is that administrators, in the USA, Britain and other societies afflicted with the welfare state mentality tend to accept welfare need as a *given*, and to take it for granted that in any modern society there will always be a sizable proportion of the population in need. Swiss administrators, on the other hand, tend to view their world as a place where individuals have a choice, and that if some are in need, this is because they have made a wrong choice, or because they have been unfortunate in their circumstances, or because of a combination of these factors.

WELFARE STATE – OR REAL WELFARE?

What is to be done for and with the poor? Welfare administrators (in welfare state societies) see the solution as perfectly simple. Because they define poverty as a lack of money, the way to solve it is to redistribute some of society's funds to the poor. Swiss welfare administrators by contrast define poverty as a condition of multiple causation, and seek to solve the problem by determining the individual causes in each case and to take steps accordingly.

In a sense, the so-called welfare state deals with poverty as if it were a fated condition, while the Swiss view poverty more rationally, as a problem which needs to be dealt with carefully, according to its precise causes. Western welfare administrators, other than the Swiss, view their clients as 'receivers of benefits', rather than as actors in their own life choices. Swiss administrators view their clients as differentially able to make changes in their lifespace and circumstances once they have been helped to determine what needs to be done.

Welfare state administrators tend to emphasise the goals of efficiency in the 'delivery of benefits', egalitarian handling of clients in a massive system, and improved management of their assignment in the fulfilment of diverse regulations. Under the Swiss system, on the other hand, the emphasis is placed on individual adjustment to society (and to his surroundings) on the part of the client so that he can learn best how to live productively, and to bring his children up as self-sufficient, productive citizens.

The welfare process seems to be seen as a necessary function in the western world, apart from Switzerland, and welfarisation is viewed as inevitable in an imperfect world. In Switzerland, welfarisation is viewed as a process by which people become used to welfare dependency and it is regarded as something to be avoided.

Indeed, many Swiss welfare workers view welfarisation as an iatrogenic disease, *actually caused by professional treatment.* Thus one Swiss welfare official drew a parallel between welfarisation and excessive bed-rest after surgery. *'If the client gets used to inaction, he will lose the ability to fend for himself.'*

3 The Family and Other Limitations on Welfare Dependency

Probably the most effective of the informal controls operating in Switzerland is the family structure. From an early age, Swiss family socialisation, at almost all levels of social stratification, operates to shape children into functional citizens and workers. Community attitudes reinforce the authority of the family over children, and children soon learn that their behaviour must conform to a standard of consideration for others. Each child is impressed with the assignment of picking up after himself, of doing the work assigned to him, and of preparing himself for self-sufficiency. Children soon learn that as members of a family they must care for their siblings and be responsible for their well-being. Because of effective family socialisation, few individuals find themselves in need of community aid.

THE SWISS COMMUNITY

Still another reinforcement of this effect derives from Swiss community planning. After the Second World War, the planning of communities, the location of factories, and the construction of residential development was based on a policy of modern industrialisation without urbanisation. This was not due to national planning, but was the result of strong local initiative and decentralised political power.

Aside from Zurich, which is not a megalopolis when compared with other metropolitan areas in the world, there are few large cities in Switzerland. Most of the population live in small villages and towns, which are easily reached by an effective network of suburban trains, trams and buses. The residents of these towns may work elsewhere, but they participate actively in communal decision-making.

Many communities function on a town-hall basis, and most decisions regarding expenditures, as well as schools, housing and welfare

78

policies, must be ratified either by an election or a meeting of all electors. The social distance in these communities is minimal, and news about individuals travels fast. In this way, people hear about jobs, informal community help is given to the aged and sick, and there is a high level of informal mutual aid.

In such a setting, a considerable degree of neighbourly aid is frequent, as is the operation of numerous voluntary social service programmes. In consequence, public dependency is minimal, and people are more readily helped to settle their problems of employment and economic independence.

In the Swiss community, voluntary activity flourishes, and indeed is expected. All able-bodied men, for example, are required to participate in their volunteer fire department (there are only three professional fire departments). Those who cannot do so, because of their jobs or situation, are permitted to pay a tax instead of serving. There is discussion in some cities of broadening the volunteer service responsibility to other realms of community service. The tax structure and informal, unofficial social control combine to ensure broad participation by almost everyone.

COMMUNITY YOUTH PROGRAMMES AS A CONSTRAINT ON WELFARISATION

Still another pattern of welfare dependency prevention operates out of the community youth authorities in each town. The *Jugendamt*, as it is called, is a publicly supported recreation, social service, supervision and career programme which serves a high proportion of young people in each town. In no other country are such extensive and intensive efforts made to aid and direct a nation's youth into prosocial activities and away from self-destructive and wasteful 'sidetracks'.

The degree and amount of services given to young people and the attempt to tie recreation to character and career development are both effective and unusual. There is a close working relationship between public welfare services and the *Jugendamt* which ensures that families given financial aid are also provided with supervision of their parenting methods when this is appropriate. The ease with which *beistand* (supervision by locally-appointed guardians) is established, and the frequent local emphasis that such services shall include *Rat und Tat* (advice and action) is not matched outside Switzerland.

SWISS DIVORCE COURTS AS WELFARISATION CONSTRAINTS

Still another informal or preventive control of welfarisation can be found in the Swiss divorce courts. Welfarised poverty has become largely feminised in many Western nations, as an aftermath of divorce and unmarried motherhood. These problems are trivial by comparison in Switzerland.

The reason is to be found in the policies and effectiveness of Swiss divorce and family relations courts. In each of the welfare agencies we visited, we found no complaints about divorce courts. On the contrary, we found considerable respect among welfare administrators for their contribution to preventing the growth of welfare. Apparently husbands who are divorced from their families must provide substantial amounts for child and spousal support, and those who do not do so have their wages attached. Funds are advanced automatically to divorced wives with children by the welfare agency, which then secures reimbursement from the fathers by legal mechanisms.

The fact that most fathers do pay what has been specified by the courts makes it more probable that they will also visit their children, and thus serve as a parental influence on them. The only exception to the fulfilment of paternal responsibilities occurs among those few families where the father is a foreigner, so that enforcement of court actions is ineffective. If he leaves the country, the active involvement of the courts in matters of paternity where marriage has not taken place also serves to prevent family dependency. The Swiss rate of paternal determination and paternal support (outside the marriage) is also much higher than in most other nations.

The Swiss rate of children born out of wedlock is reported at 5 per cent in 1982. This has been a relatively static figure (it was 3.8 per cent in 1970) and the effect of this figure is lessened by the fact that over one-third of such births are quickly followed by marriages. In the United States, data in comparison indicate a 1980 figure of 18.4 per cent, and the 1982 estimate is closer to 23 per cent. In contrast to the Swiss pattern, most American out-of-wedlock births are not followed by marriages which would lessen their impact on welfare aid. Similarly, high levels of out-of-wedlock births are found in many other industrialised nations. Probably the low Swiss rate is occasioned by high levels of informal social control, and this has contributed in the pattern of low welfarisation rates. If the father is not available,

then the community requires support by the woman, or her parents and siblings.

WHY THE LAW WORKS

Divorce and Family Relations Courts thus have a direct effect on the prevention of female welfarisation. What is less apparent is the frequent informal effect of such court processes. For example a Swiss banker reported in conversation that he had recently provided a bond to guarantee child support. This happened when a divorced man from a small town in Switzerland was summoned to meet the divorce judge. The judge was concerned, not as a judge but as a citizen of the community, that the man's publicly announced betrothal and eventual marriage to a second wife might result in his non-payment of the scheduled child and spousal supports. He did not want to see the community having to support the man's first family, and said that he planned to appear at the impending marriage to protest that this new marriage was fundamentally immoral, in that the man intended to develop a new family at the community's expense. The judge was dissuaded from his plan to protest publicly against the marriage only after the man had posted a bond, participated in by his brothers, sisters, and parents, which guaranteed continued child and spousal support until the children reached maturity.

Most Swiss judges probably do not involve themselves to this extent in the enforcement of their decrees, but this incident provides us with an indication of the informal community controls which serve to limit or prevent welfarisation.

The job of the Divorce and Domestic Relations Courts is eased in many ways by the operation and structure of Swiss society. Each individual votes (elections are frequent as compared with other societies), pays taxes, registers for military duty (up to the age of 55), and may carry out a number of voluntary activities at the offices of his commune (or quarter in the city) where he resides. If he wishes to move to another commune, he must de-register at the offices of the commune where he lives, and then register at the offices of the commune which he is joining. Not to keep one's registry up to date is a violation of tax regulations, compulsory military duty, voting regulations and police regulations. Thus, no errant father can be lost in the system unless he actually leaves Switzerland.

Similarly, the operation of the court system is such that collection

of child and spousal support can be enforced by the withholding of wages, by the establishment of liens on property, and by a variety of informal and social constraints. It must also be noted that, by contrast with the practice in many other countries, divorce is not always granted by judges. There is no 'no-fault' divorce in Switzerland, divorces are more difficult to secure, and people work harder to make their marriages work.

SWISS SCHOOLS AS A CONSTRAINT ON WELFARISATION

Unlike the view of education as 'a continuous questioning of the existing world' held by many liberal educators in other western societies, Luscher and his colleagues (1982) found a fundamentally conservative ideology at the base of Swiss education. Under the Swiss model, *'education is seen as a means of integrating children into the "system" and helping them to internalize the norms of the existing order.'*

Schooling is viewed in Switzerland, more than in most other countries, as 'the job of the child'. Just as failure on the job for an adult is more serious in Switzerland, where work has priority over many other activities, so failure in school becomes a matter of concern, not only for the school personnel, but also for the child's family, relatives, family friends, diverse affected agencies, and interested people in the community.

Because of the concern for the family's *'Ruf'* (family reputation in the community), and because in Switzerland more than in many other countries, completion of basic education is the path to economic success and self-sufficiency, parents and children both take the educational process very seriously. Observers of Swiss education have referred to the heavy emphasis placed on scholarship and discipline in Swiss schools, the high status of teachers, and the well-established role obligations and social distance traditionally specified for student–teacher contacts. The Swiss school has few extra-curricular activities and group programmes, and it imposes a heavy academic load.

Integration of children into the system by Swiss schools includes not only academic assignments, but intertwined with these the critically important norms and values of the society. Among these values and norms, a key item is the *'Principle of Subsidiarity'*. Under this principle (according to Luscher, *et al.*): 'Only those tasks which cannot be fulfilled on the initiative of the individual should be taken

away from him and given to the community. The same is true of the relationship between smaller groups, such as the canton and the federal state.'

Thus, the family is primary, and after that, the community has priority, and only after that can the canton or federal state make a claim on the loyalty of the individual. Similarly, private and voluntary institutions have priority over state institutions. As a result, loyalty to family and community are instilled early in schoolchildren.

This is accompanied by a concern for the effect of one's behaviour on the rights of others, based not only on the Golden Rule, but also on the concern for what others will think of oneself and one's family. The norms are taught to Swiss schoolchildren, including adherence to local authority, to the consensus, to amicable agreement, and the responsibility of the individual to the group.

VALUES REINFORCED IN PRACTICE

These values are also enforced in the schools. Traditional models of behaviour, respect for and adherence to the wishes of elders, teachers, and parents are all required of Swiss schoolchildren. By contrast with Riesman's model in *The Lonely Crowd*, each child is taught to carry individual responsibility for his actions, whether they occur in groups or alone. Finally, each child has instilled within him the importance of doing his work and of seeking its completion at a level of the highest quality.

Gruner (1982) has indicated that, from early to late age, 'the true Swiss is ready and willing to work, rising early and working late' as if for the joy of it. During interviews with school officials, the same theme was repeated again and again, that Switzerland has no real resources, except for its people. People are valuable to society only to the degree that they are competent, trained and eager to do their best work.

Finally, each child is taught to rely only on himself, or herself, thus providing a lifelong general commitment to economic self-reliance, postponed gratification and conserving one's assets for one's own self-protection. Swiss citizens have one of the highest rates in the world of savings in banks, and one of the highest rates of voluntary health and other insurance, with almost 95% coverage.

Closely tied to the values taught to Swiss children at home and in school is the norm of reciprocity. This essentially states that, in any

society, there is 'no free lunch'. It means that people cannot get 'something for nothing', and that if anyone secures something without effort, someone else must have made the effort for him, whether he wanted to or not.

Thus, Swiss children are taught at home and in school that if they are to expect goods and services, they must, in turn, do their work well (which is learning), as well as to carry out the chores assigned to them. Children soon learn that such a *quid pro quo* arrangement amounts to an ethic of not relying on others to do your share of the work. This ethic is reinforced in school, in the community, on the job in the workplace and in the Swiss Army, which embraces all adult able-bodied males.

Because almost all children are adequately socialised for school, and because the Swiss schools are generally effective, its products are not only academically competent, but also fully imbued with the values described above. The Swiss is a self-reliant, work-addicted, proud member of his community, with a secure place in a society which Clinard (1978) observes 'has never had the marked disparities in distribution of wealth that characterises many other European countries. The position of the Swiss worker today is generally more favourable than that of workers in most other countries.' Such an individual could hardly become chronically dependent upon public aid.

EMPLOYMENT AS A CONSTRAINT ON WELFARISATION

More than in most other societies, what an individual does for a living defines him as a person in the Swiss setting. However it is not merely what he does, but how well he does it, that determines the degree of respect he earns from his neighbours and community.

We have already described the importance given to career preparation, vocational training and professional education in Swiss society. Because work is so highly valued people usually seek to perform well at work. Despite the high level of employment, the loss of a valued job can have a devastating effect on a person. The turnover rate for employment is relatively low, and many employees tend to remain in the same job with one firm until retirement. More than in many other countries, the Swiss worker gains social, as well as economic, benefits from his job. Thus, the employment setting serves to keep people from public dependency, not only in a direct sense, but also

in terms of influencing their behaviour and performance both at work and away from work.

MILITARY SERVICE AS A WELFARISATION CONSTRAINT

As mentioned above, all adult males in Switzerland are subject to compulsory military service until the age of 55. Every able-bodied young adult is required to spend some months in basic training, followed by annual service in a unit near his home. Employers are required to fund the wages of employees while on military duty, and many companies are glad to do so because military contacts are often helpful and good for business.

If the norms and values of Swiss society and the loyalties of the locality were not fully absorbed by young Swiss males, military service with a local unit will usually complete the process. Each soldier in the Swiss Army is required to operate with a group and is also called upon to do his share within the group and on individual assignments. Thus, Swiss Army experience serves to reinforce those qualities which prevent and operate counter to the welfarisation process. An individual who 'goofs off' at the expense of his unit has to cope with criticism not only during the annual encampment, but in his rifle club where he is required to maintain his shooting record along with other men who know him.

Thus, to request welfare without adequate reason, or to fail to support his wife (or ex-wife) and children, would serve to stigmatise a man in his community. Because a person's reputation in the community is critically important to most Swiss men, it is carefully guarded in terms of appropriate behaviour in the community. Such behaviour is not conducive to welfare dependency.

4 The Extent of Welfare Dependency in Switzerland

We have described the formal and informal constraints on the welfarisation process in Switzerland. Are these constraints effective in limiting welfare dependency? It is important to note that welfare experience over decades indicates that the optimum outcome is achieved by making welfare available adequately for those unable to help themselves, while also controlling it carefully to avoid interference with the labour market.

To constrain welfare too much by formal and informal methods may create hardship for people who have no alternative but to seek it; to make it too freely available, with too few controls, will lead to its spread in the population and over time. This is likely to create problems in the employment market, and other unhappy effects in terms of inflation, immigration and a variety of social ills.

What about the Swiss experience in this regard? Have they been too harsh or too permissive? An examination of the estimated dependency caseload may help to answer the question.

In our search for transgenerational dependency, we sought evidence of dependent welfare in each of the public agencies in the four major localities and one smaller industrial town. In each of these cities and towns, we learned that a major part of the welfare load is made up of what would be described in the United States as the 'medically needy'.

These are people who have insufficient income, either from current earnings or from assets, such as earned social insurance benefits, to be able to meet their basic needs. They include many aged, handicapped, and infirm people. Because there is 95 per cent medical insurance coverage in Switzerland, and because there are some duplications of medical insurance, conservative estimates of those adequately covered for medical care ranges from 78 to 90 per cent. The remainder are provided with medical coverage and reimbursed medical care as needed by their local public welfare agencies. This makes up a sizable amount of the work of the Swiss public welfare agencies, ranging from 20 to 30 per cent of the caseload.

Because there is no central agency to collect information on caseloads, statistics are only available for each locality, and there is no generally uniform statistical format employed in each of the agencies. Thus, we were forced to supplement whatever data was available with estimates gathered from social workers and public welfare officials.

We did not gather data on the temporary caseload, which was made up primarily of people who had used up their unemployment compensation or whose unemployment compensation was less than sufficient to meet immediate survival needs. This group also contained a high proportion who were employed on a part-time basis. In almost all of these cases, the families were intact and were seriously searching for additional employment. Most of the unemployed or partially employed were in areas of industrial recession and were discussing with their social worker possible occupational retraining programmes or moving their families to areas where appropriate employment was becoming available. Many of these families were on the rolls only for continuation of payment of their interim medical insurance and were otherwise self-sufficient.

In all of the agencies visited, we learned that there was a small part of their caseload (aside from the temporary clients, aged, and handicapped, or medically needy), amounting to about 5 to 10 per cent, who represented dependent cases of long duration. These were described in terms which would normally be characterised as multi-problem families.

In each instance, there were such factors as inadequate employment conditioning or training, psychiatric disturbance, a disorganised family life, disorganised handling of family funds, anti-social or incompetent role models for the children, divorced parents, parental neglect of children, distancing of the individuals from their extended families, excessive gambling and so on.

In our analysis of these cases, it appeared that their number was few in proportion to the total welfare load, and that measures were being taken by the public welfare agency either to resolve the dependency in the present generation or to prevent it in the next. We noted that great care was being taken to ensure that children in such multi-problem families were being carefully observed and protected from the destructive life patterns of their parents. In some instances we noted that aid for such families was being maintained only as long as the parents accepted supervision and guidance in relation to their child-rearing patterns. In other instances, we noted

that *Beistand* (guardianship or supervision) actions were taken in co-operation with the *Jugendamt* (youth authority) to ensure that parental responsibilities were fulfilled. In still other instances, children were placed in special homes and institutions, where reportedly more than a majority succeeded in maturing into responsible productive citizens.

In discussions of this portion of the public welfare caseload in the agencies we visited, we learned that the use of placement of children in institutions is very much on the decrease. Instead, families with children are currently being given a combination of aid, advice and supervision to ensure that the children are appropriately reared to fit into an employed, self-sufficient population.

In attempting further to identify transgenerational poverty, we sought out the representatives of the *ATD-Vierte Welt* and interviewed the author of a book on poverty in Switzerland (Meyer, 1974). ATD-Vierte Welt representatives estimate that 3 to 5 per cent of the entire Swiss population are transgenerationally dependent. They believe that as unemployment rises, more people fall into structurally-caused poverty and remain there because of an inability to rise from the aided population level.

We questioned this because, at most, the Swiss unemployment rate is not over 3 per cent, and this includes many of the partially unemployed population.

Many of the unemployed are individuals in a family where one or more persons are employed. Thus, it is hard to believe that few of the unemployed ever become self-sufficient again. We learned that the ATD-Vierte Welt organisation had contact with some 2500 Swiss families whom they have hosted in their country-farm vacation programme over the past 15 years. They believe that these families are continually in need.

Both partners in most of these families, they believe, were themselves brought up in poor families. In each of these families at least one of the partners has been or is under *Vormundschaft* (legal supervision), after a period of alcoholism or psychiatric care. Many of the children in these families have been placed in children's institutions or foster homes, usually against the wishes of the parents, but based on their reported inability to provide an appropriate rearing of the children. The parents are said to be unable to find adequately remunerative employment and unable to help their children to use the school and apprenticeship system adequately to become self-

sufficient when they reach adulthood. Many of these families have more children than they know how to deal with.

The ability of these families to deal with the realities of everyday life is at best marginal. Some are ex-offenders of the criminal system. They find it impossible to avoid recurring problems or to learn from previous difficulties. They have constant problems of relating to community institutions. Their relations generally are in turmoil. All have problems of *Ruf* (reputation), which makes employment, housing and so on difficult. From the perceptions of these clients, the community and its institutions seemed threatening. Many are the victims or causes of accumulated unpaid debts and instalment payments for items purchased and no longer used.

AN UNDERCLASS?

The Vierte Welt portrayal of these problem families fits the description of *The Welfare Mother* described by Sheehan (1976) and many of *The Underclass* described by Auletta (1982) in the American welfare scene.

Although claims of a larger recurring dependent population were made by the ATD Vierte Welt representatives, it became apparent that in the listing of 2500 families found over 15 years this might be a fair estimate of the number of such families in all of Switzerland. In interviews with the major public welfare agencies, it became clear that no more than at most 3000 to 4000 families in Switzerland are intergenerational multi-problem families.

These multi-problem families can, we believe, be properly designated as 'individual poverty', rather than 'welfare dependent', in the terms of Strang's typology (1970, 1984). Our reason for this conclusion is that there has been little politicisation of the welfare issue in Switzerland, a condition which exists in most of the countries where the welfare clientele and the welfare administration have become symbiotically perpetuative. Similarly, we observed almost no 'bending' of Swiss welfare policies or administrative procedures, but rather a constant and firm adherence to the welfare agency goals of client self-sufficiency.

In a population of approximately 6 500 000, a residual welfare dependency figure of even 4000 represents only 0.06 per cent (less than one-tenth of one per cent). This compares very favourably with the estimates for most other nations.

IS THE SWISS EXAMPLE STABLE?

Our conclusion is that in Switzerland residual public dependency is limited and not welfare-interactive. We have also concluded that this desirable condition prevails because of a combination of interacting factors involving almost full employment, a stable social structure, local responsibility for welfare, a robust and carefully shaped social insurance system, responsible labour and management co-operation, controlled immigration, effective education and apprenticeship programmes, effective youth-serving programmes, effective follow-up of paternal support, welfare policies and cultural reinforcement. We now need to examine the probability that these favourable conditions will continue in the future.

There are a number of strengths in the Swiss situation which portend well for the future in the constraint of prolonged dependency. The continued work interest of the population, as evidenced by the population's work-week referendum and the indication found by Ruth Gurny and associates (1983), that Swiss youth intend to work rather than be maintained by others, lends support to optimism. Recent unrest among young people, as evidenced in 1980, need cause little concern for welfare dependency since these actions were, in general, remarkably responsible when compared with the youth unrest experienced in other countries. Evidence of the responsibility of youth, even in periods of unrest, is provided by the fact that most of them had weapons available to them, but these were not brought into play at all. Events in Britain in 1981 and more recently were far more violent. The levelling off of the divorce rate, the rising age of the newly married, and the current rising rate of marriage all serve to reassure one of the continued restraint of prolonged dependency.

5 Negative Factors

There are a number of other factors, however, which may serve to weaken Switzerland's prevention of prolonged dependency. These include the loosening of family controls as exhibited by the growth of 'coupling' (couples living together without marriage), and the loosening of community involvement of young adults as evidenced by the low rate of voters exercising their franchises in recent elections. The problem of 'coupling' is, of course, offset by the high rate of marriage in this group soon after pregnancy. The problem of apathy among young Swiss voters has been reported to be shrinking as issues of concern to youth have appeared in the elections.

ALCOHOL AND DRUG ABUSE

Of particular concern in relation to the possible growth of chronic dependency are the factors of alcohol and drug abuse. Alcoholism has long been a problem in Switzerland, and it is probably explicable in the light of Swiss social control. For decades, each of the cantons has expended efforts relating to this problem. A special voluntary agency was established to promote non-alcoholic beverages and to educate the public about the dangers of alcohol. The special drug subcommission of the federal government estimates that about 10.5 litres are consumed annually per resident (somewhat over two gallons). This indicates that Switzerland is about tenth in Europe in the overall consumption of alcohol. It is largely concentrated in the male population. The *Swiss Almanac* of the Zurich Sociological Institute indicates that about 26 per cent of the population were heavy drinkers, with the highest consumption between the ages of 25 and 54 years. The alcohol problem was found to surpass the drug abuse problem. The Institute did find that many of the heavy abusers of alcohol and drugs at the age of 19 learn to abstain or to become light- or middle-range consumers of alcohol by the age of 22. Only 26 per cent of the heavy users of alcohol remain heavy users by the age of 22. Similarly, only 23 per cent of the drug abusers remain abusers by that age. It is estimated by Reist and Wagner (1982) that between 130 000 to 140 000 people are serious alcoholics in Switzerland. This is about 2 per cent of the population.

Clinard (1978) reports that 82.2 per cent of the drug cases involved males under the age of 25. He views drug use as a form of protest by some Swiss youth against the more conservative society, much in the same way that some youth will use unusual or bizarre hair and dress stytles to indicate their differences with their elders.

Trimborn (1982) reported that 107 drug-related deaths occurred in Switzerland in 1981, which represents about 1.7 such deaths per 100 000 people. In the United States, the rate is closer to four per 100 000 people. Reist and Wagner's report estimates 13 000 to 15 000 drug abusers in Switzerland. Clinard (1978) believes that 'although these figures may alarm the Swiss, they show far less drug use than in the United States and many other countries.'

For example, in a sample of over 4000 Swiss Army recruits at the age of 22, 77 per cent in 1975 were found never to have used drugs. Follow-up studies on these young men during military service showed little change in the abstinence rate. Victor Reidi of the Berne Youth Authority also believes that drug abuse among a sector of Swiss youth is a form of protest against Swiss conformity and performance requirements. Those who succeed in meeting the society's requirements and standards are less likely to become abusers. In a society such as the United States, non-conformity and inadequate competency would be more easily tolerated. For example, chronic drug and alcohol abusers who are young adults, and who are, thereby considered 'totally disabled', receive a monthly grant in the Supplementary Security Income Program in the United States (in California, the grant is $440.00 per month, tax free, plus medical care). It is as if, in the United States, society, the state, and the federal government had legitimated drug abuse. Reidi views the Swiss situation as more demanding of youth. 'I think there is no country in the world with more rules, more intolerance [of deviance]. Everybody in Bern is a village policeman and in Zurich it is even worse' (or, in some important respects at least, better).

Clinard indicates that the pattern of Swiss drug use rationale by youth is different from that in other societies. In other countries, drug use by youth is often tied to crime, including violent offences. The drug addict will steal, rob or assault others in order to satisfy his habit. Much of the American drug culture is also tied to crime and delinquency. Swiss youth, according to Clinard, use drugs primarily as protest; they will 'generally not steal the property of another as this would harm someone, [but] they believe that their use of drugs is a personal decision.' Thus, the Swiss drug problem is less tied to

the drug use patterns experienced elsewhere in the world, where the drug addict has few or no internalised social controls.

However, alcohol and drug abuse problems in Switzerland, while relatively light in comparison with other western nations, are still a serious concern to Swiss policymakers. Although Swiss external controls are probably more effective in detecting and reaching users, and in seeking treatment and rehabilitation for those affected, the problem is growing. The Swiss drug problem is compounded by contagion by visitors and cultures from other lands where drug abuse is more common.

Thus, Swiss youth who have difficulty in conforming to Swiss standards of behaviour and competence are more likely, as time goes on, to learn about the drug culture of young people in other lands, and may see this alternative life pattern as an attractive way of escaping daily pressures. However, as long as Swiss families hold together, as long as Swiss schooling continues to influence youth, as long as the community concerns itself with social problems, and as long as apprenticeships are completed and jobs are secured, it is likely that the vast majority of Swiss youth will continue to conform and perform in the society. The same factors which tend to prevent welfarisation also tend to constrain the alcohol and drug problems.

DIVORCE AND SEPARATION AS COUNTER FACTORS

Yet another potentially negative factor is found in the divorce rate. Divorce often leaves children with only one active parent, and no matter how competent that parent may be, one is usually not enough. This is especially a problem if the custodial parent does not have an adult support group with whom the child and parent can interact (such as the extended family), and if the custodial parent is entirely dependent upon welfare aid. This kind of dependency often locks the parent and child out of adequate contact with others in the social mainstream, and thus provides the children with an incomplete role model.

Where the single parent is employed, the problem is aggravated further because the children are deprived of consistently available parenting in the home, and their role models are often drawn from less than mature leaders in their peer groups. In either instance, although quality day-care facilities do help, there are dangers in terms of inadequate and incomplete socialisation evident in the rearing of

children in single-parent families. This, in turn, places such children
at risk of encountering problems and becoming dependent during
adulthood.

The Swiss have both a low marriage rate and a low divorce rate as
compared to other nations. In 1980 and 1981, that rate was 5.6
marriages for every 1000 population. The rate for those same years
in the United States was 10.6 per per 1000 population. Swiss divorces
in 1981 amounted to a total of 11 131, which calculates at fewer than
1.7 divorces per 1000 population. This compares favourably with the
American divorce rate for 1980 of 5.2 divorces per 1000, the Swiss
rate being one-third of the American rate. In 1981 there were 311
Swiss divorces per 1000 marriages compared to the American figure
of 490 divorces for every 1000 marriages. It may be that the low rate
of marriages is due to the greater care and preparation required for
a Swiss marriage. In Switzerland, more than in other western
countries, marriage is a matter not only for the young couple, but
also for agreement or approval by the two extended families.
Similarly, Swiss young people are less apt to get married before the
groom, at least, is well established economically. Delayed marriage
is also a positive factor in restraining the divorce rate, since the
people involved are more mature.

What worries the Swiss is that from a total of 4977 divorces in
1965, the number of divorces rose to 11 131 in 1981. These divorces
affect almost two children each (1.8 per divorce). However, the
number of children living in one-parent homes or step-homes in
Switzerland is quite small, namely 20 036 in a population of 6½ million
(3 per 1000), as compared to the American figure of approximately
one in every three children in the United States (100 times the Swiss
rate). It is, nevertheless, a matter of serious concern to the Swiss.

AN OVERVIEW OF THE NEGATIVE FACTORS

An overview of the negative factors we have examined indicates that
neither alcohol and drug addiction, nor divorce and separation are
of sufficient gravity to lead to increased welfarisation of the population. In general it appears that the Swiss experience in relation to
welfarisation can be accepted as a positive exception to experiences
in other developed nations, particularly the welfare states.

Observation of other social ills also indicates lower levels in
Switzerland than in other western nations. With low inflation, low

unemployment, low crime levels, comparatively lower drug and divorce rates, lower school failures, lower unemployability, and lower rates of illegitimacy, it can be concluded that the volume of Swiss social problems is much lower than in other western nations, and yet it provides well for its entire population without the economic debilitation of the welfare state.

Part III
What are the Lessons?

1 Is Switzerland a Special Case?

We have demonstrated that Switzerland has avoided many of the problems of the welfare state. Is that because Switzerland is a special case, a fortunate accident, a small exception? Hardly so, when one considers that Switzerland is as large as, or larger than, many other European nations, including many welfare states, such as Holland, Belgium, and Norway, where welfarisation and its related social ills have become a serious problem.

Another argument might relate to Swiss culture, indicating that Switzerland is so imbued with the religiously-oriented Protestant ethic as to repress welfare dependency. However, one can point to other countries with similar or even stronger Calvinist influences, which have failed the welfarisation and dependency test, among them the Netherlands, Norway and Sweden.

Still another explanation for Switzerland as a special exception might be founded in its historical development. This argument would hold that Switzerland has not yet caught up with the 'ills' of the rest of the industrial world, and that, in time, the Swiss can be counted on to drop their inhibitions against dependency and pride in self-reliance. This argument can be countered by the fact that, apart from some restrained youth protest and some sign of increased 'coupling', there is little other serious evidence of social disorganisation.

The social institutions of Switzerland are intact. There are almost no slums. The social structure is stable. The family is still important. Open adultery is unknown, whereas in many other countries it is condoned. The Swiss work hard, and their children live lives firmly directed toward the goals of self-sufficiency and social responsibility. From these indices, it would be difficult to predict a breakdown of Swiss society, such as is already in evidence in many other countries.

A final argument against accepting the Swiss example relates to Switzerland's alleged homogeneity. The claim is made that Switzerland is composed of a homogeneous population, unlike other nations plagued by welfarisation problems. But is Switzerland really homogeneous? With four different languages, with two major religions, and many schisms appearing within them, with a multiplicity of political parties, and opinions at least equalling the variability

99

existing in many other nations? The answer must be in the negative.

We are forced, therefore, to accept an alternative explanation – namely that Switzerland presents us with an unusual set of welfare policies, reinforced by an effective pattern of schooling, employment and local governmental structures, supported by an involved and concerned population. These add up to an effective instrument for prevention and management of welfare dependency and its associated ills.

2 What Really Makes Switzerland Different?

What does Switzerland have that makes it immune to the problems of the welfare state which we have described in Part I of this book? We have chosen to focus on welfare dependency as one key problem, but careful analysis suggests that welfarisation is only one of a whole complex of inter-related social problems which Switzerland apparently has avoided. It is as if all the Swiss had got together and agreed to do everything possible to make their members maximally productive.

What are the norms, values and methods by which Switzerland has achieved this success? First we should note that Switzerland's constitution was modelled after that of the USA as it was originally. Thus Switzerland is a confederation of states, as was the USA at first. When difficulties between the autonomous states arose, the Americans chose to revise their country into a central Federalist model. In America, the federal government limits the legal and taxing rights of the states. Hardly anything of importance is undertaken by the states or localities unless they have the approval and support of the federal government. Power has shifted to the central government on almost every conceivable issue. The same centralised power model exists in almost every other western nation, including Britain, France and Scandinavia.

The result is that local and state government has less status and power and fewer able people are drawn to these levels of government to make them effective. On the other hand, attempts at influencing central government by local people are very difficult. Regional and local government policies are, to a great extent, results of centralised decision-making. By and large, except for periods of crisis, most communities do not try to solve their own problems, and could not do so if they tried, except by appeals to the central government. In many of the larger cities an aura of apathy prevails. Even where a city or town operates an effective government, it is often because its leaders have influence in the capital.

The general picture in the western nations is one of huge social, fiscal and governmental problems, problems which cannot be resolved by the participation of its local citizens, and eventually become unmanageable, even with the involvement of the best minds and

leaders. A general apathy pervades most local and regional capitals.

ACTIVE LOCALISM

The Swiss scene is very different. Recognition of problems is first made at local level. If the problem cannot be resolved at a strictly local level, then representatives of other nearby localities who may be affected by the same problem are consulted. Most area problems are resolved by inter-communal compacts.

A group of towns in the Swiss hinterland, for example, considered the problem of how to develop a multi-service centre to deal with multi-problem families. The costs could not be borne by one community alone, but by the writing of an inter-communal compact the multi-service agency became the responsibility of the four communities together.

In general, the atmosphere in Swiss towns seems very different from the towns of other countries. Swiss people seem proud of their towns and almost all the citizenry are involved in their operations.

LOCAL LEADERSHIP

In many other western nations, there is often a sense of distrust of the local leader, as if he represents the lowest level of goodwill for the unfortunate; as if his only interest is in tax savings or in political one-upmanship, and as if he were the least informed among those involved in social planning. In Switzerland by contrast, the best informed people are elected to local government, and it is usually the least corrupt and most concerned who become the local leaders.

Again, the pathway to local leadership is comparatively open in the Swiss community. Because everyone is watching everyone on the local scene, and because accounts are legally open, there is very little fraud. In an interview with Professor Hans Tschudi, former president of Switzerland, we learned that he had got his start in Swiss politics by working as a commissioner in the Basle Town community on their Buildings and Works Programme. *In over 20 years of service on this commission, not one instance of fraud was reported.*

Apparently, only at the local level is it possible for everyone to know each other. It is also possible at this level to ask relevant questions and to receive clear answers. It is possible at the local level

to understand the issues and the people affected. And, at the local level, the citizen either gets involved in the issues or, if he does not, he has to suffer with the results of someone else's activity.

LEGAL POWERS

Another basic difference between Switzerland and other western nations relates to the power of the federal legislature and the federal courts. On the Swiss scene, the federal courts have never entered into the question of the validity or invalidity of legislative or executive actions. The Swiss federal courts serve only as a final arbiter in individual conflicts, but do not enter into the creation of law by class action decisions. That, the Swiss believe, is the job of the legislatures and, in the last analysis, it is up to the voters either by referendum or initiative.

The Swiss federal court does not permeate into the localities and courts. Thus, a community or canton may act in accordance with the will of its voters, and as long as it does not interfere with other communes or cantons, it may continue this policy despite the fact that its actions do not parallel those of other communities and cantons.

Local autonomy is based on local financing and on local responsibility. Swiss legislation always has a central test question asked before it is submitted to the voters for approval. *Does this law grant rights for something without holding the beneficiary responsible for his actions? Does this law hold someone responsible for some act or behaviour without matching that responsibility with its related rights?*

The Swiss, by long experience, have learned that to grant rights without responsibility or to require responsibility without commensurate rights will only end with unanticipated, distorted and counterproductive consequences in the behaviour of the affected persons.

RIGHTS AND RESPONSIBILITIES

Thus, the grant of public welfare requires certain responses on the part of the client which will limit the extent and duration of public aid benefits. For each of the rights or benefits granted, there is an established *quid pro quo* to be performed.

Moreover Swiss elected officials at all levels of government are

closely attuned to the complex of Swiss ethics, involving honesty, self-reliance, hard work, the norm of reciprocity, local control and family responsibility. No law or regulation is passed which may, in any way, operate counter to the above ethics, except in the instance of the aged or sick who cannot, for the present, fend for themselves.

Even in these instances, the government seeks to use private programmes of aid if possible, and great care is exerted to prevent federal or cantonal intrusions into local affairs. For example, the problem of 'concubinage' (persons living together without marriage) was seriously considered by all levels of government because it poses a possible threat to family life and adequate child socialisation. But, after much discussion, it was left to the cantons to act, and in seven cantons, the practice is still illegal.

The Swiss have learned that culture can operate counter to the law, in which case the law becomes vacuous, or the ethic is weakened. Culture can also operate to support the law, in which case the law is strengthened and the society remains stable. This latter is apparently the fortunate condition of Switzerland. Had the Swiss society passed laws which operated counter to the prevalent ethic, counter-productive social change might well have occurred, and Switzerland would today be faced with many problems which are common elsewhere.

ORGANISING WELFARE

In making a comparison between the Swiss model of social control and social welfare and the welfare state models of other nations, a number of hypotheses can be offered. The larger the system or programme of social welfare or social control, the greater the disparity between the intended purpose of the programme and the actual effect; the more likely it is that some people for whom benefits were intended will not be included; the more likely it is that some people will be accepted for whom benefits were not intended; the more likely it is that the system will be impersonally operated, in terms of the perception of the clientele, as well as intrinsically; the more inflexibly will the system be operated and the more unresponsive the system will be to the clientele; the less concerned the disbursers of resources will be about the scarcity of funds; the more likely it is that errors will occur; and the greater will be the operational cost per unit. Only in large-scale systems will the administration be required to adhere to a mindless equality among clients when differential treatment may actually be appropriate.

AVOIDING BUREAUCRACY

It may well be that industrial methods of operation are efficient in the production and distribution of mechanical objects, but the experience of the welfare states suggests that this is not the case where welfare or other human behavioural factors are involved. Probably a highly centralised social insurance system is also efficacious if adjudication and distribution can be related to objective unalterable processes. In the matter, however, of issues relating to human behaviour and socio-cultural values, it is only in the small unit of local government that such human questions can be resolved in a consistently humane manner.

DANGERS OF OPPRESSION

The centralised welfare state also presents 'dystopian' dangers, which most people have not considered. As the mechanisms of the welfare-cum-rights-without-responsibility state proceed to promote permissive behaviour without adequate childhood socialisation, increasing concern for high levels of crime and other social pathologies may raise a clamour for improved social control. This, in turn, can lead the way towards highly centralised government and the danger of dictatorship.

We are beginning to see elements of this in the obtrusive investigations of child abuse, child neglect and child incest, under which children have been removed from their homes without court action or recourse, with parental control of children nullified. Cornish for example (1986) discusses licences for parenting! He justifies this proposal by citing studies which have proved that children from homes with strong and supportive parents learn even in a 'bad' school with poor teachers. He notes the great damage done to many children by ineffective parents. He, therefore, presses for parent training and licensing. If a license is needed for driving a car, why not limit the unrestricted freedom to have a child to 'appropriate' parents? He argues that there is already growing central government authority to trace missing fathers and hold them for support and to hold parents responsible for their children's babies. There is already government authority to hold parents responsible for their children's behaviour. It is only rarely enforced, but under Cornish's proposal, this would be more stringently applied. By the use of computerised control it could operate across the whole country. One can reasonably expect

then that unless the informal social control of the functional local community can be re-established 'big brother' government is likely to become even more powerful and dangerous.

GEMEINSCHAFT AND GESELLSCHAFT

In order to understand why the Swiss system works, it is essential to examine the differences between the 'objective industrial community' and the 'empathic local community'.

Ferdinand Tönnies (1963) was the first to make the distinction between the commercial community and the organic community. The *Gemeinschaft* community is one in which relationships are intimate, traditional, and informal – a 'folk' society. The *Gesellschaft* society refers to relationships which are contractual, impersonal, voluntary and limited. *Gemeinschaft* relationships represent the 'glue' in our society which hold us together. *Gesellschaft* relationships represent the business processes governed primarily by the economic market.

For a parent to rear a child, *Gemeinschaft* relationships are required. In order to build a factory, *Gesellschaft* relationships are required. If one allows *Gemeinschaft* relationships to shape one's decisions in an industrial programme, one can look forward to bankruptcy. If one seeks to deal with one's close friends strictly on the basis of *Gesellschaft* relationships, one would soon be friendless.

Helping a person to become self-sufficient from a state of dependency requires a kind of relationship which involves a combination of the caring of the *Gemeinschaft* and the businesslike rules of the *Gesellschaft*. Using the rules alone will not work, nor can 'caring' alone be effective. The problem with the welfare state is that it has sought to use only *Gesellschaft* methods, with a purported claim of 'caring' for the clientele in an impersonal, socially distant, rule-ridden relationship.

It is hardly likely that a huge national, centrally organised or centrally controlled welfare system can provide the individualised mix of *Gemeinschaft* and *Gesellschaft* relationship needed by the welfarised clientele or by the unsocialised or deviantly socialised children of the welfarised family. It is equally unlikely that a centralised, nationalised programme, can relate itself to helping with the creation of families, to helping to preserve families, or to helping families accept the disciplines and constraints necessary for their own rehabilitation and for the rearing of their children.

3 The Autonomous Local Community

Only in the autonomous local community can individual rehabilitation goals be addressed; can necessary exceptions be made with specific clients without creating national precedents; can welfare services be arranged providing for local conditions without, at the same time, affecting the rules by which other clients are served in other locations; can a welfare programme be carried out according to the cultural and value patterns of the community – the same cultural and value patterns which the client will have to adhere to after he has attained self-sufficiency. Only in the autonomous local community can a welfare programme be designed which can provide for a prompt appeal mechanism without bureaucratic impediments to resolution of disagreements; can voluntary welfare programmes be integrated with public welfare programmes for rehabilitation; can the total information and resources of the client and community be quickly known and used effectively for rehabilitation; can help be rendered to a citizen by his concerned peers, rather than by some impersonal agency.

In the autonomous local community, it is hardly likely that a person would get lost in the system – as long as the local unit is small enough for *Gemeinschaft* to prevail. Only in the autonomous local community can social work professionals be made responsible for their decisions and accountable to local officials and neighbours. In such a setting, professionals are more likely to be concerned with speedy rehabilitation and client self-sufficiency. Only in a local autonomous community, which carries full responsibility for its citizenry and which has to raise its own money by local taxes, will funds be spent in a manner which is accountable to local taxpayers.

In centralised welfare programmes the community dollar is worth less than 80 cents after it has made the trip to the capital and back. In the autonomous local community this dollar would be worth the entire 100 cents, and even more when one considers the contributions of local volunteers.

Only in the autonomous local community can the norm of reciprocity be enforced under which citizens are expected to serve others as they themselves expect to be served. Only in the autonomous local

community can each citizen be called on to do his share of the community's work, and each citizen in turn can receive the benefits of a welfare programme which does not contribute to social unrest. The *Gesellschaft* has *never* been able to deal adequately with issues of personal relationship. Only if we retain the *Gemeinschaft* in our home communities can we retain an atmosphere of economic freedom along with communal and personal responsibility and control.

The complexity of life brought on by the industrial revolution and the new technological revolution make it difficult for us to be concurrently businesslike and humane. It seems increasingly likely that the only alternative to either an inhumane world where we are all subject to an impersonal 'big brother' government managed by universal fear, or an anarchic jungle in which no one is safe, is the development of a society of small, autonomous, and self-reliant communities. Until such an association of autonomous communities and regions can be achieved, we might at least grasp some of the cues offered to us by the Swiss.

4 What the Swiss Have Taught Us

The Swiss have taught us the importance of altruism as a locally effective motivation for good citizenship. We have always known that altruism is related to love, but not too clearly. We know that love for others begins with self-love, in the baby for himself, and, in time, for his parents, his siblings, his playmates, his classmates, and others known to him (or her). Empathy for others is seldom found unless there is human interaction. It expands from self to family, to neighbours, to fellow citizens in one's small community, and, finally, to one's region, to the people in one's nation, and then to other unmet humans.

The force of this concept is brought upon us when disaster strikes a community or region. Only then do many people come forward with help. Often, many of these people have held themselves apart from mutual aid, but when there is a demonstration of a 'common fate' they come forward and provide generous offerings. By tying each citizen to a home community and by keeping these communities small, the average Swiss has achieved a close, direct tie to others. Only when the nation is at war or threatened by external problems are all citizens involved and roused to concern. But, at the local level, such immediate altruism, the attitudes of Swiss citizens to their fellows in need, is similar to one's feelings towards one's siblings – a desire to be realistically helpful and generous, without irresponsibly promoting dependency through licence.

The Swiss have also helped to demonstrate that social problems begin when authority and responsibility are relinquished to central authorities. The Swiss have rejected the theory prevalent in other western nations that the welfare client is always the victim of the system; that in the matter of crime, the culprit is merely a victim of the system; that the user is a helpless victim of the drug supply system; that in workers' compensation cases the employees are always the victims and never responsible themselves for industrial accidents; that in divorce and family break-up, there is anything such as mutual-'no-fault'; or that in relation to social behaviour the deviant is never at fault.

The Swiss seek to examine each individual case, and endeavour

not only to help the helpless, but to prevent recurrence by identifying the causes of the problem.

Another lesson of the Swiss experience is that widespread interventionism in social and human services by central government is not necessary in order to resolve and prevent social problems. Instead the proposal of the Bergers (1984, p. 210) for restoration of family autonomy and responsibility as much as possible, as soon as possible, is already firm policy in Switzerland.

A further lesson to be learned from Switzerland is that problems can be resolved only by directly facing them where they occur. The different outcomes in Switzerland compared with the welfare states demonstrate that problems cannot be solved by simply re-defining them. Re-definition of problems, as an alternative to facing up to them, has occurred for example in relation to unmarried motherhood, which has been re-defined as the father-free family. Alcoholism has been re-defined entirely as a disease, rather than as a problem caused by individual behaviour. Aberrant sex has been re-defined as acceptable and even normal behaviour. The need for welfare has been re-defined as mere lack of money, rather than as a condition which needs positive attention. At times indeed even crime has been re-defined as a psychiatric condition, rather than the consequence of individual choice and inadequate socialisation which it is.

The Swiss, by contrast, have shown that these and other problems *can* be controlled effectively – but only by facing them, and holding the basic institutions responsible for teaching socially appropriate and acceptable behaviour. *Constant re-definition of social problems is nothing more than avoidance behaviour, and can do nothing to solve them.*

Moreover, the Swiss experience has demonstrated that it is only at the local level that citizens and decision makers alike can view problems from what DuWors (1952) describes as 'the principle of first definitions'. Only at the local level is it possible for people to arrive at congruent and common definitions of recurring life situations. Poverty, crime, drug addiction, familial dissolution, and other crucial problems can be examined for cause only at the level where common definitions are achievable, and only then is it possible to arrive at effective solutions.

Another important lesson that can be learned from the Swiss is that no one social problem — welfare, unemployment, school dropout, crime, drugs and so on, can be resolved separately. Each of these problems must be attacked in combination at the local level,

so that provisions can be individualised and local citizenry involved. Other nations which seek to resolve these problems as effectively as the Swiss can start by returning to local communities their right to tax their citizens and to authorise communities and regions to attack all these problems without national interference.

In the case of problem communities with insufficient resources, some modest mechanism can easily be devised for regional and inter-community support.

The first priority for community work should be prevention of further dependency by training parents and teachers to work toward maximum academic and/or work-ready education. In the emergency period, with thousands of unemployable youth, a plan would need to be devised in each community to prepare youth for employability, with finances for a time provided by the national government. Unearned welfare grants and dole payments, and even unearned social insurances, should be phased out over a period of time, with the goal of eventually returning welfare responsibilities, and authority to local communities.

All in all, what can we learn from the Swiss? Fundamentally this: that human programmes do not function without incentives, and that incentives differ with people and places. The best place (perhaps the only place) where human programmes can be fully effective is in the local community, where people care about each other, where they depend upon each other to keep the peace and to promote each other's well-being, and where children can be brought up to consider their neighbours and to be considered by them.

What the welfare states should learn from their own experiences is that national and central government cannot solve social problems. It is no more able to solve the problems of individuals than are parents able to solve the problems of grown children who live away from home. Parents of grown children know only too well that, even when it is asked for, their help often ends disastrously. Similarly, national government, no matter how well-intentioned, cannot provide the socialisation that only a father and mother can deliver.

Central government everywhere should learn at least that part of the Hippocratic Oath which says '*Above all, do no harm*'. The welfare state and its policies are doing grave harm by making the fathers of many families obsolete and by distorting or destroying the socialisation of children. We should put a stop to this immediately. In *Rebuilding America*, Alperovitz and Faux show conclusively that a large and disparate nation cannot plan centrally without doing serious harm

regionally and locally. This is a lesson the welfare state nations should take to heart, as they look perhaps to Switzerland for an alternative approach.

Part IV
Towards Reform of British and American Social Policy

Part IV

Towards Reform of British and American Social Policy

1 Welfare State Societies in Decay

Britain and the United States share many fundamental characteristics which serve in combination to distinguish them even from other free societies:

Both countries are stable democracies. Established political institutions are positively supported by the mass of their populations. Anti-democratic forces have little scope for success, and – even in times of severe economic recession – find negligible popular support.

In both countries the independent institutions of the law occupy a central position within the social structure and the established social value system. They operate effectively and equitably, for the most part, in the maintenance of social freedom and public order.

In both countries the institution of private property is securely established, and access to income and wealth is broadly distributed.

In both countries the other key institutions of capitalism are equally well established and broadly supported. These include in particular the competitive pursuit of profit, a free labour market, and restraints on interference with free enterprise either by state organisations or by powerful corporate agencies.

In both countries the population as a whole is intelligent and educated.

In both countries systems of communication and information transmission are powerful and remarkably open. Freedom of opinion, freedom of speech, freedom of association, and the freedom of the press are powerfully institutionalised and intensively utilised. The scope for new and heterogeneous ideas and for consequent social and technical innovation is large.

In both countries GNP, living standards, and quality of life are by historical and contemporary standards alike very high.

However, even with these and other important social characteristics in common, these two great free societies are also enormously different the one from the other. Britain, for example, remains much more ethnically homogeneous than the United States. America is rather less centralised than Britain, with less power available to

the central state apparatus. Interference in the economy, through nationalisation or regulation, is trivial in the United States by comparison with Britain. The power and influence of trade unions is much greater in Britain than in the United States. The American population at all levels is much more enterprise-oriented than are British people, and so on.

Not the least of the differences between the two countries is in the extent and nature of state welfare provision. Apart from Bismarck's Prussia, Britain has been the historical pioneer in state welfarism. From the late 19th century onwards, and with explosive escalations in the early 1900s, the 1940s, and during the 1960s and 1970s, British social policy has followed a consistent movement towards increasingly comprehensive, homogeneous and centralised welfare provision. Only in communist societies are there to be found anywhere in the modern world state bureaucracies of the scale created by the British welfare state.

In America, by contrast, despite the New Deal and the Great Society, commitment to State Welfare provision has always been tempered by scepticism about its side-effects and its implications. The strength of faith in market mechanisms and self-help has remained almost as firm in America as it has been weak in Britain since the mid-19th century.

From a certain perspective, the welfare systems of these two societies can only seem dramatically different – the USA representing the archetype of 'residualism' with public welfare provision kept to an absolute minimum, and Britain providing a more complete exemplar of the welfare state in all its Byzantine glory than even Scandinavia.

However, this polarised comparison conceals at least as much as it discloses, and in the last resort it provides a completely inadequate and inaccurate account of the state of welfare in the two societies. For, although the United States may have come much later and for the most part reluctantly to state welfare, in the past 30 years it has moved very rapidly on most social policy fronts in the same dangerous directions as other welfare state societies. In health, housing, social security, poverty management and the rest, US social policy and administrative machinery are now in all essential respects identical with those of older established welfare state societies. In each case, small beginnings restricted to the poorest and weakest sectors of society have expanded to encompass in their bureaucratic tentacles ever broader segments of the population (Hasenfeld and Zald, 1985).

In consequence, what we find in the late 1980s in both these societies is a condition of welfare sclerosis. In both of them bureaucratic state welfare is progressively choking off individual enterprise. Bureaucratic centralism is increasingly preventing the autonomous growth of local initiatives and sapping personal responsibility. Welfarist policies are continually generating more and more dependency, and in consequence escalating the level of apparent need for yet more welfare (Murray, 1984; Seldon, 1981).

As the corporatist and pseudo-socialist ramifications of state welfarism extend their hold, the free institutions of democratic society are progressively undermined, and the chances of maintaining freedom and democracy are inexorably diminished. With ever larger proportions of national wealth and income devoted to state welfare expenditure, real standards of living begin to dwindle, and even in the midst of potential prosperity the objective conditions of beggary are being constructed to suit the beggar-state mentality which state welfarism inevitably creates (Segalman, 1986).

It is in the context of this frightening scenario of free societies driven by irresponsible state welfarism towards economic, social and moral bankruptcy that the electoral triumphs of Mr Reagan and Mrs Thatcher in the 1980s should be seen. Both were elected and re-elected to challenge and reverse the long-term trend we have been describing. Both of them have had some success in relation to this goal. But few even among their most loyal supporters would claim that either of them has so far had anything better than a marginal effect.

Bureaucracy still flourishes. Central state organisations remain dominant in welfare. Public expenditure continues at very high levels. New pauper dependents are being created daily even under their allegedly libertarian auspices in thousands. In Britain and America, as throughout almost the whole of the free world, state welfare is continuing its destructive progress. Some more powerful, more subtle, and more systematic approach than has so far been tried is needed urgently, or soon it will be too late. In the following pages we offer the outlines of such an approach, based on the investigations reported earlier in this book.

2 Reform of Taxation, Incentives and the Work Environment

Our analysis suggests that the major damage caused by state welfare provision is the creation of welfare dependency. As a consequence of the principles, scale, mode of organisation and practical procedures of state welfare provision, large numbers of people who are fully capable of supporting themselves and their dependents effectively cease to do so, and progressively become incapacitated for future independent participation in social life in a free society. This individual dependency is almost inevitably generalised to whole families, and transmitted by inadequate and inappropriate socialisation from one generation to the next.

The antithesis of welfare dependency is social autonomy – the capacity to support oneself, and one's dependents through one's own efforts in the labour market. Fundamental changes in the ways in which work and work incentives are currently handled are essential elements in the reforms which are required to reduce welfare dependency.

It would be foolish of us to suggest that the requisite reforms can be easily or uncontroversially specified, or that, even if a programme of reform were agreed, it could be implemented without difficulty. For example, even among experts convinced, as we are, of the urgent necessity of reforms in the socio-psychological environment of work, there is disagreement about the effects of minimum wage regulations, about the advisability of central state involvement in social insurance, and other important issues (Parker, 1984; Wiseman and Marsland, 1987).

Again there are few, even among those most sceptical about current welfare arrangements, who are unaware that belligerent political resistance to reform is inevitable, given the many vested interests and ideological prejudices involved. For example, a recent examination of attempts since 1979 at welfare reform in Britain interprets them with a cavalier bias as 'the politics of greed' (Loney, 1986). The author can rely on a sympathetic reading of his implausible arguments by many thousands of committed socialists and office-

118

holders within the welfare system. We shall be surprised if resistance to welfare reform in Britain and the USA is significantly easier to overcome than the reactionary bureaucratism faced by Mr Gorbachev in the USSR!

Nonetheless, it seems to us feasible and potentially useful to spell out here our own suggestions about the key reforms we believe are necessary in this sphere. We plan to take up the arguments about their desirability and feasibility in a later publication (Gilder, 1986; Murray, 1984; Parker, 1982 and 1984):–

amendment of tax thresholds to eliminate 'poverty traps';

introduction in the longer term of a negative income tax system;

progressive reduction of all income tax;

elimination of all income support in kind;

complete separation of social insurance (for health, pensions, and unemployment) from social assistance to those in unpredictable need;

encouragement of private and co-operative social insurance for health, unemployment and pensions. Eventually federal or central state involvement should be limited to legal requirement of insurance by all persons and to supervision of private and co-operative schemes;

reduction of all welfare benefits in relation to available wage levels. It should be in no one's financial interest to remain on benefit unnecessarily;

elimination of minimum wage regulations (Marsland, 1984);

gradual replacement of benefit grants by loans. This will both reduce dysfunctional stigma and encourage a quicker return to self-reliance;

coupling of all welfare benefits, whether grants or loans, to the requirement of involvement in appropriate rehabilitation programmes. The aim should be to restore to welfare recipients their capacity for independent participation in social life. This may involve, for example, further education, job training, health care, or counselling (Segalman, 1986);

obligatory workfare (useful work in return for benefits) and retraining for the unemployed. Abandonment of unemployed men and women to purposeless inactivity on the dole is as cruel to them as it is destructive of society;

obligatory requirement for families to support young unemployed people (see the next section for more concerning the family);

improvements in education to encourage enterprising, self-reliant attitudes in young men and women. Currently teachers often have the opposite effect (Brophy, 1985);

financial and administrative responsibility for support and rehabilitation for those in need of help to be delegated to the local community level. Only local responsibility can ensure personal attention, prevent abuses and inhibit the irresponsible 'rights' mentality which depersonalised, large-scale systems invariably produce (on the role of the local community in reducing welfare dependency, see page 125 below);

retraining of social workers and other welfare personnel to adopt attitudes to those in genuine need of help which are supportive of enterprise, self-help, and self-reliance. Currently social workers' anxieties about stigma, their ideological commitment to state welfarism, and their ignorance about the world of work have the effect of actively discouraging their 'clients' from trusting their own capacities and resources and from finding ways of retrieving their autonomy. Welfare personnel are a major cause of welfare dependency (Wiseman & Marsland, 1987, Appendix on social workers).

Without reforms along these lines, the welfare systems of Britain and the USA will continue the inexorable drift which is bringing an increasing proportion of their populations into the state welfare net. Already this has gone a long way towards creating an under-class of merely pseudo-citizens who constitute a dangerous reservoir of apathetic and potentially disaffected serfs. Only the restoration to them of the opportunities for autonomous self-reliance – which all citizens are owed in any genuine democracy – can rescue them from self-destructive subservience, and save our two societies from paralysis and decay. Above all this requires changes such as we have proposed here to provide effective incentives for all citizens to work hard and to encourage in their children enterprising, self-reliant attitudes and a commitment to work as a primary source of identity and worth.

3 Support for the Family

Our reports in earlier pages of this book demonstrate graphically that, if the main direct destructive effect of state welfare is through its impact on work and work attitudes, the primary arena in which its long-term damage is done is the family. If welfare dependency is to be reduced, reforms of the work environment must be accompanied by measures designed to strengthen and support the family as a social institution.

For the family is the crucial – indeed indispensable – mechanism in producing autonomous, self-reliant personalities, capable of resisting the blandishments of welfare dependency. It is apparently only in the context of loving support and rational discipline which the family offers – provided it is intact and functioning effectively – that children can be reliably socialised into the values and skills which social autonomy requires (Gilder, 1981).

Thus anything – be it the welfare dependency of parents, social policies which set a premium on family disruption, or permissive cultural attitudes and irresponsible social role models – anything at all which weakens the fabric of families inevitably generates and escalates welfare dependency. In particular, social policies which make the role of the father redundant, or weaken the legitimate authority of parents in the socialisation of their children, are likely to create environments in which only exceptional children are capable of growing up into genuinely mature, autonomous adults. The vast majority of children reared in broken or inadequate families are headed for welfare dependency in one form or another, and also for other social problems.

Already post-war developments in social welfare policy and trends over the same period (and more especially since the 1960s) in cultural values and life-styles have gone a long way towards destroying the family as a social institution (Anderson & Dawson, 1986). Fundamental changes are required if this process is to be reversed and if the escalation of welfare dependency attributable to the weakness of the family is to be prevented in the future.

Even in communist Russia, it seems, the essential role of the family in the socialisation of children to constructive values and to the social skills required for effective independent participation in social life is being recognised. A recent report (*The Times* (London), August 13,

1987) on homeless children in the USSR concludes as follows:

> Time was in the Soviet Union when the family was considered a
> subversive unit, because families offered a loyalty that could
> compete, and might conflict, with loyalty to the state and the
> Communist Party. Now it is being recognised officially that family
> life is the foundation of a stable society and state requirements
> that might conflict with family obligations are being re-examined.

It would be strange indeed if a renewal of awareness about the crucial
value of the family were achieved under communism – which is in
principle an enemy of the family, rather than in Britain, the USA,
and the other democracies – where the family's indispensable significance as a buffer between individual and state, and as the primary
source of secure identity and personal autonomy has, until recently,
always been emphasised. Sadly, we have been too much and too
easily deceived by the family's many ideological enemies, and far too
naive about the destructive effects on the family institution of many
of our social welfare policies.

Much needs to be done. The following is a short-list of what seems
to us crucial. It will be obvious to the reader that our proposals
concerning the family are more contentious and more difficult to
achieve even than the measures suggested earlier in relation to
welfare and work. For the most part they are better classified as
cultural changes than as policy reforms, and in the nature of things,
the latter are much more amenable – even in the face of resistance –
to rational implementation than the former.

Our programme for cultural change with respect to the family is
therefore perhaps better read as an agenda for debate than as a
programme of reform. This, however, renders it not one iota less
important. We are convinced, on the basis of the investigations
reported in this book, and our broader studies of the destructive
effects of recent changes in family relations, that the problem of
welfare dependency cannot be addressed adequately unless the level
and nature of support provided for the family by the state is
transformed dramatically. For four decades and more, public energies
and resources in Britain and America have been devoted to the
destruction of the family. This must be halted and reversed if
democracy is to be preserved, to which end the following are essential:

> implementation of the reforms of work and welfare described
> earlier (pages 118–20). The family cannot survive and thrive unless

its natural and necessary economic responsibilities and moral authority are restored to it by these reforms;

careful reconsideration of policy in relation to one-parent families. Avoiding unnecessary stigma is one thing; providing positive incentives for the proliferation of incomplete and inadequate families is another;

amendments in legislation designed to reduce the rate of divorce. Despite re-marriage, divorce is a major source of inadequate socialisation of children, and therefore of welfare dependency;

improvements in marriage and family education, and in support services to help married couples with difficulties;

critical analysis of school and college text books and teaching which are prejudiced and subversive in relation to the family as an institution;

serious attention to damaging role models in the media and public life in relation to promiscuity, adultery and homosexuality. The re-moralisation of social life need neither be a merely reflex response to AIDS, nor an authoritarian and reactionary expression of fundamentalist 'Ayatollism'. Re-moralisation in a modern and democratic form is absolutely vital if the family's health is to be restored;

as a further and broader aspect of this same endeavour, analysis of the values, attitudes, and life-styles associated with the so-called 'permissive society';

research and policy development in relation to youth peer groups and their role in influencing young people's sexual behaviour, moral attitude and work values (Marsland, 1982);

innovative thinking about the scope for retrieving three-generation family units (for example, in relation to house-building patterns and tax incentives for family care of the elderly);

research to identify measures which, without blocking the career aspirations of women, would limit the damaging effects on children of dual careers, overtime working, and 'workaholism', e.g. tax rebates for child-caring wives;

tax incentives and other encouragements for family enterprises. As Gilder's analysis suggests, joint family involvement in business is a major stimulus to entrepreneurial action, and by the same token a powerful antidote against falling into welfare dependency. (Gilder, 1981 and 1986). The case of Greek Cypriot immigrants to Britain demonstrates the effectiveness of family businesses in

providing even disadvantaged people rapidly with the capacities and resources needed for self-reliance (Oakley 1982).

We believe the agenda constituted by these proposals may offer a useful framework for the thorough-going debate about the family which is needed. For far too long the family has been subverted and dismissed on grossly prejudiced and scientifically inadequate grounds by influential Marxist, socialist and feminist critics. Far from being, as its enemies argue, a repressive 'bourgeois' institution – responsible for patriarchal oppression of women, unjust subjugation of children, and inhibition of social change and 'liberation' – *the family is the indispensable seedbed of genuine freedom*. It is from the care and discipline which the family reliably provides, if it is not sabotaged by wrong-headed social policies, that mature, autonomous people grow, men and women with the capacities for living as free people, immune to welfare dependency.

4 Reinvigorating the Local Community

Our analysis of the Swiss case – the only major exception in the free world to the general descent into welfare dependency – suggests a third major dimension in the framework of social characteristics necessary to the maintenance of social freedom and personal autonomy. To sensible welfare policies which encourage economic self-reliance by protecting work incentives, and to powerful cultural support for the autonomy and authority of the family, must be added delegation of real independence and power to local communities.

Localism is an indispensable bastion against state welfarism and welfare dependency, while centralism provides the normal, and perhaps necessary, context for the elaborated and oppressive bureaucracy on which state welfarism feeds. Only in a context of close interpersonal interaction and extensive mutual acquaintance is it possible to maintain that sense of common identity and shared responsibility which prevents people from becoming mere passengers in social life, parasitical and subservient 'free riders' on the efforts of others.

Where, on the contrary, the conditions of 'mass society' prevail, with individuals atomised, and mutual bonds of acquaintance and dependence diminished, where social relations are wholly bureaucratised and depersonalised, and initiative, power, and responsibility are located in a distant centre – these are the conditions in which state welfarism and welfare dependency flourish, and the freedom and self-reliance of genuine democracy are threatened by the multiple problems which welfare dependency invariably causes.

Now of course there is no way that large-scale, industrialised societies can turn back the clock to retrieve the conditions – in any case largely mythical – of Tönnies' *Gemeinschaft*. This, however, is no reason why societies such as Britain and America should not seek to organise social arrangements so as to minimise the extent of gross centralism and guarantee to local communities major responsibilities. Among the many benefits of thorough-going localism not the least would be effective control of welfare and a substantial reduction in welfare dependency.

In this respect, the USA is already at a great advantage compared

with Britain. For the federal constitution reserves considerable real power for the States, and in and of itself this prevents the worst excesses of centralised societies such as Britain and France. It is no accident that Switzerland has a federal structure, as to a lesser extent does West Germany, which is also a prosperous country with a lesser dependency problem than most advanced societies.

We believe it would make a good deal of sense – in relation to welfare policy as much as in other fields – for Britain to move towards a modest degree of federalism by devolving power to Scotland, Wales and five or six English provinces. This is not a novel proposal and indeed it has figured in the manifesto of the Alliance parties for some time. Moreover, political support for devolution is potentially strong at present as a result of widespread feelings of discontent in several of the provincial regions.

Even this degree of devolution is not, however, likely to be sufficient to answer the problems of centralism in relation to welfare arrangements. California has a population of more than 20 million. English regional provinces might have populations as large in some cases as 8 to 10 million. The key issue is at a much lower level of population, and concerns local government proper, and the mode of organisation adopted in the conurbations.

In the rural areas and other areas of low population density, this problem is not too difficult. Here coherently bounded areas with reasonably small populations are readily enough identified. It is in the heavily urbanised, densely populated zones of the big cities and the massive conurbations that argument and political dissension about the optimum boundaries for local government seem almost beyond rational resolution (Hall, 1979).

One thing at least seems certain in the 1980s. The days when big was assumed to be best, and the alleged economies and efficiencies of scale were taken glibly for granted, have gone for good. In relation to welfare as much as in relation to education, health, housing and perhaps even planning and transportation, maximum devolution of power to real communities of not more than a quarter of a million is what we would prefer to see.

These local community units – the equivalent of Switzerland's cantons – ought to be financially self-supporting to the maximum possible extent. The routine payment by central government in Britain of 60 and 70 per cent of the expenditures of local authorities has done more than anything else to destroy genuine localism. Only financial autonomy and responsibility can guarantee local initiative

and enterprise, responsible local policies and the sort of local community authority which the excision of welfare dependency requires.

If responsibility for welfare – with the vast bulk of current provision transferred first to private and co-operative institutions – were reposed entirely in the authority of these small local communities, the whole texture of its administration would be radically changed for the better. Instead of the current exclusive emphasis on 'rights', the balance would shift towards responsibilities. Where currently many benefits are doled out unthinkingly on an impersonal basis, there would be a move towards working out personalised programmes for particular individuals and families. Where at present problem individuals and families are typically ignored until their difficulties have become too serious for much to be done about them, the close, informal supervision of the local community would instead identify problems early, and ensure that useful steps were taken to help. Instead of the current homogeneous blanket system of welfare provision, providing universal benefits regardless of real need and without proper attention to their appropriateness in different situations, we should see much greater variability from one community to another. It would be much healthier if different policies with varying levels and types of provision were established by different communities, allowing comparison, competition and evolutionary change.

However, this last point also suggests an apparent danger which local community autonomy might threaten. Since the 1960s in Britain, it has been particular local authorities – the Greater London Council, extreme left-wing councils in the north of England, such as the so-called 'Socialist Republic of South Yorkshire' – which have installed the most profligate policies, and done most to increase the extent of welfare dependency. It could be argued that with increased freedom and power for local communities, there would be even more such damaging folly.

While the danger is certainly real, we believe the risk is worth taking, and indeed must be taken. If local people are required to pay for their own policies, *with no chance of being baled out by central government*, they will soon recognise mischievous nonsense when they see it, and elect different leaders. Our whole approach presumes – and it is an assumption backed by considerable evidence – that where people have a real and visible stake in their community, they will involve themselves seriously, and take action to ensure that local resources – their own money – are not wasted, and that the lives and

energies of their neighbours and fellow citizens are not squandered by destructive welfare arrangements. This strategy requires that local communities should be restored to genuine autonomy. Without the risk of error this involves, there is no chance at all of transforming them into the nurseries of personal initiative and individual self-reliance they need to become.

5 Reform in Housing and Education

There are two further areas of social policy where radical reform is necessary if the British and American people are to leave welfare dependency well and truly behind them. These are *housing* and *education* – two fields in which the seeds of welfare dependency currently grow and flourish profusely.

Ironically, both housing and education have long been favourite targets for well-meaning philanthropists and over-confident social engineers. The history books and reform bills are full of graphic descriptions of the squalid housing conditions of the poor, and their ignorance has been blamed for much of the suffering they have had to endure. New housing and good schools have been the recommended panacea of the interfering classes for generations. Yet what do we find in the inner cities of our two countries as the century draws to its close? Sprawling, high-rise tenement projects with doors and windows boarded up, on streets which even policemen visit nervously at best; where addicts, muggers and burglars roam freely, and nullify for thousands the security which home and only home can provide; where litter, graffiti and vandalism on every hand display the careless unconcern of residents for their own neighbourhoods (Coleman, 1985).

And in the schools? Truancy exists on a huge and grossly underestimated scale. There is sullen disaffection against every educational ideal. Bored and bullied or bullying pupils are common. Domination by the nihilistic culture of pop and rampant permissivism is prevalent. Broken teachers are becoming the norm. The educational dream has become a hopeless nightmare (Anderson, Marsland, and Lait, 1981).

In these two areas of the neighbourhood and the school, new welfare dependents are being created month by month and year by year. Individuals and families are having the spirit of enterprise and the will to organise their own lives knocked out of them. Hundreds of thousands of our fellow citizens are being shaped for nothing but subservient pauperism, and all in the name of planning and progress. Even the radical changes in work and welfare, the family and the local community we have recommended earlier will fail unless they are accompanied by a new approach to housing and to education.

In New York, Detroit and Los Angeles, as in London, Liverpool and Glasgow, public housing built as recently as the 1960s and 1970s is being demolished: from slum to slum in 15 years. If these breeding grounds of crime and welfare dependency are to be eliminated once and for all a whole new strategy for housing is needed:

> outlaw absolutely any building or administration of housing by public authorities;
>
> eliminate all funding of housing by public authorities except in the form of tax rebates or loans to individuals, co-operatives, or private companies;
>
> eliminate all housing benefit grants and housing aid which leaves residents unaware of the real costs of their homes;
>
> encourage, by the provision of protected loans, the establishment of small-scale co-operative home building, home purchase, and home renting schemes, and self-help housing;
>
> encourage, through tax rebates, the establishment of home purchase loan schemes for employees and members of companies, trade unions and so on;
>
> phase out rent controls – a primary cause of homelessness (Tucker, 1987);
>
> local communities to provide loans for home maintenance and improvement;
>
> increase expenditure on local policing and community self-defence;
>
> increase expenditure on local youth service and youth involvement programmes, and youth employment training schemes.

If housing policy were transformed along these radical lines, the whole quality of neighbourhood life in our inner cities would be rapidly improved. It would offer to poorer citizens a real stake in their local communities, and an opportunity for them and their families to gain for the first time the benefits of a genuine home in which they could rationally invest care and pride.

The main role of the family in preventing welfare dependency is to provide a context of care, support and discipline within which children can learn the attitudes and skills required for self-reliant living. The role of the schools is to build on this foundation and carry it further. In Britain and America they are patently failing in this role abysmally, especially with children of average and less than average ability. The evidence of this failure is extensive and indisputable (Brophy, 1985; O'Keeffe, 1986).

Here let it suffice to consider a report of two recent studies (*Mail on Sunday*, 16 August 1987). A study of 15-year-olds, given mathematics tests involving decimals, fractions and percentages, found that West German children did twice as well as British children. Indeed many of the British children could not answer the questions at all. In a follow-up study:

Three papers for GCSE Arithmetic were set in a German school for the lowest ability range. A staggering 40 per cent of 15-year-old 'low ability' Hauptschule pupils sailed through the test with marks of 80 to 100 per cent.

That is the equivalent to an O-level grade C pass in this country, achieved by only the top 15 per cent of 16-year-olds. And Hauptschule are the lowest of the three grades of German senior schools, roughly the equivalent of our old secondary modern.

For their six-part programme, Educating Britain, which starts next Sunday, LWT tested British pupils in a similar ability range on the mathematics paper for the Hauptschule leaving certificate. All ten questions on fractions, percentages and decimals have been covered in lessons in the comprehensives.

The 170 British childrens' average mark was 33 per cent compared to the Germans' 61 per cent. Most Germans easily divided 543.75 by 12.5 whereas few of the British pupils knew how to start.

Amazingly a British expert is reported as criticising the German leaving exam as 'too mechanical', and aimed merely at 'cramming mathematical techniques'. Invited to provide an alternative:

. . . she devised her own test, designed to measure pupils' underlying understanding of mathematical principles and how to apply them to practical circumstances.

Again Britain lagged behind. The average German score was 62 per cent compared with 44 per cent in this country.

In Britain and America alike it has fortunately been recognised at last that the fashionable educational platitudes of the past three decades are failing our children. Experiments in tightening up educational objectives and school management; better training of teachers; re-introducing discipline and competition; linking school work with the real world; and involving parents and the local community in the educational process are going ahead rapidly on many fronts.

It is our view that these reforms must be pressed hard in the face

132   *Reform of British and American Social Policy*

of the educational establishment's predictable defensive protestations.
Substantial improvements in education are essential if welfare dependency is to be reduced, and if a new generation of young people is
to be produced which is better capable of independent, self-discip-
lined, self-reliant living. Comparisons between American schooling
and Japanese, and between British schooling and German, should
be continued systematically until the shameful gap is closed. And
even then we shall need to make comparisons with Switzerland,
where, more even than in Japan or Germany, excellent schooling
makes a major contribution to maintaining the mature capacity and
personal freedom of Swiss people of all ranks.

6 Towards a Culture of Freedom

The damaging consequences of the welfare policies adopted all over the Western world after the Second World War are now apparent. Governments of left and right alike are reaching around for solutions to the decay and chaos which increasingly characterise all our major cities. Our argument is that nothing less than a reversal of these policies is necessary if we are to avoid a deepening crisis. The welfare state has proved a damaging distraction and shown itself dangerously counter-productive wherever it has been tried. Instead, we should follow the clues provided by the Swiss, by common sense, and by principles long established in free societies, to reach beyond the welfare state towards real welfare.

In this last part of our book we have briefly outlined a strategy which could lead our two countries in this direction – away from dangerous fantasies towards real welfare. It will require bold political leadership at national level, and both courage and trust on the part of the people. It will demand skill and patience from administrators and local community leaders.

However, the alternative to these difficult challenges is an imposition which, for free people, is infinitely worse – a vicious circle of growing welfare dependency, increasing state control, deepening poverty, worsening anarchy in the inner city, and inexorably diminishing freedom.

If this fate is to be avoided, all the reforms we have proposed are urgently necessary:

fundamental changes in the structure of work and welfare, to increase personal self-reliance (pages 118–20);

restoration and augmentation of the autonomy and authority of the family (pages 121–24);

delegation of central state power and responsibilities to the local community (pages 125–28);

reform of housing and improvement in the quality of local neighbourhoods (pages 129–30);

radical changes in education to improve its effectiveness (pages 130–32).

In combination, these reforms will inaugurate a qualitative transformation of the culture of British and American society. Their motivational effects will facilitate a radical shift from the culture of serfdom, into which we have gradually sunk since the Second World War as a result of state welfarist policies, political ineptitude and moral blindness, towards the culture of freedom, in which our two countries have long been pioneers (Marsland, 1988).

Even in the heartlands of socialism in the USSR and China, the past decade has seen a reluctant recognition that all-enveloping state provision from cradle to grave is inefficient and morally dangerous. Here in the powerhouse of freedom and democracy, this is a lesson we should not have needed to learn at all, since it is a corollary of freedom and an axiom of democracy.

For while democracy can restore freedom to people who have been robbed of it, freedom and democracy can neither grow spontaneously nor survive successfully except, and unless, men behave as free men must – that is, freely, independently and with brave self-reliance. The apparatus of state welfare, with whatever beneficent intentions it may be established, necessarily and inevitably inhibits the responsible, adaptable behaviour which freedom requires. Its bureaucratic structures strangle the natural, spontaneously developing co-operative institutions on which freedom depends, the family, the market and the local community foremost among them. Its tangled systems of rules and obligations destroy the capacities of free men and women to choose freely for themselves and to pursue rational interests. Its illegitimate seizure of moral control abandons the people to purposeless drifting, subservient dependency, and aimless incapacity to choose and act for themselves morally, responsibly and freely. Its grip on our two countries and our people must be broken once and for all.

Bibliography

Alperovitz, Gar and Jeff Faux (1984) *Rebuilding America: A Blueprint for the New Economy* (New York: Pantheon Books).

Anderson, D. C. and G. Dawson (eds) (1986) *Family Portraits* (Social Affairs Unit).

Anderson, D. C., D. Marsland and J. Lait (1981) *Breaking the Spell of the Welfare State* (Social Affairs Unit).

Auletta, Ken (1982) *The Under Class* (New York: Random House).

Berger, Brigitte and Peter (1984) *The War Over the Family: Capturing the Middle Ground* (Garden City, N.Y.: Anchor-Doubleday).

Besharov, Douglas J. (1986) 'Unfounded allegations: A new child abuse problem', *The Public Interest*, no. 83, Spring, pp. 18–33.

Bethell, Tom (1985) 'British views and prospects', *The American Spectator*, July, pp. 7–9.

Bethell, Tom (1986) 'Das kapital ideas: II', *The American Spectator*, July, pp. 11–13, 48.

Bourdieu, P. (1980) 'Cultural reproduction and social reproduction', in J. Karabel and A. H. Halsey (eds), *Power and Ideology in Education* (New York and London: Oxford University Press).

Brophy, M. *et al.* (1985) *Trespassing: Businessmen's Views on the Education System* (Social Affairs Unit).

Brown, Muriel and Nicola Madge (1982) *Despite the Welfare State: Studies in Deprivation and Disadvantage* (London: Heinemann Educational Books).

Caldwell, Taylor (1965) *A Pillar of Iron* (Greenwich, Connecticut: Fawcett) p. 572.

Carlson, Allan C. (1983) 'What happened to the family wage?', *The Public Interest*, no. 83, Spring, pp. 3–17.

Clinard, Marshall (1978) *Cities without Crime: the Case of Switzerland* (London: Cambridge University Press).

Coleman, A. (1985) *Utopia on Trial* (Hilary Shipman).

Coleman, J. S., *et al.* (1966) *Equality of Educational Opportunity* (Washington, DC: US Office of Education, Dept. of HEW).

Cornish, Edward (1986). 'Will "parent licenses" protect children?', *Los Angeles Times*, 10 Oct., pt. V, p. 14.

Daniels, A. M. (1986) 'National health goes sick', *The Spectator*, 9 Aug., pp. 8–9.

Davis, Stan Gebler (1986). 'The caring state that ruins us', *The Spectator*, 16 Aug., pp. 14–15.

Dornbusch, Sanford M., Michael J. Fraleigh, Philip L. Ritter, *et al.* (1986) *A Report to the National Advisory Board on the Main Findings of our Collaborative Study of Families and the Schools* (Stanford, CA: Sociology Dept., Stanford University, 27 Feb).

DuWors, Richard E. (1952) 'Persistence and change in local values of two New England communities', *Rural Sociology*, vol. 17, no. 3, Sept., pp. 207–17.

Eisenstadt, S. N. (1985) 'Introduction', in S. N. Eisenstadt and Ora Ahimer, *The Welfare State and Its Aftermath* (Totowa, N.J.: Barnes & Noble).

Forman, Rachel Zinober (1982). *Let Us Now Praise Obscure Women: A Comparative Study of Publicly Supported Unmarried Mothers in Government Housing in the US and Britain* (Washington, D.C.: University Press of America).

Fondation pour la Recherche Sociale (1980) *Poverty and the Anti Poverty Policies: The French Report Presented to the Commission of the European Communities* (Paris: Fondation pour la Recherche Sociale, Dec).

Freeman, Roger A. (1981). *A Preview and Summary of the Wayward Welfare State* (Stanford, CA: The Hoover Institution Press) p. 102.

Gallagher, Maggie (1986) 'Gimme shelter: Children on the run', *National Review* 10 Oct., pp. 38–40.

Gilder, George (1981) *Wealth and Poverty* (Buchan and Enright).

Gilder, George (1986) *The Spirit of Enterprise* (Penguin).

Gilder, George (1986) 'The sexual revolution at home', *The National Review* 10 Oct., pp. 30–4.

Glazer, Nathan (1983) 'Towards a self-service society', *The National Interest*, no. 70, Winter, pp. 66–90.

Green, D. G. (1985) *Which Doctor?* (Institute of Economic Affairs).

Gress, David (1982). 'Daily life in the Danish welfare state', *The Public Interest*, no. 69, Fall, pp. 33–44.

Gruner, Erich (1982) Private correspondence with Segalman, 26 March.

Gurny, Ruth *et al.* (1983) *Careers and Blind Alleys: Paths to Professional Life in the City of Zurich* (Soziologisches Institut der Universität Zürich).

Hall, P. (1977) *The Containment of Urban England* (London: Allen & Unwin, 1973).

Hasenfeld, Y. and M. N. Zald (eds) (1985) *The Welfare State in America: Trends and Prospects* (Annals of the American Academy of Political and Social Science).

Hinde, R. A. (1980) 'Family influences', in M. Rutter, (ed.), *Scientific Foundations of Developmental Psychiatry* (London: Heinemann).

Hirschi, Travis (1983), 'Crime and the family', in James Q. Wilson (ed.), *Crime and Public Policy* (San Francisco: Institute for Contemporary Studies) pp. 53–68.

Jencks, C., *et al.* (1973) *Inequality: A Reassessment of the Effect of Family and Schooling in America* (London: Allen Lane).

Levenstein, Aaron (1964) *Why People Work: Changing Incentives in a Troubled World* (New York: Collier).

Loney, M. (1986) *The Politics of Greed* (Pluto Press).

Luscher, Kurt (1982) 'Fifty years of family policy in Switzerland', in *Profamilia* (Report of the Family Conference of 21 Nov. 1981) (Lucerne: Profamilia Eidgenössischen Verband).

Luscher, Kurt K., Verena Ritter and Peter Gross (1973) *Early Child Care in Switzerland* (London: Gordon & Breach).

Marsland, D. (1982) *Youth, Freedom, and Authority* (Problems of Youth, no. 4).

Marsland, D. (1984) 'The Wages Councils and Unemployment', *Economic Affairs*, vol. 4, no. 2.

Marsland, D. (1988) *Seeds of Bankruptcy: Sociological Bias against Business and Freedom* (Claridge Press).

Meyer, Jürg (1974) *Armut in der Schweiz* (Poverty in Switzerland) (Zurich: Theologischer Verlag).

Mitscherlich, Alexander (1970) *Society without the Father* (New York: Schocken Books).

Mount, Ferdinand (1986) 'Hippies, workfare and the myth of total mobilization', *The Spectator*, 14 June, p. 6.

Murray, Charles (1984) *Losing Ground: American Social Policy, 1950–1980* (New York: Basic Books).

Newhouse, John (1986) 'The gamefish', *New Yorker*, 10 Feb. pp. 68–99.

Nisbet, Robert (1986) book review of *The Rise and Fall of New York City*, by Roger Starr (New York: Basic Books, 1986), in *The American Spectator*, July pp. 43–4.

Oakley, R. (1982) 'Cypriot Families', chapter 10 in R. Rapoport (ed.), *Families in Britain* (London: Routledge & Kegan Paul).

O'Keeffe, D. (ed.) (1986) *The Wayward Curriculum* (Social Affairs Unit).

Parker, H. (1982) *The Moral Hazards of Social Benefits* (Institute of Economic Affairs).

Parker, H. (1984) *Action on Welfare* (Social Affairs Unit).

Pavalko, Ronald M. (1971) *Sociology of Occupations and Professions* (Itaska, Ill.: Peacock).

Reist, W. and Regula Wagner (1982) 'On the Drug Problem in Switzerland', *Zeitschrift für Öffentliche Fürsorge*, Feb., pp. 162–6.

Riesman, D. (1950) *The Lonely Crowd* (Yale University Press).

Rydenfelt, Sven (1981) *The Rise and Decline of the Swedish Welfare State* (Lund, Sweden: Nationalekonomiska Institutionen, Lunds Universitat).

Schaber, Gaston (1980) *Pauvreté Persistant / Grande Région (Project #20)* (Walferdange, Grand Duché de Luxembourg: Group Etude pour les Problèmes de la Pauvreté, July 7).

Segalman, Ralph and Asoke Basu (1981) *Poverty in America: The Welfare Dilemma* (Westport: Greenwood).

Segalman, Ralph (1986) *The Swiss Way of Welfare* (Praeger).

Seldon, A. (1981) *Whither the Welfare State* (Institute of Economic Affairs).

Sharff, Jagna Wojcicka (1981) 'Free enterprise and the ghetto family', *Psychology Today*, vol. 15, no. 4, March.

Sheehan, Susan (1976) *A Welfare Mother* (New York: New American Library, Mentor).

Starr, Roger (1986) *The Rise and Fall of New York City* (New York: Basic Books).

Strang, Heinz (1970) *Erscheinungsformen der Social Hilfebedürftigkeit: Beitrag zur Geschichte, Theorie und Empirischen Analyse der Armut* (Stuttgart: Ferdinande Enke Verlag).

Strang, Heinz (1984) *Sozialhilfebedürftigkeit: Struktur- Ursachen- Wirkung unter besonderer Berücksichtigung der Effektivität der Sozialhilfe* (Forschungsbericht), (Hannover: Institut für Sozialpädagogik der Hochschule-Hildesheim).

Tönnies, Ferdinand (1963) *Community and Society: Gemeinschaft and Gesellschaft* (C. P. Loomis (ed.), New York: Harper).

Trimborn, Harry (1982) 'Switzerland Faces Up to the Growing Problem with Hard Drugs', *Los Angeles Times*, 15 Dec., pt IB, p. 1.

Townsend, Peter (1979) *Poverty in the United Kingdom* (Berkeley: University of California Press).

Tucker, William (1986) 'The landlord's tale', *The New Republic*, 7 July, pp. 14–16.

Tucker, William (1986) 'Moscow on the Hudson', *The American Spectator*, July, pp. 19—21.

Tucker, William (1987) 'Where do the Homeless come from?', *National Review*, 25 Sept.

Van der Vat, Dan (1980) 'Sunderland: Where unemployment is a way of life', *The Times*, 9 June, p. 11.

Van Doorn, Jacques (1978) 'Welfare state and welfare society: the Dutch experience', *Netherlands Journal of Sociology*, 14, pp. 1–8.

Waugh, Auberon (1985) 'Runcieballs revisited, or what to do with the Beveridge Boys', *The Spectator*, 21/28 Dec., p. 9.

Wilensky, Harold L. (1975) *The Welfare State and Equality: Structured and Ideological Roots of Public Expenditures* (Berkeley: University of California Press).

Wilson, William Julius (1985) 'The crisis of the ghetto underclass and the liberal retreat', annual *Social Service Review* lecture, University of Chicago, May.

Wiseman, J. and D. Marsland (1987) *The Social Welfare Programme of the Republic of China* (Taipei: Council for Economic Planning and Development).

Zellman, Gail and Steven L. Schlossman (1986) 'The Berkeley youth wars', *The Public Interest*, no. 84, Summer, pp. 29–41.

Index

absenteeism 4
aged and infirm, social insurance
    package, Switzerland 70
AIDS 47
alcoholism 4, 18, 37, 44, 91, 93,
    110
altruism, importance of 109
anti-social behaviour 33
apprenticeship/educational
    completion rates, Switzerland
    67
avoidance behaviour 110

behaviour, civilised 39
Beistand 79, 88
benefits 5
    extended to the relatively
        deprived 57
births out of wedlock 80–1
Blue Cross 20, 22
Blue Shield 20, 22
borrowers, selection of 27
Britain
    comprehensive schooling 16
    federalism through devolution
        126
    low achievement in maths 131
    the NHS 23–5
    shift to self-help in the housing
        field 58
    some fundamental
        characteristics 115
    and state welfarism 116
broken families 4

California, an example of the
    welfare state 59–60
central goverment
    complexity of 58
    harm done by 111–12
    interventionism not necessary
        110
centralisation of power 54
centralism 117, 125

charity health programmes 24–5
cheap labour 34
child abuse/incest/neglect 47, 105
children
    inculcation of acceptable
        behaviour 40
    and mother-love 48
    in multi-problem families 87
    perceptions of parents 41–2
    in single-parent families 50
    socialisation of: discouraged 7–
        8; by the family 121;
        inadequate 44; loss of vii,
        7
    in Switzerland: reared for self-
        sufficiency 72; following
        traditional models 83
    in a welfare family 10, 11
    of the welfare state 45
    without families 51
citizens, dependency on
    bureaucracy 59
civil rights 45, 46
client co-operation required in
    Switzerland 74–5
client rehabilitation, Switzerland
    67, 72
cohabitation, favoured by Swedish
    tax system 7
community involvement, loosening
    of, Switzerland 91
community life, invidivual's
    investment in 33
community youth programmes, a
    constraint on welfarisation 79
'concubinage'/'coupling', in
    Switzerland 99, 104
confidentiality issue, welfare
    workers and clients,
    Switzerland 74–5
crime 4, 36, 37, 105, 110, 129
    and the family 43–4
cultural change, with respect to the
    family 122–4

cultural life patterns and health
  care 23

daughters, in a welfare family 12
de-centralisation, movement
  towards 58
decision-taking in Switzerland 78–
  9
delinquency 4, 33, 44
  child 43
  hard-core and welfare
    dependency 14
  juvenile 52
democratic masochism, and the
  NHS 24
Denmark, schools 18–19
Department of Housing and
  Preservation and
  Development, New York 31
dependency
  collusion with 13
  ghetto 11–13, 45
  as a norm 7
  prevention of, Switzerland 67
  psychosocial 15
dependency pattern, perpetuation
  of 13
desegregation, results of 16
dictatorship, danger of 105
disability, Swiss definition 66
divorce 90
  acceptability of 46
  difficult to secure 82
  easy 51
  reduction in rate of 123
divorce and desertion rate 4
divorce and family relations courts,
  Swiss, as welfarisation
  constraints 80–1; why the law
  works 81–2
divorce laws, relaxation of 46
divorce and separation,
  Switzerland 93–4
doorkey children 55
drug abuse, Switzerland 91–3
drug addiction 4, 14, 18, 22–3, 33,
  36, 37, 44, 47, 129
drug culture 92
drug problem, the 22–3

early learning years 15
economic changes, effects of 4–5
Edsel's Law 3
education
  collapse of in USA 19
  dependent on parental attitude
    23
  efforts to reverse the decline
    131–2
  elsewhere in Europe 18–19
  failures of 15–16, 130–1; in
    Sweden 17–18
  impasse in 16–17
  importance of 14–15
  improvement needed 120
  loss of commitment and
    professionalism 18–19
  preparation for an occupational
    role 14
  responsibility for 15
  and social skills 14
  state vs. private 16
  in Switzerland 82–3, 84
elderly and handicapped, Swiss
  public welfare policies 71–2
empathy, for others 109
employers, constraints on 34
employment
  as a constraint on welfarisation
    84–5
  destruction of 34–5
  part-time 87
  in the welfare state 33–7
employment market 36
employment patterns, change in 5
employment placement 36
expectations of the less educated,
  poor 14–15

familial life, denigration of 51
familial rights for children, few 52
families
  female-headed 10–12, 37;
    welfare dependency and
    education 14
  legitimated, non-formation of 37
  limited-income, provision of
    housing 26

families – *continued*
  supporting young unemployed 119
family advocate 12
family enterprises, encouragement of 123–4
family formation, declining rate of 4
family relationships, necessary 41–2
family structure, Switzerland, operates against welfare dependency 78–9
family, the
  and crime 43–4
  endangered by sexual liberals 50
  and genuine freedom 124
  support for 121–4
  and the welfare state 38–55
Farm and Home Administration 27
fatherhood, sacrifices of 49
fathers
  absent 42, 44, 47, 50
  crucial role of 48, 49
  economic function eliminated 45
  made redundant 121
  position in family weakened 7
  in a welfare family 11
federal constitutions, advantages of 126
federal housing projects 28–9
female-headed families 10–12, 14, 37
feminist delusions 50
financial management, in a welfare family 11
France, social services and welfare income administration 6
freedom
  need for 58–9
  without reponsibility 57
future, the, planning and working for 38

Gammon Law of Bureaucratic Displacement, and the Health Service 24
gang membership 12, 44

gangs and gang alliances 12
Gastarbeiter, apprenticeship / educational completion rates 67
Gemeinschaft 106, 107, 108
gender equality 7
gentrification, not found in New York 32
Gesellschaft 106, 108
ghetto dependency 11–13, 45
grants / benefits, desocialising effects of 33
Greek-Cypriot immigrants, effectiveness of family businesses 123–4

health care delivery system, Britain 23–4
health, and education 15
health insurance, Britain 23
health maintenance organisations 21
health standards, Britain 23
health in the welfare state
  controlling costs 20–1
  the drug problem 22–3
  health care for welfare dependents 21–2
  NHS: problems with 23–4; as a monopolistic monster 24–5
heavy industry, lost to Third World 4
Holland, schools 18
home loan system, reasons for success 27
housewife, role of 48
housing bureaucracy, unnecessary 31
housing reform 130
housing, in the welfare state
  central state intervention 26–7
  destructive rent control 30–2
  a more direct method of intervention 28–9
  transformation of the system 29–30
husbands, divorced, providing support in Switzerland 80

immigration, control of 68
income, guaranteed minimum,
    damaging consequences of 7
income redistribution 5
individual enterprise, choked off
    117
'individual poverty' 89
individual rights 52
    and needs of society 50–1
individuality 33
industrialisation without
    urbanisation 78
industry
    movement to newly-developing
        countries 34
    in New York 35
inflation 3
informed consent 47
inner cities, possible improvement
    of neighbourhood life 130
insurance programme, self-earned
    66

job losses, New York 35
jobs, new, require more education
    and technical training 4–5
Jugendamt 79, 88

key money 31

leadership, local, Switzerland 102–
    3
left-wing councils 127
legal powers, Switzerland 103
loan programmes 27
loans
    reinsurance of 27
    replacing benefit grants 119
local autonomy, Switzerland 103
local community
    decline in power of 54
    early identification of problems
        127
    importance of in Switzerland
        70–1, 78–9
    possible dangers of autonomy
        127
    reinvigoration of 125–8
    responsibility for support and
        rehabiliatation 120

serious involvement of local
    people 127–8
local community, autonomous
    107–8
local community units, financially
    self-supporting 126
localism
    active, Switzerland 102
    benefits of 125–6
low-rent housing projects 28
    dilapidation of 30
    rights of 'undesirables' to a place
        in 29

markets and states 57
marriage
    automatic dissolution of 46
    delayed 94
marriage and family education,
    improvement in 123
mathematics, studies 131
means test, Switzerland 70, 73–4
Medicaid 20, 21
medical care coverage,
    Switzerland 86–7
medical insurance, commercial 20,
    21
medically needy 86
Medicare 20, 21
mediocratisation of American
    public education 16
middle class, exodus of from New
    York 35
military service, as a welfarisation
    constraint 85
minimum wage regulations 119
minority families, dependent,
    results of influx of 36
minority unemployment 34
modern life, complexity of 108
mortgage arrangements, for poor
    families, USA 27
motherhood, sacrifices of 48, 49
mothers
    lacking authority 11
    role of 48–9
    unmarried 44, 80, 110
    in a welfare family 10–11
    working 44

multi-problem families 87–8, 89, 102

National Health Service (NHS) 23–5
need, different views on 76
needy, deserving 60
negative factors, Switzerland 91–5
New York City
   decline in industry 35
   destructive rent control 30–2

occupational retraining 87
oppression, dangers of 105–6

parental non-involvement 44
parenting 40
   by peer group 51, 93
   effective 43–4
   inadequate 44
patrents
   authority weakened 121
   committed to society 42–3
   competency of 42–3
   ineffective 105
   necessity for two 42
   and social mainstream 42
   to be seen as competent 41
peer parenting 51, 93
permissive behaviour 105
permissiveness 19
personal rules of behaviour 38–9
political change, 1980s 117
poor
   aid for and self-help,
      Switzerland 65
   shown as victims 9–10
poor families, Switzerland 88–9
poverty
   and affluence, affecting child
      supervision 43
   causes of 76
   evidence of 9–10
   as a fated condition 77
   Swiss approach to 65–8
   welfarised, feminised 80
poverty and dependency, European
      studies of 9–10
poverty traps 119

Preferred Provider Organisations 22
pregnant women, lack of self-care 47
private schools 16
problem school districts 17
problems
   development of behaviour for
      solving 39–40
   tendency to re-definition 110
production costs 34
productivity
   discouraged by welfare 7
   and the welfare state 7–8
productivity problem, W.
   Germany 34
professional accountability 58
promiscuity or family
   responsibility 50
Pruitt-Igoe houses, St Louis 30
pseudo-family care 52–3
public assistance, Switzerland
   as a loan 74
   locally controlled 70–1
public dependency, limited in
   Switzerland 90
public housing programme, change
   in nature of 28–9
public housing projects, USA,
   lacking in safety 30
public welfare, Switzerland
   administrators, views of 76
   confidentiality issue 74–5
   policies 71–2

re-moralisation, of social life 123
reciprocity 83–4, 104, 107
regulations and counter-
   regulations 6
rehabilitation 107, 120
   and welfare benefits 119
relatives, responsibilities of,
   Switzerland 73
rent control, destructive, New York
   City 30–2; conditions
   achieved 31–2
rent stabilisation 31
rents
   low-rent housing projects 28–9

rents – *continued*
regulation of, New York 30–1
resocialisation 17
responsibility
learned in the family 57
reimposition of 17
retirement benefits, Switzerland 69
right and wrong 58–9
rights of others 83
rights and responsibilities,
Switzerland 103–4
rights without responsibility 52,
105
role models, damaging 123

schooling, 'the job of the child' 82
schools
influence of 51
position of limited
accountability 17
role of 130
Swiss, a constraint on
welfarisation 82–3
self-confidence 14
self-discipline 14
self-help, expansion of 58
self-reliance 120
Switzerland 83, 84, 104
self-restraint 14
self-sufficiency 28, 106
discouraged by welfare 7
expected in Switzerland 72
pride in 33
self-worth, sense of 33
service industries, new jobs 5
sex
aberrant 110
irresponsible 46–7
loosening of constraints on 47
sexual models 47
single-parent families 4, 37, 50,
123
and crime rate 43
problem of working parent 93
social assistance 119
social autonomy 118
social control 8, 105
social insurance 119
Switzerland 69–70; as a

prevention of poverty 65–6;
a true insurance programme
66–7
social insurance contributions,
Switzerland 69
social pathology, dynamics of 44
social problems
and central authority 109
local involvement in solutions
110–11
social services
decentralisation of 57–8
government-supported, growth
in 52–3
separated from eligibility
determination 13
social services and welfare income
administration 5–6
social welfare policy, post-war
developments and the family
121
social work, impact of 53–4
social workers
in the local community 107
retraining with different
attitudes 120
sons, in a welfare family 12
state, caring, problems of 59
state welfare
damaging to the family 121
destructive viii–ix, 117
state welfarism 125
Britain a pioneer 116
ramifications of 117
step-orphans 46
stepfathers 42
stigma 120, 123
Switzerland 69–70, 75
subsidiarity, principle of 82–3
Sweden
educational failure 17–18
guaranteed income 7
health service 25
Swiss community 78–9
Swiss culture 99
Swiss ethics 104
Swiss society, structure of 81–2
Switzerland
active localism 102

Switzerland – *continued*
  approach to poverty 65–8
  avoiding bureaucracy 105
  births out of wedlock 80
  constitution 101
  dangers of oppression 105–6
  Gemeinschaft and *Gesellschaft*
    106
  legal powers 103
  limited national resources 68
  local leadership 102–3
  negative factors 91–5
  organising welfare 104
  people as a resource 67, 83
  public aid as a loan 74
  public assistance programmes:
    local responsibility 70–1
  public welfare policies 71–2
  rights and responsibilities 103–4
  social insurance 69–70; as a
    prevention of poverty 65–6;
    a true insurance programme
    66–7
  a special case? 99–100
  welfare system 69–77

tax, open system in Switzerland 66
tax collection system, Switzerland
  73–4
tax income and cut back of
  employment population base
  5
taxation ix
  increased 54
  and medical insurance 20
  reform 119
teacher and staff morale 17
tenants, selection of 26
therapeutic goals 53
therapeutic professions, growth in
  52–3
Third World countries, cheap
  unskilled labour 4
three-generational units 123
trade union monopoly power,
  effects of 34
trade unions 116
transgenerational dependency 86,
  118

transgenerational poverty,
  Switzerland 88–9
transport, in New York 35
truancy 17, 19, 67, 129
trust, taught by parents 38–9
two-income families, Sweden 7
two-parent families 44–5
  not always satisfactory 41

under-class, creation of 120
unearned payments, phasing out
  of 111
unemployability 37
unemployment 88
  acceptability of 37
  means lack of work 34
  youth 37
unemployment bureaucracy 36–7
unemployment compensation 66
unmarried mothers 44, 80, 110
USA 6
  benefits of federal constitution
    125–6
  births out of wedlock 80–1
  drug addiction 22–3
  educational collapse 19
  federal involvement in housing
    26–32
  guaranteed minimum income
    experiment 7
  health care provision 20–2
  inadequate socialisation of
    children and schooling 16
  less state interference 115–16
  power shift to central
    government 101
  rehabilitation of the dependent
    lacking 53–4
  shift to self-help 58
  some fundamental
    characteristics 115
  and state welfare provision 116
  unemployment 34
  welfare dependency, evidence of
    suppressed 9, 10
USSR, essential role of the family
  now recognised 121–2

values
  reinforced in practice 83–4
  socially-responsible, inculcated
    by the family 40
vandalism 129
venereal disease 47
verbal and written skills 14
Veteran's Bureau 27
violence 36
voluntarism 58
  prostituted 60
voluntary social service
  programmes 79

W. Germany
  high maths achievement 131
  productivity problem 34
  studies on welfare dependency
    10
welfare 37
  availability of 45
  and local communities 127
  as a right equals permanent
    welfare 6–7
welfare administration, Swiss 72–3
welfare apartheid 54–5
welfare benefits, reduction in 119
welfare clients, seen by western
    nations as victim of the
    system 109
welfare dependency
  collusion with dependency 13
  creation of 118, 129
  destructive effect of 10–11
  evidence of poverty 9–10
  ghetto dependency 11–13
  in Switzerland 86–90; limitations
    on 78–85
welfare dependency vii–viii, 40,
    121, 125
welfare dependents
  health care for 21–2
  an influx of 36
welfare dependents vii
welfare family 106
  characteristics of 10–11
  children: adjusted to welfare
    dependency 12; unable to

  re-enter society 45
  and education 15
  family relationships 10–11
  housing of, USA 29
  learned roles 12
  relations with the community 10
welfare issue, little politicised in
    Switzerland 89
welfare organisation in
    Switzerland 104
welfare programmes
  centralised 107
  public 107
  voluntary 107
welfare reform
  in Britain, suggestions 118–20
  resistance to 118
welfare sclerosis 117
welfare state
  assumptions of 56; proven
    invalid 57
  Californian example 59–60
  children of 45
  complex and uncontrollable 5–6
  employment in 33–7
  and the family 38–55
  and feminist vision 50
  health care 20–5
  impersonal 6
  interference in lives of the
    people 57
  and moral deterioration 37
  national and central government
    cannot solve social
    problems 111
  New York City as 30–2
  political support for 5
  problems in 3–4
  and productivity 7–8
  or real welfare 76–7
  seen as destructive 60
  socialisation of children
    discouraged 7–8
welfare state nations, client
    rehabilitation concept given
    up 7
welfare state societies, in decay
    115–17

welfare workers, role of in
    Switzerland 74–5
welfarisation 77
    constraints on in Switzerland:
        community youth
        programmes 79; divorce
        courts 80–2; employment
        84–5; military service 85;
        schools 82–3
    female 80, 81
    Switzerland 94, 101
work
    benefits of 33
    preparation for, Switzerland 67
workers, discouraged 36–7

workfare 119

young people
    dependence of 4
    preparation for employability
        111
    unprepared for employment 3–4
youth, lack of occupational
    training 34
youth culture, dominance of 51–2
youth peer groups 123
youth unemployment 37
    Sweden 18
    USA 34